DOOLEY!

The Autobiography of a Soccer Legend

Derek Dooley

with Keith Farnsworth

Derek Dooley

DOOLEY!

The Autobiography of a
Soccer Legend

Derek Dooley

with Keith Farnsworth

 The **Hallamshire** Press 2000

©2000 The Hallamshire Press

Published by The Hallamshire Press Limited

Typeset by The Hallamshire Press Limited
Broom Hall
Sheffield S10 2DR
England

Printed by the Cromwell Press, Trowbridge.

British Library Cataloguing in Publication Data:
  A catalogue record for this book is available from the British Library.

ISBN 1 874718 59 8

Contents

Introduction

By Tony Pritchett, former chief sports writer with the Sheffield Star, *a man who worked closely with Derek Dooley for thirty years and who has known author Keith Farnsworth as a fellow football writer on the South Yorkshire scene since the late 1960s. Tony became one of the Sheffield region's best informed journalists and travelled extensively with Dooley at both Sheffield Wednesday and Sheffield United.*

No writer of fiction would ever have dared to dream up a story like this. The Derek Dooley story is a unique and tremendous tale, and every word of it is fact.

It is the chronicle of events which has as its focal point one of the most remarkable men of our time. It is by no means just a tale of a famous football star, rather an inspiring account of triumph over desperate adversity, of success despite overwhelming misfortune, and of achievement stemming from cruel circumstances which would have destroyed the will to survive in anyone of lesser character.

In the closed world of professional football the bare facts of Dooley's career are the stuff of folklore. A raw kid from the wrong side of Sheffield with no privileges, except that he was born into a strong and loving family environment, who became the most prolific goalscorer of his time. He was at his peak and on the brink of greatness and worldwide fame when it all came to a sudden and cruel end on St Valentine's Day 1953.

Dooley lost a leg and his playing days were over at the age of twenty-three. What was seen initially as a straightforward broken leg which would mend within a month or two, proved to be something much more lethal when an infection in a minor cut unexpectedly turned gangrenous. Surgeons had to amputate the limb to save Dooley's life.

The impact the news made on the people of Sheffield, and especially the local sporting public which loved him as they have loved no other football hero before or since, was unforgettable. It is no exaggeration to say that the heart of this great city stopped for a moment when word of Dooley's million-to-one misfortune was relayed from Preston Infirmary.

That could have been the end of Derek Dooley as a public figure. Instead he made a joke of his artificial leg, forged a new career in the game which was always his greatest passion, and became the first professional footballer to rise to the chairmanship of a top club.

More than that, he earned the total respect of everyone in sport. Professional football has become a cesspit of intrigue and cynicism, but Dooley's standing has never been higher and he remains a symbol of all the good things in the game. He is the true sportsman with an unblemished reputation for honesty, integrity and fair play. Moreover, he remains the archetypal modest hero, a guy who is simply grateful to have had the chance to spend a lifetime in football and enjoy such warm and lasting public support.

Over the years he has proved an inspiration to so many people. He has been a source of fresh resolve to those who have suffered the blow of losing a limb and with it their livelihood, while on so many occasions his courage and great character have left us all feeling humble and counting our blessings. There was the time, for instance, when a massive heart attack threatened his life and we feared that at the very least it might finish his career in football. However, Dooley, not for the first time, proved us wrong. Such spirit and determination served only to warm the hearts of those who watched him bounce back.

When the City Fathers decided to make Dooley a Freeman of his beloved Sheffield, the first sportsman to be so honoured, the news was greeted with widespread acclamation. It spoke volumes for the esteem in which Dooley was held that there was not a single dissenting voice raised when the subject was discussed by rival parties within the City Council.

It has been one of the great privileges of my lifetime in journalism to have witnessed so much of the Derek Dooley story at first hand and to have been able to do so as his friend.

Derek's co-author in this book, Keith Farnsworth, has also been a friend as well as a colleague in the days when he was on the *Sheffield Morning Telegraph* and I was with the *Star*. When I arrived in Sheffield, from Nottingham, Farnsworth was following the fortunes of the local football clubs as a writer and he later served as sports editor. In more recent times he has become an author of growing stature, with such works as *Sheffield Football: A History* (in two volumes) and *A Sheffield Boy* among his many books.

Dooley has often said he has been lucky in life, not least in the choice of his wife, Sylvia, a very remarkable lady who has been a constant source of strength and encouragement. He has, too, been fortunate in his choice of collaborator in this venture, for Farnsworth is a writer renowned for meticulous research and impeccable detail. As co-author of this volume he not only has the advantage of having known Dooley for many years but the two of them grew up in the same part of Sheffield and share a similar background and sense of values. Farnsworth not only cheered Dooley from the Hillsborough Kop back in the early 1950s but in later years they became good pals and collaborated on a manuscript entitled 'Dooley the Centre Forward' which, sadly, never achieved publication. They have compensated in style with the present book and I am sure it will be greeted with great enthusiasm by the public of Sheffield.

It is a gripping story about a great guy. Dooley is such a credit to himself, to football and to Sheffield. Never once have I heard him lament the wicked hand that fate dealt him. Never once has he looked back in anger and cried 'Why me?' It is a measure of the man that he has only one regret about his life as a footballer, being disappointed even to this day that the last time he touched the ball before breaking his leg at Preston he didn't put it into the net. Instead it trickled just the wrong side of the post. If only his final touch had brought a goal, he would have been content.

I cannot repeat often enough that this is the remarkable story of a remarkable man, a book for football supporters to treasure. I congratulate Dooley and Farnsworth on taking the time to place it all on record in such a readable style and I give praise to Pauline Climpson and The Hallamshire Press for having the wisdom to support this venture and ensure publication of such a worthy addition to the sporting literature of Sheffield. I am sure people will be reading and enjoying it a hundred years from now, and they will still be saying that this guy called Dooley really was a sporting legend of whom Sheffield is very proud.

Acknowledgements

The authors wish to thank Sheffield Newspapers for permission to reproduce copyright photographs spanning Derek Dooley's career, and are grateful to the individual photographers for specific pictures. Thanks also to those journalists whose work has been quoted from original match reports and features, and to our good friend Tony Pritchett, former chief sports writer of the *Star*, for writing a special introduction.

Thanks also must go to Sheffield United FC and Sheffield Wednesday FC, to everyone who has made a contribution to this work in any way, but especially to Pauline Climpson and her staff at The Hallamshire Press for their help, support and patience—and, of course, their expertise.

Derek Dooley thanks Keith Farnsworth for undertaking this collaboration with typical enthusiasm and dedication.

Chapter One

Pitsmoor Boy

When I was a boy growing up in the Pitsmoor and Firth Park districts of Sheffield, I lived for sport. I loved running and swimming, but football was my greatest passion. I was never happier than when kicking a small rubber or tennis ball about on the steep, cobblestoned streets of Pitsmoor. We used coats or jumpers for goalposts, but, in our imagination, we thought we were playing at Wembley.

As there were very few reasonably flat stretches of road near where we lived, we got used to playing on a slope. Montfort Street, which ran from Andover Street and cut across Nottingham Street, was more level than most, but it had the disadvantage of being within sight of a Police box. We grew tired of being chased by a bobby and having to retrieve our coats from his box at the cost of a severe ticking off!

Sometimes we might go up to the Danville Street or Pye Bank 'rec' but, as these weren't proper pitches with grass, we invariably ended up with gravel rashes on our elbows and knees. Even so, I revelled in pretending to be my favourite Wednesday hero, the legendary Jackie Robinson.

Of course, like all the other kids, I sometimes dreamed of playing for Wednesday, but a dream is all it was, and making a career in football was the last thing on my mind, I doubt if I ever gave it a thought. I could not have imagined I was destined to be involved in the professional game in my home city for more than half a century, and if anybody had predicted I would serve Wednesday for twenty-six years and United for almost as long, and end up being made a Freeman of Sheffield for my services to local football, I would have thought they were barmy. If someone had suggested I would play for and manage Wednesday, and later become the first paid director in the history of Sheffield football and be managing director and chairman of United, it would have sounded like pure fantasy.

The reality, of course, is that all this did happen—and much more—truth, as they say, is often stranger than fiction. In 1951–52 I had the good fortune to establish a Wednesday record which still stands, for the most goals scored by an Owls player in a season, but less than a year later the loss of a leg 'in action' at Preston at the age of twenty-three meant a premature end to my playing days.

Twenty years on, having rebuilt my Hillsborough career and graduated from the club's pools office to become Wednesday's team-boss, I was sacked on, of all days, Christmas Eve. That was a blow that hurt even more than losing my right leg but, again, I bounced back and made a contribution across the city at Bramall Lane. Happily, United's appreciation even extended beyond my retirement, and on three occasions they called me back to help the cause. It was good to still feel needed even though I was approaching seventy!

No, as a cheeky-faced kid I might have known I would always want to play football, but, even in my early teens, I never aspired to become a professional. When it happened, corny as it might sound, it was as if a miracle had occurred. The sheer joy I felt when I was invited to sign for Wednesday, in June 1947, is a memory I have never forgotten, and I don't think I have ever lost that sense of wonder. Hard experience may have subsequently ensured I was always a realist, but I have invariably remained the essential romantic at heart. People may remember me as a fearless centre-forward, tough as steel and ready to run through a brick wall, but I'm blessed with the kind of sentimental streak that means I am easily moved and often get very emotional when I look back and remember with gratitude the good things that have happened in my life.

Most of us tend to forget the setbacks when we start counting our blessings. For me, the greatest blessing of all is my wife Sylvia and our family, then, of course, I have always been grateful to have been a football man. I might regret some of the things that have happened along the way in my career, but I wouldn't have wanted to be anything other than a football man.

I have known some great people, and had the luck to have most of them as friends, it has also been my good fortune to have enjoyed the respect and support of a local public whose loyalty has been remarkable. I consider it an honour that I am one of the few people in the history of Sheffield football to have gained acceptance by both Blades and Owls fans.

Fame was never my spur and I am still constantly surprised by small incidents which remind me that I continue to be touched by it, even well beyond Sheffield. For instance, in a television play a few years ago, one of the characters had a dog called Dooley. It transpired that the author, based in the south, had been an avid fan of mine as a youngster and gave the dog my name by way of tribute.

I never cease to be surprised at how often I travel abroad and come across people who not only know my name but are genuinely thrilled to meet me. Considering it is nearly fifty years since I last played, it is moving to meet someone in a distant corner of the world who isn't just delighted to recall having seen me in action but insists I was his hero.

Once, when Sylvia and I were in the Algarve, a man came up to me and said he remembered watching me play against Doncaster Rovers in 1951. 'Derek' he said, 'I just wish my father was still alive so I could go home and tell him I have met you. It would have meant so much to him.'

My journalist pal Tony Pritchett, who served the *Sheffield Star* so well for many years until his retirement in June 1999, used to pull my leg whenever we went on foreign trips with United, invariably wondering as we travelled to some faraway corner of the globe whether we might at last have found a place where nobody would know me. Once, as we flew into Beijing, he said: 'Well, I'll bet China is one country where you can be sure they've never heard of DD'. To his astonishment, when we got into the official car taking us from the airport to our hotel, the Chinese chauffeur turned to me and said: 'Mister Dooley, I am honoured to meet you, for I once saw you play at Tottenham many years ago when I was stationed in London'.

Such small moments probably don't mean much to anyone else, but they are incidents which give me a feeling of fulfilment that money cannot buy, and sometimes I'm prompted to wonder what the cheeky-faced kid from Bramber Street would have said had he known what the future held. I can well imagine him saying: 'I don't believe it'.

As I have said, my playing career ended when I was twenty-three but, in fact, my footballing days might easily have finished at the tender age of eleven. I suffered a playground accident typical of the sort of scrape I often got myself in as a lad, and so badly damaged my left ankle that at one stage there was talk of amputating the foot!

At school, I was nicknamed 'wild young Dirk' because I was such a dedicated daredevil and seldom stayed out of trouble for long. Kicking a ball about and fighting were the things I most enjoyed. If football was my great passion, I loved a good scrap almost as much, and I never hesitated when someone suggested a fight on the local quarry to challenge my 'crown' as 'cock of the school'.

I was a red-haired bundle of unbridled energy and enthusiasm. I suppose like most young lads, I just wanted to pack as much excitement and activity as possible into every day. I had so much spirit and such a love of life that I gave everything I tackled every ounce of myself. I wasn't an unruly kid, and didn't get into trouble for being a bad lad, my upbringing ensured I didn't lack respect for my elders, and I knew and accepted the difference between right and wrong.

Most of the problems came about because I would often go where angels feared to tread. Certainly I was always ready to stick up for myself against bigger lads, and I could never resist fighting other people's fights, especially if a big lad was bullying a small pal of mine.

I was always in trouble at school. Roy Slack, one of my teachers at Owler Lane, described me as 'a born scamp', and I think I held the school's record for the most cane in a day. I used to go home and tell my mother—not without a sense of pride: 'I've had eighteen strokes of cane today'.

*The date on the back of this photograph is February 1932,
so when I posed for the camera with my elder brother Alan
I was only three months past my second birthday*

However, if I was expecting sympathy, I didn't get it. Mother would say: 'Well, I suppose you deserved it'. I know that nowadays people tend to frown upon the kind of punishment that was commonplace in schools then, but I don't think the cane I had did me any harm. Once the pain wore off, it was soon forgotten. Alas, it was seldom long before I got myself into another scrape!

I mentioned earlier the Pitsmoor quarry where we used to stage fights, and this reminds me of how, as kids, me and my pals were totally oblivious of the dangers inherent in some of the games we played on that site. Times many we risked life and limb just to prove how brave we were, and how we lived to tell the tale still remains a mystery to me over sixty years later!

The quarry was situated in an area bounded by Andover Street, Catherine Street and Kirton Hill, and there was a cliff we used to call Elephant's Back. In one spot there was a ledge about ten-inches wide above a sheer drop of thirty-feet, and many was the time we dared each other to walk across it. Later, we would adjourn to an old derelict property we knew as 'the haunted house'. The quickest way into the building was along a precariously-placed plank which extended across a steep gap and into a window. One false step and you were sure to fall and probably break a leg, but nobody would admit to fear in front of his mates.

One benefit of a trip to that old house was the chance to strip some of the floorboards and chop them up for sale as firewood. We supplemented our spending money for months in this way. Of course, as the property grew more and more desolate and dangerous with our removal of whole floors, so the risk of an accident increased. Happily the gods protected us.

It is intriguing to reflect on the little twists of fate that, with hindsight, appear to have spared one from possible disaster and, in this context, I must mention how the Dooley family escaped the worst of the Sheffield Blitz on the night of the 12th and 13th of December 1940.

I spent the first eleven years of my life living in Pitsmoor and, probably about halfway through this period, we moved from the house at 82 Bramber Street to a larger rented property at 110 Nottingham Street. Around September 1940, my parents negotiated another removal to 34 Addison Road, just below Firth Park, little knowing that, within less than three months, the old Nottingham Street house would suffer a direct hit from a German bomb. The new people at number 110 were in the air-raid shelter in the yard at the time, but they and their pet dog still had to be dug out from beneath the rubble of the shattered house by an army of ARP wardens.

It was after the move to Addison Road that I had the accident which nearly led to me losing my left foot. I had gone up to Concord Park with a pal called Peter Brooks and, dashing between the swings and roundabouts, I jumped on a fast-moving roundabout without noticing a missing board in the broken platform. My foot went straight through the gap, a rivet pierced my ankle and, after being dragged round and round for several minutes, the back of my ankle was in shreds.

I was a big lad for my age and, in carrying me all the way back to Addison Road, my pal performed an heroic feat for which I have always been grateful. I remember it was a Saturday evening and my parents had gone off to see the latest 'turns' at Pitsmoor Working Men's Club. Peter got me settled in the living room and then went to fetch Mum and Dad home. I ended up at the hospital, where a doctor inserted twelve stitches in the wound. Unfortunately, it subsequently turned septic, and at one

This is me sometime around my third birthday.

point the medical experts said there was a possibility the foot might have to be amputated.

Happily, that didn't happen, but the scare was not enough to stop me flirting with danger once I had recovered. My next setback was a broken arm, and then came a day when, for a dare, I jumped over a wall on Sicey Avenue while carrying a bicycle on my back. It didn't seem much, for the wall was only two-feet high, but what I didn't realise until it was too late was that on the other side of the wall there was a fall of eight feet. I finished up beneath my bike with a pedal impaled in my head. I don't think my mother ever believed me when I told her all that happened was I had simply fallen off the bike!

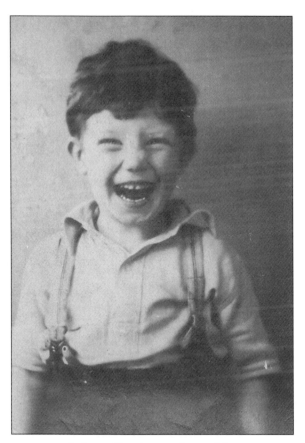

A picture of happiness at the age of four.

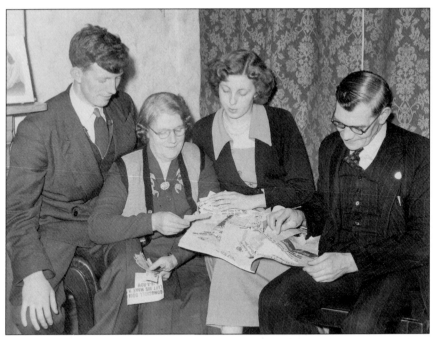

Mum and Dad set me a good example from my earliest days and were always delighted in my progress as a player. Here they are reading a few headlines and helping Sylvia arrange my cuttings book during my early career with Wednesday.

Chapter Two

Charles and Jennie: My Parents

My parents, Charles and Jennie Dooley, were married for fifty-six years until my father died in November 1978. They were a devoted, happy and hard-working couple who, while never having much money, created a warm, comfortable and contented family home in which my brother, Alan, and myself were able to grow up in a secure and stable atmosphere. They endured some lean times over the years, but Alan and myself never lacked affection or any of the essentials of a happy childhood. If our parents couldn't always afford life's little luxuries, they ensured we were never neglected or went without what we needed. It would be an understatement to say they were a major influence on us in terms of setting the right example in how to live and conduct ourselves.

They were, I suppose, a typical working-class couple of their generation. Their priority was to provide for their family and, in their era, that meant both had to turn out to work to make ends meet. Mother never expected nor wanted to be a lady of leisure and, like thousands of women in similar circumstances, she would come home after a long day at the factory and start on the cooking, cleaning and washing. She never complained and, like Dad, she didn't ask for or need much by way of amusement or entertainment to make her happy. As a couple they liked nothing better than a night out together, usually about twice a week, with the highlight watching the latest 'turn' at Pitsmoor Working Men's Club. The club meant a lot to them, and one benefit of their membership which their sons appreciated was the annual club trip, to Cleethorpes or Skegness, which I can never remember coinciding with anything but fine, sunny weather. Apart from the club, Dad's favourite relaxations were fishing and gardening, they cost little but gave him a lot of pleasure.

Mother made sure that, unlike many other families in our neighbourhood, we always had an annual holiday at the seaside. While Dad was more easy-going, Mother was the dominant one, the organiser. What money was put by for the holidays was down to her ability to manage the family budget and ensure, even when finances were tight, that something was saved for a week at Blackpool. Our places at the boarding house were booked well in advance and, weeks ahead of the traditional Sheffield holiday fortnight, Mother would join the long queue to book train or coach tickets. In those days, if you didn't book early there was no way you could expect to get on a train or bus to any seaside resort at the peak of the season.

I remember we always had bed and breakfast booked at the boarding house on Exchange Street on the North Shore, and it was typical of Mother that, each day, she would buy some ham so we could have a salad tea. I recall that, at the start of the holiday, she would give me and my brother half-a-crown (12¹/₂p) each and say: 'Don't spend it all at once—make it last the week'.

I was still in short trousers when this picture was taken, but brother Alan and myself look very smart, being on one of our annual holidays at Blackpool.

Dad, who at the time of my birth in December 1929 earned £3 a week for an eleven-hour morning, afternoon or night shift as a leverman at a local forge, worked in a number of similar, manual jobs until he was sixty-seven. When Alan and I were small boys, he endured a succession of spells on short-time or unemployed and, with little money about, Mother, who had started her working life at the age of thirteen as a file-cutter at Firth's, went back to her old trade.

Mother was employed by Ralston's in Rockingham Street, and she often recalled that, in the thirties, she had to fight to get a job because, in the economic climate of the slump, firms preferred to employ men. 'I had to persuade them I needed the work as much as any man' she said. She made arrangements for her brother Dick, who was then unemployed, to look after Alan and myself while she was at the factory. Uncle Dick, incidentally, later lost a foot in an accident at Sanderson & Newbould's where he eventually got a job. During the war, Mother gave up her job, but insisted on returning in 1946, and though she went part-time in later years she did not finally retire until shortly before her sixty-fifth birthday.

Dad, born in October 1897 and a product of the Park district, was the son of a miner who played in the Salvation Army band. He was one of five children, having two brothers, Joe and Albert, and two sisters, Mary and Cilla. When I was a boy, every Sunday, Dad used to take me to visit my grandparents in Ruben Street. I especially remember winter weekends when I would sit beside the coal fire and watch my grandmother take the seasoned Yorkshire puddings out of the oven. She always left them to cool on top of a coal-scuttle in the hearth and, when her back was turned, I would help myself to a piece. That was how I acquired my taste for seasoned pudding!

Of Dad's brothers, my great hero was Uncle Albert, whom I regarded as one of the bravest men I knew. During the war, while serving with the Royal Engineers at Dunkirk, he was left behind to blow up a bridge and was one of the last British soldiers to jump into a boat. He had been in the boat for only a few minutes when it was sunk by the Germans but, miraculously, he survived a long spell in the water and eventually came home to tell us the story. At the time, I remember how his heroics so captured my imagination that I readily forgave him for being a Unitedite!

As a boy I always used to think that Dad's sister, Mary, was the richest of my relations because she worked in a sweet shop in Charles Street, and, whenever I called in, she not only gave me some chocolates but half-a-crown (12½p), which seemed a fortune to me in those days.

Dad, unlike his brothers, always leaned more towards Wednesday than the Blades. Even so, for many years, he was a regular spectator at both Hillsborough and Bramall Lane—I think it was only after I started playing for Wednesday that he chose to concentrate on Wednesday. Of course, when I started playing, he always went to most of my games, and, from the earliest days, I welcomed his company and support.

As a youngster, Dad had been a notable full-back in local amateur football and, had circumstances not been a problem, he might have become a professional. Those who saw him play insisted he was good enough to make the grade, but when Bradford City offered him a trial he had to turn it down because it meant taking time off work. It was just his luck that, after some months without a job, he had recently found one in which he was expected to work six days a week. 'There was no way I was going to put a secure job at risk and gamble my future on football' he told me many years later. His consolation was in retaining a deep interest in football. He understood the game and, always down to earth and full of practical commonsense, was a constant fund of good advice and wisdom when he began following my career.

He was fiercely proud of my progress, but at the same time he was a bit of a taskmaster. I wouldn't say he never gave me any praise but he kept my feet on the ground with criticisms whenever he felt them appropriate. In the early days, on the journey home from a match, he would talk about the goals I had missed, rather than the ones I had scored. Even when I was playing in Wednesday's first-team, and during the famous 1951–52 season when I claimed the club's scoring record, he seldom openly enthused about my performances. Looking back, I can see that his pride didn't blind him to the need to ensure I didn't get carried away by my successes. There was no way he would let one of his sons become big-headed.

Mother, of course, knew nothing about football, and she would listen without comment when Dad was being critical. Once, however, when I had scored five goals against Notts County and I walked into the house to be greeted by Dad's comment 'Well done, son', she couldn't resist remarking: 'Bloody hell, he must have played well today!'

Dad was a keen angler and inspired my passion for the pastime. He was a trustee and secretary of the fishing section at Pitsmoor WMC, and the club's annual match was a high point in his year. Even though I was always teetotal, when I was old enough I joined the club so I could fish with Dad at these events.

Very early in my life, Dad introduced me to the ritual of getting up at five o'clock on a Sunday morning to catch an early train from the Victoria or Midland station into Lincolnshire. Over the years we spent countless hours together on river banks and the shared interest brought us closer together. On those occasions we talked in a way that was different from when we were at home but, looking back, I often think that the long silences contributed just as much to the development of our mutual understanding.

I treasure the memory of those fishing trips. We maintained the ritual right up to the end of his life. In later years, I used to take a day off from work to fit in a weekly visit to Albert Bramall's pond at Thurgoland, and I remember it was during this period that I suddenly realised how the years were starting to catch up with Dad. He was then well into his seventies and, for the first time in my experience, he began showing a tendency to get into a bit of a tangle on the pondside. We had some fun sorting out his problems! After his death I missed him, and fishing alone in that pond was never the same. Indeed, for a while I lost a bit of interest but, happily, in recent times my grandson Del has revived my enthusiasm. The way Del has taken to the pastime and so enjoys going fishing reminds me of the days of long ago when Dad was teaching me how it was done.

Dad's other great interest was gardening. I recall how, in the days when we lived in Bramber Street and lacked a garden of our own, he used to take me along to the allotment he rented in Roe Woods, which was just a short walk from our house. In later years, the greenhouse he built in the yard of our house in Addison Road was his pride and joy. For him it was a symbol of independence. It stood on the site of the old air-raid shelter we inherited after our move from Nottingham Street. Incidentally, I have never forgotten how, when we first moved in, Dad noticed the shelter had not been fitted deep enough into the ground, so he took it to pieces, rebuilt it at a lower depth and covered it with earth and his favourite plants.

Mother, born Jennie Wilkinson in February, 1900, was one of six children. Her brothers were Harry, Dick and Benny, her sisters Ada and Doris, and, growing up in the Lopham Street area of Pitsmoor, they all continued to live on that side of Sheffield for the rest of their lives. Aunt Ada, in fact, eventually lived next door to us in Addison Road, and her husband, Uncle Joe Hopkins, was one of my staunchest supporters when I became a professional footballer. His praise tempered some of Dad's keenest criticisms!

It is interesting to note that the month of Mother's birth coincided with a famous marathon derby duel between Wednesday and United. It took the Owls and Blades three games to settle a bitter FA Cup battle which finished with only seventeen players on the pitch in the last match. At the time Wednesday were in their first season at Owlerton, as their ground was then known. However, I don't imagine too many members of the Wilkinson family were aware of the fact, though it would be no surprise to learn that my grandfather, George Harry Wilkinson, listened to a good deal of football talk in the steelworks where he was then working as a furnaceman.

As I have mentioned, Mother knew little about football, and I think she only ever saw me play once. This I recall was on a day when I played for the YMCA against our greatest rivals, Oaks Fold. Before the kick-off, she overheard an Oaks Fold official saying: 'The bloke we've got to stop is Dooley. If we stop him, we can win'. She thought they were plotting to kick and injure me, and could not resist telling them: 'You'd better leave my lad alone, or you'll have me to deal with!'

She was always very protective of her sons, and her pride in our success knew no bounds. I'm sure she must often have reflected on how different Alan and I were, chalk and cheese being the phrase she probably used, but she treated us both the same, with equal affection. That, between us, we were destined to give her five grandchildren was a source of great delight to her. I think she was pleased, too, that while Alan and I were never great mates in the sense of always seeking each other's company, we were always pals. There was a bond between us which grew stronger the older we got, and we always knew without ever needing to spell it out that we could depend on each other.

Alan, two years and three months older than me, had black hair, while mine was ginger. He was the studious type, while I had no enthusiasm for anything remotely academic, and when I was out playing football or getting into some sort of scrap he would either be doing his homework or practising on the piano.

I remember once when we were boys he was playing his party piece, 'Bluebells of Scotland', and sucking a ballbearing at the same time. When I patted him on the back rather over-robustly, he swallowed the ball, which caused a huge panic in the Dooley house. Needless to say, I got a stern rebuke from Mother!

As lads we both started our schooling at St Catherine's in Andover Street, not because we were a Catholic family but simply because the school was conveniently situated just up the hill from our house. When Alan passed his Eleven-Plus exams in 1938 he was so comfortable with the religion that he elected to formally convert to the Catholic faith, which also offered the bonus of qualifying for De La Salle College. On leaving there five years later he joined the famous firm of Firth Brown's and eventually made his mark as an outstanding metallurgist.

Apart from National Service in the Fleet Air Arm, Alan spent all his working life with the same company until taking an early retirement which, sadly, he was unable to enjoy for long because he died suddenly at the age of fifty-eight. Mother had died only three months earlier, in late December 1985, and our only consolation was that she had been spared the pain of losing her elder son in such unexpected circumstances. Alan left a wife and three children.

Chapter Three

Schooldays

I spent the first eleven years of my life in that part of Pitsmoor situated immediately north of the Wicker Arches. The Bramber Street area I knew as a boy ceased to exist a long time ago when the district was redeveloped but it remains vivid in my memory. In reality I suppose it was rather a grey place but I remember it as a bright and colourful corner of a world in which, as kids, we found plenty to stimulate our imagination and keep us amused.

Bramber Street, off Spital Hill, was one of the many steep, cobblestoned streets in the district, and our house, number 82, was up towards the top in that section where, unlike those back-to-backs further down the hill, the properties boasted four rooms and a back door as well as one at the front. This is where I was born at eight o'clock on the evening of Friday the thirteenth of December 1929.

At the time of my birth, Wednesday were the current Football League champions and well on their way to regaining the title. The day after my arrival they beat Blackburn Rovers 4–0 at Hillsborough, with Jack Allen scoring two of the goals. Allen went on to finish the 1929–30 campaign with thirty-nine, and it is intriguing to note that the tally was not equalled by an Owls player in any season until I managed to better it in 1951–52.

As I have already mentioned, because St Catherine's School was almost within sight of our house, this is where I started my schooling in the mid-1930s. It meant that although I was not a Catholic I was more or less brought up as one in this period and, apart from during my first term, I was taught by nuns. Pye Bank and Ellesmere Road were the nearest 'ordinary' schools, but the convenience of St Catherine's made it an automatic choice and, as far as my parents were concerned, the religious aspect never came into the equation.

Of course, later, when I went to a Church of England school, I had to adapt to a different service at assembly, and for a short spell my lack of familiarity with the different customs probably prompted some people to think I had been raised as an atheist!

Frankly, I was never a great lover of school, but I remember St Catherine's with affection. This could be partly because I always associate that phase in my life with a time when I had so much fun on the old quarry and the days followed an endless pattern of adventure in which football, fighting and being fearless and brave were the themes of my boyhood. Saturday mornings were synonymous with joining the 'penny rush' at the Coliseum cinema on Spital Hill, but we were never short of drama and excitement on the other days of the week.

If I am honest, the big attraction of St Catherine's was having the facility to play football in the school yard instead of on the street. It was a welcome bonus to be able to concentrate on playing instead of having to keep an eye out for the arrival of a policeman who seemed to delight in emerging suddenly from his box in Nottingham Street and scaring the pants off boy footballers. Unfortunately, the school had no organised sports, so the best of our football matches were the makeshift ones we staged on Danville Street or Pye Bank 'rec'.

It was typical of my attitude towards school that the phase I enjoyed the most came late in my time at St Catherine's. After the outbreak of war in 1939, there was a spell when normal schooling was suspended, and we had periods of what was known as 'home service'. This meant the pupils were split into groups of ten or twelve, each group being joined by a teacher who conducted lessons in the house of one of the pupils. The idea was to ensure everybody was not in the school at the same time in case of a sudden air raid on Sheffield. In the event, the school buildings survived the war so the exercise in preventing a possible disaster proved unnecessary. However, I only remember thinking how brilliant it was to escape from the classroom!

Considering my lack of enthusiasm for all things academic, I cannot have done so badly when I sat the Eleven-Plus examinations because I was accepted at Owler Lane Intermediate School. This was a happy coincidence because at around the same time we moved from Pitsmoor to Firth Park and Owler Lane was just a short walk from our new home in Addison Road, which, incidentally, was another steep hill.

As my brother, Alan, had earlier qualified for De La Salle, a Catholic establishment with high academic standards, there was a suggestion I ought to aim for a place at Firth Park Grammar School, which had a similar reputation for excellence and was also conveniently close. However, as I recall, I viewed myself as a modest pupil with limited ability and interest in all things academic, and it seemed to me rather over-ambitious to expect to get into a school where the requirements might be beyond my scope.

As far as I was concerned, Owler Lane was an ideal choice. I was especially attracted by the fact that, though a pupil could elect to stay on at the school until the age of sixteen, if he wished he could leave at fourteen. I have to admit I had no intention of remaining a schoolboy any longer than was absolutely necessary!

I was fitted out with a blazer, a blue and gold cap, and my parents also had to equip me with shirt, shorts and plimsolls for physical training lessons. However, the real bonus was the other compulsory item of equipment, my first pair of football boots. Here at last was a school which boasted organised sport, and nothing ever quite matched the thrill of wearing my new boots and the green shirt of Newton House for the first time.

Sports day was Wednesday, so every Wednesday morning there was a mass exodus from Owler Lane as we all climbed aboard the tramcar bound for Stubbin Lane and the sloping sports field opposite Firth Park Grammar School.

I should perhaps mention that ahead of my football debut in house colours I got into the first of the many scrapes which littered my Owler Lane years. However, in the event the episode influenced my progress in school football, for, had we first-year boys not been the target for third and fourth-year bullies and had I not reacted by fighting and beating one or two of the biggest culprits, I might not have been chosen as captain of form 1B.

It was unfortunate that this initial scrap in the school yard led to my first taste of the cane from the deputy head, Mr Frost. As I recall I only got involved because I was sticking up for a smaller boy, but the incident probably identified me as a lad always likely to be in trouble. At least it gained me the respect of my classmates, who, recognising my readiness to fight their battles as well as my own, did not hesitate to elect me as form captain.

The man who was in charge of first-year sport at that time was a geography teacher called Leonard Hancock. Most of the teachers combined some sports duties with their main school subjects and I think Mr Hancock just happened to be given responsibility for our group on Wednesday mornings because he had no geography classes. On the first Wednesday we went up to Stubbin Lane he told me to pick a team. Naturally, I chose all the lads who played with me in the school yard and I made sure I was the centre-forward.

Within a week or so, our 1B team faced a 1A side and, as I bagged two goals in our win, I quickly gained a place in the school's second eleven.

*I am second from the right in the middle row of this Owler Lane School first eleven line-up.
As you can see, most of my team-mates were bigger and older than me—
and so were the majority of our opponents!*

*I made a mark in school athletics, and as a star sprinter I qualified to represent Owler Lane.
I am second from right in the back row of this school group.*

Within a few months I graduated into the first-team, which was then considered something special for an eleven year old. They said I was one of the youngest first-teamers in the school's history. Most of the other boys were four years my senior and one or two were already sixteen. Moreover, the majority of the teams we faced were packed with older boys. If I was tall for my age, I was still a 'titch' compared with some, but I was determined to prove I could match anybody and, if I took a few knocks, I made sure I gave a few, too!

The pals and team-mates I still remember from those days include Peter Horsefield, Donald Sheriff, Derek Pagden and Roy Dearden, and I recall lads called Mitchell, Hobbs, Hunt and a good little footballer by the name of Crowther.

It was all great fun, and a bonus I particularly enjoyed was attending school assembly on Monday mornings and hearing the headmaster, Mr Jeffries, read out short reports of the school matches. My proudest moments came when he mentioned that Derek Dooley had scored. A taste of fame!

I cannot remember the first time I enjoyed the experience of watching a professional match, but it was in my Owler Lane years that I got into the habit of going down to Hillsborough on Saturdays with some schoolpals. We used to walk to and from Firth Park and were often in the ground more than two hours before the kick-off. We might sometimes claim seats on the front bench of the old North Stand, but I often stood immediately behind the railings in the area in front of the seating. Whether sitting or standing our enthusiasm for Wednesday and all things blue and white knew no bounds.

My great hero was Jackie Robinson, the inside-forward with the wavy hair, the wonderful body-swerve and a knack of scoring memorable goals. Another big favourite was Charlie 'Happy Feet' Napier, a brilliant Scottish inside-forward. In truth, the entire team were all my idols then and I could not begin to imagine that some of the players I watched, like Redfern Froggatt, Hugh Swift and Joe Cockroft would one day be my fellow professionals at Hillsborough.

Walter Millership, who had helped Wednesday win the FA Cup in 1935, was still a member of Wednesday's team in those wartime years and, though I didn't know it then, within a few years I would not only find myself playing against him, but he would be the man who persuaded Wednesday I had the potential to become a professional.

This Wednesday team, which reached the League North Wartime Cup final in 1943, included some of my earliest heroes, not least Jack Robinson (front row, second from left), while the back row includes Eric Taylor (on the extreme left) and Walt Millership (fourth from left), who were involved in signing me for the Owls in 1947.

Jackie Robinson...
a great Wednesday goalscorer
and my boyhood idol.

Chapter Four

'Pop' Bennett and the YMCA

I always intended to finish my formal schooling as soon as I was fourteen and legally entitled to start work. So when this major milestone began to draw nearer I started looking for a club or team to join in order to be sure of continuing to play competitive football once my Owler Lane days were over.

Frankly, I had no idea what I wanted to do by way of a career, and at that stage I was not particularly concerned about making a choice. In the event, shortly after I turned fourteen in December 1943, I became a fifteen shillings (75p) a week trainee deaf-aid mechanic with a firm called Alfred Peters & Son on Fargate.

However, in my final year at school, what mattered more to me than getting a job was choosing the right club to join and play football for. I did not aspire to make a career in football, indeed the thought never entered my head, but I could not envisage life without playing the game that was my passion.

My enquiries led me to the Fargate premises of the YMCA, and it was there that I met a remarkable man called 'Pop' Bennett. Dear old Pop was friend and guide to hundreds of youngsters over the years and, although he is all but forgotten now, many lads of my generation had cause to be grateful for his wisdom and generosity. By day he ran a small cutlery firm which he owned, but the YMCA and the cause of youth were the cornerstones of his world.

Pop was a brilliant youth leader, and the YMCA was his life. He was always there, wandering round the Fargate premises and keeping an eye on what was happening. On Saturday afternoons he would invariably be up at Crimicar Lane, where we played our football matches. A man called Sam Weston acted as Mr Bennett's right-hand man but, whenever or wherever we played, you would always find Pop on the touchline at some stage during the game.

There were many boys who could not afford the bus fare to Lodge Moor but Pop ensured they were never left behind. Some boys from poor families even had their subscriptions paid by Pop, and one of the secrets of his success was that every single boy mattered. You knew you didn't need to be a star performer at a sport to be regarded as an essential part of Mr Bennett's team. Yet Pop was always self-effacing and ever the epitome of modesty and he neither sought nor expected plaudits. Indeed, he would be embarrassed by this small tribute, but no man deserves it more.

Pop knew I had joined the YMCA solely in order to play football, but he soon got me involved in a range of other activities. I became a regular at the Tuesday youth club nights. I developed a keen interest in table tennis and went on to represent the YMCA in local tournaments, but those Tuesday sessions were intended to ensure that everyone had a go at all the games and pastimes, not just those one liked. You might start off playing snooker but, after half-an-hour or so, Pop would blow his whistle to signal everyone to switch to something different, perhaps draughts or chess. Looking back I can see that his system meant lads who might not be able to get onto the snooker or table tennis tables because of the heavy demand were given the same opportunity as everyone else.

Pop also inspired my enthusiasm for the PT class and I got a physical training badge and certificate for this. It proved useful later when I joined the Royal Air Force on National Service, even though, as I will explain in due course, it did not persuade them to give me the role for which I thought the certificate might help qualify me.

Another activity which I might not have got involved in without the encouragement of old Pop was athletics, and I have fond memories of the times when I ran for the YMCA in the regional NAYC sports at the Sheffield University sports ground. I have never forgotten the occasion when I won both the 100 and 200 yards titles, beating a lad called McGhee, whose father was a dentist at Firth Park. McGhee, who ran for St Vincent's Youth Club and was something of a star in junior athletics, went into the races as the firm favourite. He had a smooth and natural running style, while I was one of those 'up and at 'em' types, but I delighted in proving I could run the fastest!

In fact, I found myself really enjoying those sports days and I have not forgotten my disappointment when, after I became a part-time professional footballer, I found myself barred from amateur athletics. However, what was a greater blow in the first months after I joined Wednesday was not being able to turn out for the YMCA on those days when I hadn't been picked in any of the Owls' teams.

I shall always remember my first meeting with Pop Bennett and the pattern of events by which I persuaded him that I didn't want to play anywhere but centre-forward in the YMCA team.

'You're a big lad, Derek' he said. 'What position do you play?'

I told him I was a centre-forward at school. 'Ah, but we've got a good centre-forward here already' he said. 'Do you fancy centre-half?'

'No' I said. However, keen to impress, I confirmed I was happy to play anywhere. The upshot was my debut in the YMCA 14–16 Intermediate League side came at centre-half. Alas, I could not resist going up front whenever we were attacking, and the lad I was supposed to be marking finished up scoring four goals. I think we lost 6–4.

'Well' said Mr Bennett, 'we shan't make a centre-half out of you. Let's try you at left-back.'

I protested that I only used my left foot for standing on but to no avail. Happily, we won the game and I scored two of our goals. Unfortunately, Pop noted the opposition's outside-right had been the best player on the pitch, obviously benefiting from my frequent excursions upfield.

'Well' said Pop, 'perhaps you're right, Derek. We'll play you at inside or centre-forward in future.'

I had some wonderful days wearing the maroon and black of the YMCA, and colleagues from this period included Arthur Bottom, who went on the play for Sheffield United and York, Charlie Kelk, Cliff Goodison, Charlie Grant and Pete Jarvis. We used to hit twelve or fourteen goals in a game as a matter of course, and it was quite common for me to notch six or eight. There was one famous occasion when we won 19–1 and I bagged eleven. We invariably walked away with both the league and cup competitions.

There were three pitches used by the YMCA teams at Crimicar Lane. The best, used by the seniors, was flat and well kept. We all aspired to play on that pitch because it was in such good condition and, somehow, it lent added status to the teams who used it. Frustratingly, I didn't get to play on it very often. Of the other pitches, one was called 'the Alps' because it was situated above the others, while another was known as 'the Jungle' because it was invariably covered in long grass. I think most of my goals were scored on the Jungle!

There was a spell when the YMCA opened a branch in a church hall at Firth Park and, as I lived at that end of town, I went there one night every week. I also played for the Firth Park YM at football and I especially remember a famous occasion when we beat our great local rivals, Oaks

Fold, 6–5 in Concord Park. I scored all our six goals. Incidentally, our goalkeeper that day was a lad called Brian Battersby, a big Unitedite who went on to work for Firth Brown's. In more recent times Brian has been a staunch member of the executive club at Bramall Lane.

Oaks Fold always had a good side in those days and a lot of their players were products of the Sheffield Boys team. The club became a nursery for Sheffield United and over the years they produced quite a number of lads who went on to make the grade in the professional game. A chap called Lol Swallow, who in his heyday had been a well-known United cricketer, was running Oaks Fold then. Lol, like so many of the local amateur club officials of that era, was very dedicated and passionately proud of his club. He was always seeking to strengthen his teams and there was a time when he tried to 'tap me up'.

In fact, as many of his players were from the Shiregreen area and I knew most of them well, no doubt they would have made me welcome. However, there was no way I was going to do anything to upset Mr Bennett. I felt I owed him my loyalty. I knew the only way I would stop playing for the YMCA was if I got the chance to try my luck at a higher level and could do so with the blessing of Pop.

By the same token, I always felt a loyalty towards the firm where I began my working life, and it is fair to say that had I not made the grade in professional football I would probably have remained with Alfred Peters & Son for much longer than I did. It was a place which always boasted a friendly and convivial atmosphere in which I felt comfortable. I remember those years with affection and have not forgotten the keen interest and pride my colleagues took in my progress in football.

The firm's office and workshop were situated in Fargate House, which then stood in that part of Fargate where Marks & Spencer later built a store. At the outset my duties were menial and I recall they mainly involved helping with the packing of deaf-aids and taking the parcels down to the GPO to be registered and stamped. Eventually, under the guidance of a mechanic called Roy Fisher, I graduated to doing repair work and became reasonably competent at the job. I worked for the firm until I was called up for National Service. Then, after I left the RAF and accepted full-time professional terms at Sheffield Wednesday, the boss, Ernest Ward, was good enough to encourage me to continue with Alfred Peters on a part-time basis, which I did until I established myself in Wednesday's first-team.

Chapter Five

A Foggy Day
at Denaby

I took my first significant step on the road to a career in football a couple of months before my sixteenth birthday when I received an invitation to play for Lincoln City reserves in a Midland League match at Denaby. My abiding memory of the game is that it coincided with one of those grey mid-autumn afternoons which grew foggier by the minute. It was impossible to see either goal from the centre circle. In modern times floodlighting might have improved the outlook, but frankly I doubt if the game would have been allowed to go ahead nowadays. My consolation was at least the conditions ensured nobody saw how badly I played!

Of course, the occasion was an exciting episode for me which began when, out of the blue, a telegram arrived at our house in Addison Road. It was probably the first time in the history of the Dooley family that anyone had received a telegram and I remember the surprise was still in my mother's face when she greeted me with the news after I arrived home for lunch. The message read:

> *Selected to play for Lincoln Reserves v Denaby at Denaby next Saturday. Report to ground 1.30–1.45 pm. Signed Joe McClelland, Secretary-Manager.*

At a distance of more than fifty years it is difficult to convey the mixture of elation and panic I felt at that moment. I was scheduled to play for the YMCA at the weekend, and, curiously, my first thought was that I didn't want to let Pop Bennett down. All the same, I didn't want to miss this opportunity.

Mother and I both felt we needed Dad's advice before deciding the next step but, unfortunately, he was at work. The upshot was that while I tried to concentrate on eating my lunch, Mother went off to a phone box to contact Dad.

As always, Dad knew exactly what to do. As it was a pre-paid telegram requiring a reply, he said he would go down to Firvale post office when he got home later in the afternoon and send a 'yes' message to Lincoln. In the meantime, he suggested I should call in on Pop Bennett on my way back to work to explain the situation. As he said, Pop would understand and, anyway, there were always lads queuing up to fill vacancies in the club teams so I wouldn't be letting anyone down.

Just to digress, I should mention that at this time I used to cycle to and from work. I did it to save a few coppers and to ensure I could get home and back in the one-hour lunch break, even though, in truth, it was invariably a hectic phase in the day. Moreover, riding up the steep Barnsley Road on a full stomach on the return trip was quite a challenge. Looking back, I often wonder that Mother, knowing how accident-prone I was, allowed me to use the bike, and all the more so after the occasion when I managed to get my front wheel caught in the tramlines in Waingate and ended up on the bonnet of a passing motor car! Fortunately, in this instance, despite my preoccupation with the prospect of playing for Lincoln I avoided any mishap while riding back to work and then home again in the evening.

Dad often recalled in later years that, when he learned about the telegram, his first reaction was 'Where's Denaby?' None of us had a clue, although we knew it was a mining town somewhere in the South Yorkshire coalfield. Fortunately, Dad had a workmate who had played for Mexborough and this chap helped in the plotting of a journey which involved travelling on three trams and a trolley bus on a route via Templeborough and Rotherham. We set out on what seemed like an all-day excursion with my boots wrapped in a brown paper parcel carefully tied with string!

Amusing as it might seem now, I remember being taken aback, shocked even, when I discovered Lincoln played in red and white stripes. Considering I had a large collection of football cigarette cards and was a regular reader of *Topical Times*, I must have been familiar with the colours of every club in the country, but until I walked into the dressing room at Denaby I had forgotten Lincoln's strip was exactly the same as Sheffield United's. That hurt a Wednesdayite, although it was some consolation to find my shirt bore a large figure nine and at least the novelty of wearing a numbered shirt for the first time in my life suggested a genuine brush with the big time!

I scored a goal and I think we had another one disallowed because I was off-side. Alas, we lost 6–1 and all I can remember is the way they kept bringing the ball back to the centre circle for me to spot off. The gathering gloom as the fog got thicker just about summed up my feelings.

I knew I had not played well and it did start to seem as if my dream was turning into a nightmare.

A chap called Eddie Dwaine was in charge of the team that day and as I came off the field at the end of the game I hoped the fog had prevented him from having a good look at me. This may well have been the case, but he didn't comment, and I admit that when we said our farewells and he promised to drop me a line I thought he was simply being kind. I told Dad: 'I'll bet that's goodbye Lincoln'.

When the following Saturday came and went without a word, I feared the worst but, happily, a letter finally arrived, and, thereafter, I played fairly regularly in Lincoln's reserves. My colleagues there included another Sheffield lad called Lol Smedley and a local product, Danny Hellings, who used to get leave from the RAF to play alongside me in the attack.

I got to know Eddie Dwaine well and found him helpful and thoughtful. I don't think he was an ex-player, but he was much more than simply the man who looked after the reserves and paid out the half-a-crown tea money. He was always there with a wise word and encouragement and his friendliness, enthusiasm and dedication to the cause were typical of the other key figures at Lincoln, Joe McClelland and Bill Anderson.

It is worthy of note that McClelland, who was the manager for most of the time I was connected with Lincoln, had once been assistant to Bob Brown at Hillsborough, while Anderson, the first-team trainer, had spent three years at Bramall Lane as a full-back. Bill, one of the great characters of football in the early post-war era, succeeded McClelland in January 1947 and remained City's manager for twenty years. Later, he served Nottingham Forest for many years and scouted for them right up to his death in 1986.

Bill, of course, was not the only man at Sincil Bank with Sheffield United connections. Others included Tom Johnson and Jimmy Hutchinson. Johnson, the captain, had played in United's 1936 FA Cup final side, and his brother, Harry, still held the Blades' all-time scoring record. Their father, 'Old' Harry, had been a member of the famous United team of the 1890s. Hutchinson was a clever inside-forward who had been with United for nine years and, of course, his son George would shortly make the grade with the club after moving from Huddersfield.

This link between Lincoln and United meant that Tom, Jimmy and a number of other City lads who were based in Sheffield were allowed to train at Bramall Lane. Once I signed as a Lincoln amateur, I, too, qualified to join these training sessions which were held on a couple of evenings each week.

My presence at one of the earliest sessions coincided with a practice match involving a United team and Oaks Fold and led to an amusing development. United were a man short, I was asked to fill the gap, and always being anxious to excel, especially against Oaks Fold, I did well enough to impress some of the Bramall Lane staff. Apparently one of the spectators was Teddy Davison, the club's secretary-manager. The upshot was that, on learning I was connected with the YMCA, Davison contacted Pop Bennett, and Pop wrote to my father to say Davison would like to have a chat with me. Davison, of course, was unaware that I had signed amateur forms for Lincoln, and because of this I never did go to see him. It is, however, intriguing to think that, had I been free to do so, I might well have joined the Blades thirty years sooner than actually happened!

It is of interest to note I have something in common with Teddy Davison in that we both played with Wednesday and later gave long service to United. Teddy's record was eighteen years with Wednesday and twenty years with the Blades. In his day he had been a fine goalkeeper and he played in over 400 games for the Owls between 1908 and 1926. He was with United from 1932 to 1952.

Playing in the Midland League at the age of sixteen was a daunting experience, for the competition boasted teams packed with seasoned professionals and some of the toughest veteran defenders anyone could expect to meet. It is fair to say I learned a lot very quickly and in the early days there were times when my courage was severely tested.

I recall one game against a works team called Ransome & Marles when I faced a centre-half called Les Bailey. He had played with Derby County before the war, and to say he frightened me to death on the pitch would be an understatement. He spent the entire ninety minutes threatening to break my legs and the way he performed that afternoon convinced me he meant it! I doubt if I have ever been so relieved to hear the final whistle.

When the return fixture at their ground came round, I questioned the wisdom of playing. I said to my dad: 'Shall I tell them I'm not fit? I don't fancy facing that chap again'. It was the only time I ever contemplated crying off for it wasn't my style to admit to fear. When Dad insisted 'Derek, you've got to play', I travelled to the game wondering if he really knew how tough Bailey was.

I hadn't been in the dressing room more than a few minutes when there was a knock at the door. 'Is Dooley there?' someone shouted. I knew the voice belonged to Bailey and before I had time to ask what he wanted, he said: 'It's a good job for thee, Dooley, that I'm injured and not playing today'.

I cannot recall whether I ever saw or faced Les Bailey again, but, strange as it might seem, I remember him with affection. Like a lot of the hard men of that era he was fearless and tough as nails, but his aggression was tinged with respect. I soon learned such threats were a way of testing your courage, and, if those lads found you were ready to stand up to them and to give as much as you took, they had more time for you than they ever admitted. Some years after our clash, when I was in Preston Royal Infirmary after having my leg amputated, I received hundreds of goodwill messages and among them was a lovely letter from Les. He was just a big softie, really!

Of course, my services were not always required by Lincoln and, when I was free to do so, I still played with the YMCA. As always, I could never get enough football and I could not bear to let a Saturday pass without a game.

There was one occasion when Lincoln sent a telegram announcing their fixture had been postponed. I made haste to get in touch with Pop Bennett and, as it turned out, the YMCA were struggling to raise a team because several key players had gone down with flu, the crisis was a big one because the club was scheduled to play in a Yorkshire YMCA cup final at Wakefield.

I was delighted to turn out and celebrated with four goals in a 6–1 triumph. Dad often recalled that game because one of my goals was among the most remarkable I ever scored. The opposition goalkeeper got so annoyed with my constant attention that he picked up the ball, threw it at me in sheer anger and frustration, and it promptly rebounded into the net! I still possess the black and maroon embroidered cloth badge which was given to me as a medal at the end of that match.

The record books show Joe McClelland's ten-year stint as Lincoln's manager ended in December 1946 and, according to a story my dad used to tell, it must have been in the same month that he tried to persuade me to turn professional. Dad once suggested McClelland had come to our house to press his case but, to be honest, I have no memory of this, though it is probably true. Certainly there were people at Sincil Bank who felt I had a future in the game and the fact that I got into the first-team towards the end of my second season with the club confirms they had faith in me.

Whatever the actual details, the plain fact was I did not want to become a professional at that stage. I was still playing for the YMCA at regular intervals and, indeed, my performances with them had earned me a place in the Sheffield & Hallamshire representative teams. I knew the county side was doing well in the regional and national competitions and, as I didn't want to deny myself the chance to help them in their bid for honours, it was essential to retain my amateur status, at least until the end of the season.

I didn't know it at the time, but my decision, coupled with the unusual circumstances of that prolonged 1946–47 season, helped create the pattern of events which were destined to change the course of my career and prompt the opportunity to become a Sheffield Wednesday player.

As a footnote to that foggy day at Denaby in 1945, it will be of interest to mention that I went back there some sixteen years later on a scouting mission for Wednesday. I was in charge of the club's youth team at the time and the manager, Vic Buckingham, asked me to attend a schools match between Don & Dearne and Barnsley at Denaby.

Vic was quite a character, and when I asked him which player he particularly wanted me to watch he said: 'If I tell you that, you'll be wiser than me. No, just do a report on the game, Derek'.

When I returned to Hillsborough after the match, I told Vic I had been especially impressed with a lad called Roger Barton.

'What about the Barnsley number seven?' he asked.

'Yes' I said, 'a boy called Alan Woodward. He scored three goals, and he takes a good corner-kick, but, frankly Vic, he didn't get stuck in enough for me. He seemed a bit nesh'.

Woodward was invited to Hillsborough but for some reason the talks broke down. There was a suggestion that Vic misunderstood a comment made by Woodward's dad or granddad. Vic thought he was being asked for some extra payment which, in fact, wasn't the case.

The upshot was Woodward signed for Sheffield United the following week and it is a part of local football folklore that he went on to play around 600 games for the Blades, scoring a post-war record 175 goals. He was at his peak in the late sixties and early seventies and most people would include him among the best United players of the past forty years. Unfortunately, I cannot claim to have given him more than a passing mention in my report!

Chapter Six

'Does Tha Fancy Playing for Wednesday?'

The 1946–47 campaign was the first season of peacetime football after the war and it was not without irony that, just when everybody was looking forward to getting back to normal with a resumption of the traditional League and Cup format, the country found itself in the grip of one of the worst winters in modern times. As a teenager, I had never seen so much snow, between January and March it just about brought the nation to a standstill with conditions prompting a national fuel crisis.

The first three months of 1947 coincided with the greatest hold-up in the history of the Football League and by mid-March there were over 200 games waiting to be re-arranged. Even if floodlit football had existed in those days the fuel shortage would have meant the lights standing idle. In any event, for a time there was even a ban on midweek matches being played in daylight because the Government didn't want people taking time off work. Naturally, thousands of minor teams were just as badly affected as the big clubs and everybody faced a huge fixture pile-up.

The football season was extended into mid-June, and as a consequence arrangements were made by the Football League for all professional contracts to be renewed to cover two extra weeks. Amateur contracts, however, were allowed to lapse, and this legal loophole explains why I was no longer formally bound to Lincoln when the opportunity arose to join Sheffield Wednesday.

For all the frustrations caused by the weather at the peak of the 'Big Freeze', I remember the 1946–47 season as one in which I knew I was making good progress and I certainly enjoyed my football. I was playing fairly regularly with Lincoln reserves and, when they didn't want me, I turned out for the YMCA. My links with the YMCA had an added bonus in ensuring I qualified to play for Sheffield & Hallamshire representative sides, something that gave me a very satisfying sense of achievement.

The Sheffield & Hallamshire team at that time was a good one. It included some very useful players. Names like Dennis Rodgers, Barry Webster, Cliff Goodison and Charlie Kelk will not mean a lot to many people now, but in those days they were well-known youngsters and were key figures as we made excellent progress in a number of competitions. We felt we had a fair chance of capturing some honours, and in that situation there was no way I was going to relinquish my amateur status before the end of the season. As a consequence I rejected all talk of turning professional even though I was flattered by Lincoln's interest in adding me to their payroll.

My first game with the Sheffield & Hallamshire side is one I recall with a smile because in the space of a few minutes I experienced extremes of fortune and learned that in football matches justice invariably prevails in the end.

In those days the county side played most home games up at the B & C ground at Shiregreen. This was then also the venue for Wednesday's 'A' team matches in the Yorkshire League. It was used, too, for some local cup finals as well as for games involving Sheffield Boys. It was here that I made my county debut against a West Riding CFA side which included a centre-forward called Len Browning, who later played for Leeds United and Sheffield United.

Early in the game I went for a cross which I could not reach with my head, so I steered the ball into the net with my hand. When the referee ignored Leeds' protests and awarded a goal, I have to admit I simply smiled and kept quiet. A few minutes later opportunity knocked again and, from close range, I volleyed the ball into the net with such venom that it hit the ironwork at the back of the goal and shot out again. The referee insisted the ball had merely hit the underside of the bar and refused to listen to my protests. Browning later scored twice for Leeds and we ended up losing 3–2.

Despite that setback we progressed in the senior cup competition but, after I had scored a hat-trick in a 4–1 defeat of Lincolnshire CFA, we fell at the semi-final stage when Liverpool FA thrashed us 4–0 at Goodison Park. My sole consolation was having my first experience of playing at one of the country's top League grounds—a venue steeped in football folklore and, of course, synonymous with the legendary 'Dixie' Dean, one of the most prolific centre-forwards in the game's history.

In between my outings with the YMCA and Sheffield & Hallamshire, I was doing well with Lincoln reserves and, though I didn't know it at the time, one Midland League game at Sincil Bank on Good Friday turned out to be particularly significant. It happened to be against Denaby, the club I had faced on my City debut in the previous season. On this occasion the opposing centre-half was none other than the former Wednesday hero Walter Millership.

Of course, I had seen Millership play in the Owls' side that went all the way to the final of the League North War Cup in 1943 and his name will always be associated with Wednesday's FA Cup-winning team of 1935. When Walter went to Hillsborough in the early thirties, I think he did so as an inside-forward but most people remember him as a tough, uncompromising defender whose fighting qualities earned him the nickname 'Battleship'.

In fact, Walter wasn't really a big chap, and even as a teenager I stood a good six inches taller than him. However, he was absolutely fearless and, like many of his breed, he had a capacity to intimidate young centre-forwards with his sheer presence. In that Good Friday game, he whispered a few threats into my ear! 'Tha might be big and fast but I'll slow thee down, don't worry about that' was a typical comment.

The great thing about Walter was if he could dish it out he could also take it. We had a right royal battle with no quarter given or expected on either side and I finished up with more than a few aches and pains. However, when we were walking off the field after the final whistle, he was the first to congratulate me. He put an arm round my shoulder and said: 'Does tha fancy playing for Wednesday?'

I told him I did, but not thinking he was serious, never gave his question another thought. I didn't know until much later about how Walter had gone down to Hillsborough the following week and told Eric Taylor: 'I played against a young lad called Dooley yesterday. Honest, Eric, he's the most awkward centre-forward I've met—just like a ruddy great tank!'.

With so many postponed matches to be fitted in, the final weeks of that extended season were a bit hectic but, as always, I revelled in playing at every opportunity and, in the last weeks of May, it was a terrific bonus to find myself named in Lincoln's first-team.

My senior debut came against Grimsby in the final of the Lincolnshire Senior Cup. I was called in to replace the injured Tom Cheetham and found myself in the same line-up as the former Blades, Tom Johnson and Jimmy Hutchinson. Grimsby were then in the old First Division and they had a very good team which included Harry Clifton, Billy Cairns and a newcomer called Tommy Briggs, who was destined to make a big name for himself as a goalscoring hero of the early post-war years.

Fifty years later occasions like that local cup final between Lincolnshire's two Football League clubs tend to be regarded as unimportant, but in those days just after the war they were considered special. There were fewer counter attractions then, and with people hungry for the colour and drama of local football these games attracted big crowds. It was certainly a big occasion for me and I celebrated with a goal. Unfortunately, we lost the match 2–1, but at least I collected a little silver cup as a runners-up prize.

The following Saturday I had my first taste of Third Division (North) football when I scored in a 3–1 defeat of Wrexham, then two days later I notched the only goal of the game against Barrow. Sadly three goals in three games wasn't enough to earn me a place when we went to Accrington Stanley for the next match and I had to settle for the role of twelfth man. Checking in the record books I note we lost 8–4, but I honestly cannot remember the match. If I'm not mistaken, it was on the day after the Accrington trip that my amateur contract with Lincoln formally expired, although I was not conscious of the implications of this at the time.

Two weeks later, on June 14th, I was back on duty with the Sheffield & Hallamshire side in what was my last game of the season but was to be one of the most significant fixtures of my early career. We were playing Doncaster in the final of the Minor Counties competition on Thorncliffe's muddy Lane End ground at Chapeltown. We won 6–0, I scored four goals and, at the end, I was approached by the former Wednesday full-back Tommy Walker. I didn't know it then but I was destined to get to know Tommy very well over the following years. Of course, I already knew he had been in the Wednesday team that won the League Championship in 1929 and 1930.

It transpired that Tommy had been sent to the match by Eric Taylor, who had not forgotten Walter Millership's comments about the 'ruddy tank' he had faced at Lincoln. When Tommy invited me to visit Hillsborough on the following Monday to meet Eric Taylor and discuss the possibility of signing for Wednesday, I didn't need asking twice.

Tommy was not the only representative of a top club present at that match. In fact, Second Division Nottingham Forest and Wolves, who were then a major force in the First Division, had someone there, and both talked to my dad afterwards. The man from Forest said his club would be in touch again within a few weeks but, by the time they made contact, they found they were too late.

The Wolves' representative was a chap called Mark Crook, whose short and stocky figure was familiar on the touchline at many grounds in South Yorkshire. In fact, he was something of a legend among football scouts in those days. He had been a winger with Wolves before the war and was later connected with a team at Wath which became a nursery for his old club. Mark had delighted his old boss, the famous Major Frank Buckley, by sending a succession of notable young discoveries down to Molineux, and he continued to find talent long into the eras of Ted Vizard and Stan Cullis.

On this occasion, in June 1947, Mark seemed to think he had arranged to pick me and my dad up on the following Tuesday to take us to meet the Wolves manager, Ted Vizard. To his dismay, when he arrived at our house in Addison Road, he found I was at work and Dad was resting up ahead of going off to start on the afternoon shift.

Dad, surprised to find Mark Crook on the doorstep, told him he knew nothing about having promised to travel to Wolverhampton, and said that, in any event, I had already signed for Wednesday. Apparently Mark was decidedly displeased, and, so I was told, he and Dad had a bit of a verbal ding-dong during which the Wolves scout, who was well known as a blunt speaker, got rather abusive.

In the meantime, I was walking about with a grin on my face as wide as the Wicker Arches for, less than twenty-four hours earlier, I had walked into the main entrance at Hillsborough for the first time, met secretary-manager Eric Taylor, and become a part-time professional with my favourite club.

I walked on cloud nine for weeks and all I can remember about the night I went to the ground is how I couldn't wait to get hold of a pen and sign the forms. Eric Taylor was the best salesman Wednesday ever had but I didn't need anyone to 'sell' the club to me. The prospect of playing for Wednesday was something I had never considered remotely possible and when it happened it was like a miracle.

Of course, like me, Dad was excited and elated but, true to character, he didn't really express his pleasure in my presence. As always, he was keen to ensure my feet remained firmly on the ground. This, he stressed, was not the end of a journey, it was only a beginning. All I had done was get a foot on the first rung of the ladder, which would be no big deal if I thought climbing it was going to be easy. He said: 'It's a wonderful opportunity, Derek, but, if you want to make the grade, now you've got to start really working at it'. He knew enthusiasm and confidence were not enough to guarantee success and was aware I would need plenty of persistence and patience to progress and overcome the inevitable frustrations along the way.

Chapter Seven

Early Trials

Of course, Dad was right. Becoming a part-time professional with Sheffield Wednesday was a tremendous milestone for a teenager with my unbounding passion for football and all things blue and white, yet it was merely a first step. However, if my education in the game was just starting and if I was well aware that I had a long way to go, the learning process proved enjoyable despite a few frustrations along the way.

The thrill of wearing a Wednesday shirt for the first time is something only a young, romantic and fanatical supporter, such as I was then, can really savour to the full. I don't think I could ever explain the pride I felt on that August day in 1947 when I made my 'A' team debut in a Yorkshire League match against Yorkshire Amateurs at Thackerey's ground, near Leeds. Not even a 5–1 defeat could spoil my afternoon.

Unfortunately, we also lost our next game, against Gainsborough Trinity on the following Monday, by a 6–1 margin and as a consequence I was one of the players dropped from the side. It seemed like the end of the world and my misery was compounded when I found myself stuck on the sidelines for four weeks. In those days if your services weren't required, you still had to report to the ground on match days, and one of the perks of being a player was being able to stand in a pen near the tunnel at Hillsborough and watch the first-team or the reserves in action. Alas, watching was little compensation when all you really wanted was to be playing.

Not getting picked was probably a blow I would have taken in my stride in other circumstances. The real shock was to discover that, unlike when I had not been required by Lincoln, I was no longer an amateur at liberty to wander off and play for the YMCA. As a professional I was tied to Wednesday. I could not turn out for anyone else, not even a local parks team. Certainly there was no way I could telephone Pop Bennett and ask for a game. When the reality of the situation hit me, I was in total despair.

It might seem a bit juvenile but playing football was all that mattered to me then and being prevented from doing something that was such an essential part of my life was sheer murder. As a part-timer I was paid a £3 match fee, and I got nothing if I didn't play. Of course, the money didn't matter and I would gladly have paid Wednesday £3 to let me play. Nothing was more frustrating than to be selected as twelfth man and forced to stand on the touchline watching the other lads play. In that era before substitutes were permitted there was no way of getting onto the pitch if you weren't in the starting line-up.

Officially I wasn't even allowed to join in a six-a-side kickabout in Firth Park but, though I probably shouldn't have done so, there were several occasions when I could not resist the lure of a makeshift game on an unmarked pitch with some of my old mates.

Happily, once my four-weeks 'exile' ended I got back into the Yorkshire League side and played fairly regularly. Indeed, the fact that I hit twenty-five goals in eighteen 'A' team appearances and gained promotion to the Central League side, for whom I scored five times in seven outings, confirms I was making reasonable progress. The only pity was finding myself called up for National Service towards the end of that first season.

Certainly it was fulfilling to be playing on Saturdays and training at Hillsborough on two evenings every week. The training sessions comprised little more than running round the perimeter of the main pitch but it seemed to me then to be a wonderful way of life and I revelled in the atmosphere. Mind you, if I harboured any romantic notions in those early days, there was always a realist called Johnny Logan to bring me down to earth.

Many people nowadays will know little or nothing of Johnny Logan, but those of us who knew him well remember him not only with great affection but as one of football's genuine characters. As the saying goes, they threw the mould away after making Johnny. He was definitely a one-off, totally unforgettable, and I would not hesitate to describe him as the first major influence on my career.

As a fan I had watched Johnny, stocky and strong, perform in his familiar role as a tough and tenacious wing-half. A product of Durham, he had served Charlton and Darlington, then played over 300 games for Barnsley between 1937 and 1946. During the war, incidentally, he went back to work as a miner. Unfortunately, after moving from Oakwell to help in Wednesday's successful battle to avoid relegation to the Third Division North in 1946–47, he was limited to only a handful of Football League outings, but he was always the kind of player respected and appreciated by his fellow professionals because he was invariably in the thick of the action and readily undertook the donkey work for players regarded as 'stars'. In fact, Johnny's senior career was all but over when I arrived at Hillsborough but he was to prove a fine servant to the club for twenty years until February 1967, with much of his best work done behind the scenes and away from the limelight.

Johnny was in charge of the 'A' team in which I started my Wednesday career and to say he was a tough taskmaster would be an understatement. He was then just past his mid-thirties but he was still playing and doing so with the fierce passion, uncompromising spirit and enthusiasm that epitomised his character. He was a one-hundred per cent performer who believed in playing it hard, expecting everybody else to do the same. His comments and frequent criticisms of those who gave less than total commitment were invariably delivered in a language I can only describe as very colourful.

Johnny was okay if you gave him the commitment and effort he demanded but he was seldom generous with his praise and not often very sympathetic. For quite a long time in my early days with Wednesday I was convinced he didn't like me. No matter how well I thought I had done on occasions, he always seemed more ready to find fault than to give me a good word.

However, in later years when I enjoyed some success at senior level, nobody took more pride in what I achieved than Johnny, and I like to think he knew I was grateful for the guidance he had given me in my early days. It's only when you look back with the benefit of experience that you identify the people who made a crucial contribution to your development. I put Johnny firmly in that category.

When Johnny joined Wednesday he continued to live in the Barnsley area, and I remember he was always especially keen for us to do well whenever we played in any of the mining districts where he was known as an old Oakwell man. Once, for instance, when we played Wombwell, who were then top of the Yorkshire League, he told us in no uncertain terms that we had better beat 'this lot' or he wouldn't be able to face his pals in his local pub that evening.

Wombwell had a few 'stars' in their team, including Lol Boyes, brother of the old West Brom and Everton man, Wally, but we romped to a comfortable win. I think the margin of our victory was 6–1 and I bagged three goals. I came off feeling very pleased with myself and expected Johnny to express delight at my hat-trick. Alas, he could only say: 'Tha should have had six goals, just look at them tha missed!'

As a teenager you tend to think this kind of reaction is harsh and unfeeling, but with hindsight I can see that Johnny, like my dad, was determined to keep my feet on the ground.

Certainly the 'Logan treatment' ensured I didn't start thinking I was doing Wednesday a favour by playing for them. I soon learned that football is a game in which you have to take the knocks in your stride—and that includes accepting verbal 'stick' when you don't deserve it. Once you endured a lashing from Johnny's tongue you couldn't be hurt by criticism from anybody else!

I have never forgotten a match against Scunthorpe when I earned a typical 'roasting' from Johnny after missing a penalty. Johnny had invited me to take the kick after I had been brought down by a centre-half called Millington but I made the mistake of letting the goalkeeper put me off with a deliberate exercise in gamesmanship.

When I placed the ball on the spot, I did so with the lace facing the goalkeeper. However, when I turned to pace out my run-up, the goalkeeper, a man called Poxon, walked from his line and turned the lace of the ball to face me. So I promptly walked back and replaced the ball as it had been before. Once again Poxon left his line and repeated his earlier act. This time I complained to the referee, who ordered Poxon to stay on his line. For a third time I placed the ball with the lace facing the goalkeeper. Then I walked back, turned, ran in and contrived to hit the ball with such force that it trickled across the goalmouth and Poxon had to walk three yards to pick it up!

Johnny, who could swear like a trooper even at his most placid, did not exactly mince his words when saying what he thought of my performance. He vowed it was the last penalty I would take as long as he was in charge of the team.

In fact, he did later have a change of heart and it was typical of him that he chose to do so in order to give me the chance of completing what I think was my first Yorkshire League hat-trick. The game was against Sheffield United at the B & C ground at Shiregreen. I had already claimed two goals when, five minutes from the end, I was brought down in the box. Johnny, jumping from the bench, shouted from the touchline that I had to take the spot-kick. There was no way I was going to risk missing this one and I belted the ball with such force that it went in even though the goalkeeper got a hand to it.

Johnny was not a man without heart or a sense of humour, but he was invariably reluctant to show sympathy, and all the more so if he felt you didn't deserve it. There was a famous occasion when I was knocked out no fewer than four times in a Yorkshire League game against Bradford Park Avenue, yet Johnny staunchly refused to feel sorry for me.

That day I came face to face with a defender called Bob Danskin, a tough and wily old-timer who had forgotten more about football than I had then begun to learn. Bob knew all the tricks and he was far too wise to let me turn our duel into a running match when he knew he hadn't the legs to match my speed. He marked me so tightly that every time I got the ball and tried to turn and go past him I simply ran smack into his fifteen-stone frame. The man was built solid as a rock! Every time I crashed into Bob I ended up on the floor nursing a sore head. On four occasions I was out for the count and it took a dose of Logan's 'magic sponge' to bring me round. At the end I walked off feeling battered, bruised and a little bit sorry for myself, but there was no consoling word from Johnny.

'Perhaps you've learned your so-and-so lesson' he snapped. 'How many times have I told you there's your inside man to lay the ball off to? But no, you've got to learn the hard way with a bloody nose every few minutes. If you've not got the so-and-so sense to use your loaf, you don't deserve sympathy.'

Johnny was not without a touch of wit, though some of the younger lads didn't always appreciate his sharp humour, especially when his comments were laced with a few choice 'blue' words.

We had a lad called Freddie Fox, who was a fair player with some clever touches. However, once when Freddie deliberately let a crossfield pass go through his legs to Johnny, who was standing behind him, the move broke down because Johnny was completely taken by surprise. 'Who the hell do you think I am, one of the **** Pinningtons?' he shouted. (The Pinningtons, I should explain, were a popular mind-reading act of the period.)

Johnny was a player-coach who continued to perform his off-the-field duties even when he was playing in the team and, amusing as it might seem, he considered it quite normal that he should switch from player to trainer and give treatment to an injured player during a match. One day, I recall, one of our lads was knocked out and Johnny shouted to the twelfth man to bring on the 'magic' sponge. Instead of simply dashing on with the sponge in its cut bladder, as was the custom, the youngster carted the water bucket on as well. He could not understand why Johnny asked him if he hadn't more sense than to see he only required the sponge not the full bucket of water!

Apart from Johnny Logan, the other key figure in my earliest years at Hillsborough was Tommy Walker, a pre-war Wednesday full-back who was in charge of the reserves. Tommy, who served the club from 1926 to 1967, was as different from Johnny as it was possible to be. While Johnny was blunt, outspoken and didn't care who witnessed his verbal blasts at an individual, Tommy was the quieter type who preferred to sit with you and discuss any criticisms privately. I found his personal touch and constant encouragement very helpful, and I had good cause to be grateful to him, especially when I had my initial taste of Central League football in my first season.

Like Johnny Logan, Tommy took great pride in my later success and he was the first member of the backroom staff to suggest to Eric Taylor, the manager, that I deserved a run in the first team. Indeed, but for Tommy's intervention, I might well have been transferred to Aston Villa before I was given my big chance, for early in the 1949–50 season, with a deal in the offing, he told the boss it would be a mistake to sell me. 'Keep the lad, you might need him' he said.

Thank goodness Eric Taylor listened to Tommy. However, before that happened, my first three years on Wednesday's books had been interrupted by a two-year spell of National Service in the Royal Air Force.

Here I am at 18, a time when I was just starting to make some progress with Wednesday but it was interrupted by the arrival of my call-up papers, which meant two years in the RAF.

Chapter Eight

National Service
1948–1950

It was not without irony that, just when I was starting to get into Wednesday's reserves and seemed poised to finish my first season as a part-time professional on a positive note, I was called up for National Service. Of course, having celebrated my eighteenth birthday shortly before Christmas in 1947 the arrival of my call-up papers was no surprise. However, like many other teenagers in that era of conscription, I resented what I saw as an unnecessary interruption in my career and went off to join the Royal Air Force with more than a little reluctance.

I still remember those two years in the RAF as a waste of time in terms of my football ambitions. I often wondered whether my Wednesday career might have developed more quickly if I had not had to do National Service. After joining up in February 1948 I think I managed fewer than ten games with Wednesday in my first year in the RAF. As only one of these matches was in the Central League side it is not difficult to appreciate why I felt my progress had come to a full stop. It only compounded my disappointment that my first posting took me to Yatesbury where for three months I never got near a football pitch and had to settle for playing hockey, while my second posting did little to improve my opportunities for football.

It is amusing now to reflect that the RAF wanted me to sign up for three years though there was no way they were likely to persuade me to serve an extra year. I ended up training as a radar mechanic although, to be honest, I rather fancied becoming a PT instructor. Unfortunately, the men who made the decisions claimed I lacked the necessary qualifications. I was probably clutching at straws when I pointed to the modest physical training badge and certificate I had gained with the YMCA and suggested this, and my experience as a part-time professional, ought to count for something. To my dismay if not to my surprise, the officer who interviewed me was not impressed.

I did my initial training and square-bashing at Bridgenorth and was then posted to Yatesbury to undertake a three-months course in air radar. As I have mentioned, my only sports activity in this spell was a few games of hockey and my solitary souvenir of that frustrating phase was a painful cut above an eye when someone caught me with his 'jolly' stick!

I did hope for better things when I was posted to RAF Kinloss, near Elgin in North Scotland, but once again it proved difficult to get a game of football. I ought to have known things weren't going to go as I wanted when I found myself on ground radar after having trained in air radar. However, the most important question I wanted answering on my arrival was what the chances were of playing football. The PTI sergeant said the station had a team but stressed it was a good one, and his tone suggested he didn't think I had any chance of breaking into it.

Blue is still the colour, but now it's Airman Dooley.

As I feared I never got a look-in and it is probably a fair summing up of my three months at Kinloss to describe it as a dead loss. Things didn't go right almost from the outset. I had not been there much more than a month when I had an accident. Running for shelter through the rain one day I slipped. Putting an arm out to break my fall, I saw my hand smash through a glass window. I ended up in hospital with a gashed thumb and forearm.

A happy consolation, however, came when, after a week in hospital, I was sent home on leave. Once back in Sheffield, I was more than content to be playing football again, even with my arm strapped up. I enjoyed myself immensely and it was a nice bonus to earn appearance money as well as being back in Wednesday's colours. Unfortunately, I made the misjudgement of believing all I had to do to prolong my leave was to keep supplying the camp with a regular doctor's note supplied by the Owls' club doctor, Andrew Stephen. Then one day, out of the blue, a telegram arrived at Addison Road bearing the stark warning that if I was not back at RAF Kinloss within twenty-four hours I would be posted AWOL (absent without leave). I doubt if I ever packed my kit bag and caught a train as quickly as on that occasion!

In fact, there was some welcome news awaiting me on my return to the camp for I learned I had been posted to RAF Leuchars, near Dundee, with immediate effect. This proved to be my last posting for I spent the rest of my National Service at this Coastal Command base. It marked the start of the happiest phase of my time in the RAF.

Amusingly, my first day on the camp coincided with an incident which, at the time, made me wonder what I had walked into. The place was deserted when I arrived—it transpired everyone was on holiday for twenty-four hours. The NCO on guard duty told me which billet I was in and, after depositing my kit there, I adjourned to the NAAFI. I decided to have an early night and I had just got between the sheets when the door suddenly burst open and three men, quite literally, fell into the room. One man was holding a corporal while the other kept hitting him with his fists. I hadn't a clue what it was all about or who this trio were but I had no hesitation in jumping to the aid of the poor chap who was outnumbered and firmly on the receiving end. It was only in retrospect that I could see how funny it must have looked. There I stood in my pyjamas, tapping on the shoulder the big lad who was hitting the corporal when, to my astonishment, he turned and pulled out a cut-throat razor!

I was always able to move pretty fast in those days but I reckon I would have claimed an Olympic record for sprinting that night. Thank goodness a nearby window was wide open for I dashed and threw myself through it, then made haste to hide in the cookhouse. Later I crept back and found the mysterious threesome had disappeared. I never did learn what the episode was all about.

After that, I found life at Leuchars eventful but fairly normal and I knew I would not find it difficult to make the best of my time there once I discovered the camp not only had good football facilities but a station team in which I quickly found a regular place.

We played in the RAF Cup and the Senior Cup, and it was a happy coincidence that in the first round of the latter competition we happened to be paired with RAF Kinloss. When the Kinloss lads flew in and I spotted the PTI sergeant who had not considered me good enough to play in his team I had all the incentive I needed to want to excel on this occasion. I have long since forgotten the name of the PTI and I doubt if I would know him if I should ever meet him again, but I shall always remember how keen I was to show him what he had missed.

On the day of the match a gale-force wind was blowing and we had the good fortune to have it on our backs in the first half. When the half-time whistle blew we were leading 5–0 and I had scored all the goals. Alas, it was a different story in the second period as Kinloss hit back to make it 5–5. However, I ensured a story-book finale when, towards the end of the game, I burst through from the half-way line and, with the strong wind almost blowing me over backwards, I somehow managed to deliver a hard shot and squeeze the ball over the goal-line from about five yards.

After the game I was still savouring the sweetness of that success when an officer who had travelled with the Kinloss team asked me why he had never seen me play during my time there. I said it was because the PTI sergeant had not thought I was good enough and had never given me a chance. I often wonder what the two of them talked about on the way home and how my old adversary explained his reasons for denying me a trial run in the side!

The Leuchars team I played in boasted some decent players. Unfortunately, I have forgotten most of the names but I do remember an inside-right called Barney Banks who hailed from Wigan. Nobody looked less like an athlete than Barney but he could certainly play football. He was one of the key figures in the side that reached the final of the RAF Senior Cup in my first season at Leuchars. One of my happiest memories of that run was a terrific triumph over RAF Weeton. As Weeton boasted seven professionals they were the overwhelming favourites, but we romped to a 4–1 victory.

As always, I could never get enough football and I was invariably frustrated whenever anything cropped up which might deny me the chance

On duty with RAF Leuchars in 1949–50. I am fourth from the left in the back row, and the officer with the ball between his feet is Group Captain Forbes.

of a game. There was, for instance, one occasion when the camp's annual sports day coincided with the same Wednesday afternoon when we had an important fixture in the Dundee Half-Day League. Happily, despite all my fears, I managed to fulfil all my scheduled races and still get away in time to play in the match. Participation in the sports day was compulsory, but to my relief the 100 yards, the 220 yards and the long jump, the events in which I had to compete, were staged early in the programme. As I recall, I won medals in all three but then forsook the chance of bidding for the Victor Ludorum by getting permission to leave early with just enough time to make the football match.

It is not generally known that I actually played for Dundee United during my spell at RAF Leuchars and they were impressed enough by my debut to start talking about signing me on. They didn't know I was already on Sheffield Wednesday's books as a part-time professional and I didn't enlighten them. I simply said I was unable to accept their offer and left it at that.

In fact, when Dundee United asked me to play for them in a friendly against St Andrew's University, I was a bit concerned about the ethics of the situation. I certainly wasn't sure about the regulations. I sought the advice of my senior officer at the camp. He said that, as at that time I was an RAF man and not a professional footballer, I had to do what the RAF wanted. I think it was regarded as something of an honour for the camp that one of their men had been invited to assist a Scottish League club.

I suppose Dundee United subsequently learned a bit more about their guest centre-forward and they were good enough to remember me a few years later when I lost my leg. One of the first telegrams to arrive just happened to be from them!

The Leuchars team again reached the final of the RAF Senior Cup in my second season at the camp but, unfortunately, by the time the game came round I was on demob leave and so didn't play. The irony of it all was that not only did the people at Leuchars want me to play but I was prepared to give up some of my leave to do so. Just before I went on leave the officer in charge of the camp, Group Captain Forbes, asked me if I could defer my demob in order to play. He promised me some stripes if I would do so. I think it was the first time the man had ever spoken to me and I was flattered. I said I was happy to leave the RAF a plain Airman and wanted to depart on schedule. However, I told him I would be happy to travel from Sheffield for the game, which was at Chester. Forbes was delighted with the compromise and arranged for travelling details to be sent to me by telegram but, unfortunately, when I put the proposal to Wednesday they made it plain they didn't want me to play. As I didn't want to do anything which might damage my prospects at Hillsborough, I wired RAF Leuchars to say I couldn't join them after all.

I said farewell to the RAF soon after Christmas 1949 with my formal demob taking effect in February, 1950. Of course, I was delighted to return to civilian life and I was especially keen to pick up the threads of my football career again. All the same I went home with many fond memories of my National Service. A spell in the Forces was not something I would have chosen, but the experience did me no harm and I think Derek Dooley at twenty was much more mature than the raw recruit he had been two years earlier.

Moreover, I had made a lot of friends in the RAF and I have never forgotten my best pal at Leuchars. He was a lad called Dickie Phelan, who hailed from Slough. I remember him as a real Cockney, a cheeky, lively chap who was a really good mate. Curiously, he had little interest in football but we kept in touch after our return to civvy street and the last time I saw him was when I arranged for him to have a couple of tickets for a Wednesday match at Arsenal in which I was playing. He brought his girlfriend along, and we enjoyed a brief chat about old times. Sadly, some six months later I had a telephone call from his girlfriend. She told me Dickie had died in a motorcycle accident.

Chapter Nine

Full-time Blues

When I came home at the end of my National Service in the early weeks of 1950, I didn't know what was going to happen in terms of my Wednesday career. I believed I was doing well enough to justify being offered a switch from a part-time to a full-time contract and that was my goal. However, initially, an air of uncertainty prevailed and it was a question of being patient and waiting to see how the situation developed.

As I had a fortnight's demob leave, I used those two weeks to experience my first taste of full-time training at Hillsborough. In the meantime, I popped in to see Ernest Ward at Alfred Peters & Sons to let him know I was back home. My parents, aware of the benefits of secure employment, urged me to resume my job as a deaf-aid mechanic and, as I told Ernest, I was anxious to keep my hand in. Happily, Ernest appreciated the position in which he knew I was hoping to get the nod from Wednesday. He told me to 'play it by ear' and turn up at the firm whenever I could. 'Don't worry, Derek' he said. 'We'll work something out.'

As I noted earlier, Ernest Ward and the people at Alfred Peters were always remarkably understanding and encouraging. Some employers would have forced me to make a choice between them and football but that was not Ernest's way. In the end we had an arrangement which lasted for the next couple of years whereby I went into work at the firm's Fargate premises on most weekday afternoons until I had firmly established myself as a Wednesday first-teamer.

Even when I got my wish to become a full-time professional, I looked forward to those sessions at the workbench because, with a footballer's training spanning little more than three hours in the mornings, it was good to have something practical and useful with which to occupy the rest of the working day.

It wasn't really a matter of earning a few extra shillings, more a case of wanting to make sensible use of the generous spare time I suddenly found at my disposal. Time could, if one allowed it, hang heavily on one's hands, and there was a lot mischief that young people could get up to when they had nothing better to do and didn't know how to fill the day. I always felt it was more difficult for the single lads, especially those without a trade or an interest outside of the game. The married players, of course, usually went off home and lost themselves in family duties.

Having another job to occupy my mind was ideal. Later, I admit, I welcomed the freedom to be able to spend some afternoons playing tennis and, naturally, I especially enjoyed those carefree Friday afternoons when a group of us would while away a few hours in Marsden's snack bar on Pinstone Street and finish up trying out all the latest 'pop' records in Wilson Peck's shop at the corner of Leopold Street.

Of course, when I became a full-time professional, it constituted a dramatic change in my routine, and while I revelled in the role it took time to adjust to a way of life which was different from anything I had known before. It was quite a novelty to have most Mondays off and to have to train only from 10 am to 1 pm on the other days. I always looked forward to the Tuesday practice matches. Naturally, being keen to improve my game, I didn't need any persuading to volunteer for an extra couple of hours in the afternoons. I was so keen that even when I was instructed to do extra training I felt the backroom staff were doing me a favour!

Incidentally, one bonus of being a full-timer was that, if you got to the ground early and had an hour or so before training started, you could enjoy a game of snooker. One of my colleagues then was Ivor Seemley, who lived at Shiregreen. Most mornings I used to catch a tram to Firth Park, walk up Sicey Avenue to Hatfield House Lane to meet Ivor, and then we travelled down to Hillsborough on the Outer Circle bus. We always ensured we were first on the snooker table!

Back in those first weeks after my demob, I wasn't too sure about my prospects of being invited to turn full-time. I knew I was doing fairly well but the proverbial question mark still hung over my head. I think I ended the 1949–50 season with fourteen goals in fifteen Central League games, and I remember that a particularly successful spell in December and January, coinciding as it did with my impending farewell to the RAF, gave me cause to think I might be on the brink of a significant step forward.

There were a couple of games in this period which especially boosted my confidence. The one in which I helped us to a 2–0 victory when facing Everton's famous veteran Welsh international centre-half, Tommy

The snooker table at Hillsborough was always a big attraction. Here I am displaying my Joe Davis style to team-mates 'Mick' Kenny, Keith Bannister, Eddie Gannon and Dave McIntosh.

G. Jones, earned me a good write–up in the local papers. Jones was just about at the end of a distinguished career in which he had collected seventeen caps but he was still a very astute and classy defender. The other game, which saw me claim a hat-trick despite the attentions of Aston Villa's experienced defender Amos Moss, prompted a headline in the *Sheffield Telegraph* which read: 'Dooley is a leader to note'.

In fact, I had already notched a treble in an earlier meeting with Villa, which no doubt explains why they were prompted to try to sign me. I believe the fee Villa offered was £5,000 and I think Wednesday were tempted. However, this was the famous occasion when Tommy Walker, the reserve team trainer, made a bee-line for Eric Taylor's office and begged the boss not to sell me.

It was probably Tommy Walker's backing that finally persuaded Eric Taylor to offer me full-time terms, though the interest of other clubs might have influenced the decision. Eric was a canny man and I wouldn't be surprised if he intended to take the step weeks before it happened but chose to see if the delay prompted any reaction from me. It was typical of Eric that he said nothing immediately after my demob but, as nobody else said anything either, I was left to sweat and wonder. Perhaps the club felt it would save them a few pounds if they delayed the decision. Anyway, one day I plucked up the courage to knock on Eric's door and ask if I was getting a full-time contract. 'Of course' he said, as if he was surprised I didn't know!

My first wage was £8 a week with £10 when I played in the first-team. Unfortunately, if I thought this development would see my career suddenly take off, I was to be disappointed. The record books show that between March, 1950 and September, 1951, I made just two first-team appearances, flopped on both occasions, and spent most of what seemed a long and frustrating phase playing with the reserves and, worse, at times finding myself back in the third team.

I was left in no doubt that becoming a full-time professional certainly did not guarantee success, and I must admit there were moments when I was in total despair.

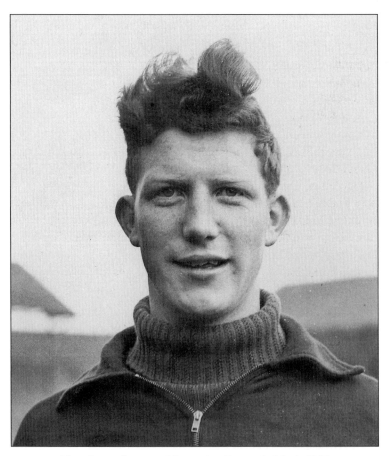

All set for my first-team debut against Preston in March 1950.

As it happened I didn't have long to wait for my first appearance in the senior side. I was called up for my Second Division debut in the home match with Preston North End on Saturday, 11th March, 1950. Unfortunately, the game itself proved rather an anti-climax, a disappointment for the team as well as me personally. Even so I have never forgotten the occasion and the circumstances surrounding it, for nothing quite compares with one's first experience of the 'big time'.

Wednesday were not doing too well at the time and, with just three points from the previous six games, their promotion push was faltering. They had slipped to third in the table, fifteen points behind the runaway leaders Tottenham and three in arrears of second-placed Sheffield United. The loss of Hugh Swift, an outstanding left-back, with a broken jaw, and winger Dennis Woodhead, with a broken leg, had hardly helped the cause, while Redfern Froggatt was having trouble with an injury that dogged him all season. Eric Taylor had sought to strengthen the team with such recent signings as Gerry Henry from Bradford Park Avenue and Hugh McJarrow from Chesterfield. Gerry and Hugh were both inside-forwards. With improvements in attack the priority, there had been talk of Wednesday trying to persuade Barnsley to part with Chilean-born centre-forward George Robledo. George went instead to Newcastle, where he was a big success.

I had been banging in a few goals in the reserves, and, on the previous Saturday, scored twice, including the last-minute winner, in an exciting 4–3 defeat of West Brom reserves in front of a 5,000 Hillsborough crowd. Tommy Walker was not the only person who felt I was ready for a run in the first eleven, but the boss was only induced to give me my opportunity when Clarrie Jordan, our regular centre-forward, suffered a knee problem which was destined to sideline him for about twelve months.

When the news broke that Clarrie might need an operation, local football writers Fred Walters and 'Dick' Sparling were soon speculating that my moment had come. I suspected they had probably been tipped off by the boss. However, I didn't dare to believe it until Eric Taylor called me into his office to confirm my selection. I couldn't wait to get home and tell my parents. For two days I walked about with my head in the clouds and my stomach churning with that nervous tension called 'butterflies'. I still remember quite vividly the events of the day of the game, from setting out from home on the tramcar, the pre-match meal at the Athol Hotel in the city centre, and the taxi ride to the ground an hour or so before the kick-off.

Riding in the taxi was a novelty I savoured and, as the vehicle reached the stadium and nosed through the large crowd outside the players' entrance, I felt like royalty. The attendance at Hillsborough that day was 49,222, and it was a long way from being the biggest of the season.

For the record, Wednesday's team featured Dave McIntosh in goal, with Vin Kenny and Keith Bannister at full-back, Edgar Packard at centre-half and Eddie Gannon and Doug Witcomb at wing-half. Jackie Marriott and little Walter Rickett were on the wings, with Gerry Henry and Redfern Froggatt at inside-forward.

Preston had a very good side at the time and their team featured the legendary Tom Finney on the right wing, Tommy Docherty at right-half, and Eddie Quigley at inside-left. Quigley, of course, had been a Wednesday player at the start of the season before Preston paid £26,000, which was then a British record fee, for him in December 1949. I should mention that the centre-half I was facing that afternoon was a man called Harold Mattinson.

I think Doug Witcomb, a Welsh international, was our captain at the time, and I recall that Doug and one or two of the other senior players did their best to put me at ease in the dressing room before the game. Incidentally, this was probably one of the first games in which trainer Sam Powell was in sole charge in the dressing room, for, sadly, Billy Knox, the club's trainer-coach, had collapsed and died at the ground only a few weeks earlier.

I don't remember much about the game other than that I didn't get many kicks and the team didn't play well. The windy conditions didn't help but I don't think that was much excuse. Tom Finney, who later suffered a fractured cheekbone in a clash of heads with Keith Bannister, cashed in on a misjudgement by Dave McIntosh to nod Preston in front from a corner-kick after only eleven minutes. It proved the only goal of the afternoon.

'Dick' Sparling said in his *Sheffield Telegraph* report that he didn't think I was ripe for League football, but the most relevant point he made was in suggesting I had lacked support. Certainly I didn't get the service I had expected and, having been so desperate to do well, it was bitterly disappointing when things didn't work out and I was unable to do myself justice.

I don't suppose I was surprised when I was dropped for the next game and Hugh McJarrow, who was really an inside-forward, was given an eleven-match run in the number nine shirt. However, I did feel it was a bit unjust to be denied an immediate second chance. Okay, I lacked polish and may have looked awkward and out of place at times, but I think a player needs at least forty-five minutes to adjust to the pace of League football on his debut, and it would have done my confidence a lot of good to have been told I was keeping my place for at least one more game.

I went back to the reserves the following week, then found myself briefly demoted to the Yorkshire League team. I knew I probably faced another long wait for a further chance, although I did figure in what was ostensibly the first-team again right at the end of the 1949–50 season when I was chosen to play in the final of the Scunthorpe Hospital Cup at the Old Show Ground. We beat Scunthorpe, then a Midland League club poised for election to the Football League in the summer of 1950, by a 2–1 margin, and I got one of the goals.

It is relevant to note that, while I was playing out the latter weeks of the season in the reserves, the first-team did go on to clinch promotion, doing so by the narrowest of margins as they pipped Sheffield United and Southampton by a .008 superior goal-average. Wednesday won five and lost only one of their final eleven games and snatched a place in the top grade for the first time since 1937 thanks to a famous 0–0 draw with Second Division champions Tottenham in the last game of the season.

I shared in the delight of that last-day triumph, watching the Spurs match from the players' pen. Wednesday had ended a thirteen-year wait for a return to the elite and I hoped it might not be too long before I got the chance to play for them in the First Division.

Chapter Ten

Second Chance

The 1950–51 campaign was my first complete season as a full-time professional and I hoped I might profit from the experience of a sustained spell of pre-season work and begin to benefit from regular full-time training. I knew I could not have wished for a better way of life and it was wonderful to be in a job in which I was paid to develop my physical fitness and play football, but unfortunately this proved to be a season in which I hoped for so much and ended up feeling I had achieved precious little.

I had to wait until January for a second chance in the first-team, but once again things didn't go well. It was little consolation that I scored twenty goals in twenty-six Central League games and helped the third team win both the Yorkshire League title and the Yorkshire League Cup.

In fact, I played for the third team only seven times that season and I suppose I must have enjoyed those games because I notched twenty-one goals, including eight in one match against Halifax. Naturally, I gave nothing less than total commitment no matter which team I played for. All the same I couldn't help feeling the Yorkshire League was a bit of a comedown for a Central League regular who aspired to a first-team place.

As I remember, the match against Halifax at Owlerton Stadium in late September came only a few days after I had played in the reserves in front of a 5,000 crowd at Hillsborough. With only about half-a-dozen spectators in the stadium the contrast could hardly have been greater, and I remember our full-back Norman Jackson, who had also been dropped from the reserves, asking what we were doing there. 'Come on' he said, 'Let's show 'em we deserve something better.'

The eight goals I scored set a Yorkshire League record which, I think, was subsequently only equalled by one man, Geoff Robinson of Sheffield

FC. Unfortunately, it didn't ensure permanent promotion back to the reserves. As I recall, I went back into the Central League team, enjoyed a decent run of success, then belatedly got another chance in the first-team. Alas, I was so dismayed by my second senior failure that it affected my game and within a couple of weeks I was back in the Yorkshire League side.

Incidentally, six of my twenty-one goals for the Yorkshire League side came in two cup games. I notched a hat-trick in a semi-final success against Norton Woodseats, at the time one of the best teams in the Sheffield area, and followed up with a treble in the final against Farsley Celtic at Hillsborough. I collected a miniature trophy to mark our YL Cup final triumph, yet, strange as it might seem, I didn't qualify for a championship medal despite bagging fifteen Yorkshire League goals! Eric Taylor said five appearances were not enough to qualify for a medal.

My second chance in the first-team, for the trip to Charlton in mid-January, came at a moment when Wednesday were struggling badly and found themselves stuck at the foot of the First Division table following a mere six wins in twenty-five games. Hugh McJarrow had worn the number nine shirt for most of the season but, in a desperate search for a winning formula, Gerry Henry had been switched into the position for a few games. When the club failed in a bid to sign Willie McIntosh, the Scottish centre-forward who was being kept out of Blackpool's team by the brilliance of Stan Mortensen, McJarrow resumed the role.

However, when Redfern Froggett's ever-present run was ended by an injury sustained against Arsenal, McJarrow was switched to inside-left and I was called up for the date at Charlton. The experience of joining the senior lads for a week at Blackpool put me in good spirits and I revelled in the prospect of my first-ever trip to London, but, sadly, by the time we were travelling home to Sheffield I wasn't feeling quite so happy.

Once again the problem was I just couldn't get into the game and it was not really much consolation that I was involved in the scramble which led to Dennis Woodhead hitting our equaliser halfway through the second half. Charlton, having led through a lad called Riley Cullum, snatched victory two minutes from the end when Hans Jepson, a Swede, pounced to shoot past goalkeeper Albert Morton.

My most abiding memory of the game is my duel with Sam Bartram, the veteran Charlton goalkeeper. Sam was not only an outstanding performer, he was one of football's biggest personalities, a great showman and certainly the finest uncapped goalkeeper of his era. Sam was a Charlton legend, making 623 appearances for them between 1934 and 1956. On that January day in 1951 he was within a week of his thirty-seventh birthday but I doubt if there was a fitter and more agile goalkeeper in the game.

He was quick to tell me 'I'm too good for you' and I had no doubt he was right. My two best shots were saved by Sam with contemptuous ease—he enjoyed frustrating and taunting a raw youngster like me. Once, for instance, he made a save, deliberately dropped the ball, and started dribbling outside his penalty area. He was clearly inviting me to make a challenge, but, when I did, he left himself with just enough time to belt the ball into touch.

Apart from barging into the referee, Bill Evans, and flattening him, I made no impact at all, and I wasn't entirely surprised to find myself back in the reserves the following week. When I was then demoted into the third team, I feared it might signal the end of my Wednesday career. Indeed, I started to fear my survival as a professional footballer was under serious threat, and, with the outlook continuing gloomy, my self-esteem was lower in the early months of 1951 than at any time in my days as a player.

While I was nursing my wounded pride, Wednesday continued to struggle in the First Division and suffered relegation despite a famous 6–0 defeat of Everton on the last day of the season. It was not without irony that my pal Dennis Woodhead, one of the best wingers in the business, was used as a makeshift centre-forward in the final nine games. In fact, Dennis didn't do badly at all in the number nine shirt for he claimed eight goals, but it was not quite enough.

Soon after my solitary first-team outing, Eric Taylor went in search of an experienced centre-forward. The club was linked with several 'big names' including Jessie Pye, a seasoned campaigner from Wolves, but the deals kept collapsing.

Around this time, too, the boss also made an audacious bid to sign Jimmy Hagan from Sheffield United. A £32,000 fee, which would have been a British record, was agreed but, in the event, Hagan, one of the finest inside-forwards of his era and a legend at Bramall Lane, rejected a move which would have been one of the most sensational in local football history.

Subsequently, Wednesday did break the transfer record by signing a young inside-forward called Jackie Sewell from Notts County just before the mid-March deadline. Jackie, who cost what was then a staggering £35,000, was unable to prevent the club from dropping back into the Second Division. However, a time would soon come when I was glad to have him playing alongside me and helping me to finally prove I could make the grade.

Of course, in the early months of 1951 I did not know my fortunes would soon take a turn for the better. Indeed, it is not without irony that, just about the time I found myself back in the Yorkshire League team within a fortnight of tasting the First Division, Eric Taylor made a 'signing' which was destined to have positive long-term implications for me.

The man Eric recruited was a new coach called Alan Brown, a former Huddersfield and Burnley centre-half who had drifted away from the game and was running a café when he was persuaded to fill the Hillsborough vacancy caused by the death of Billy Knox. 'Brownie' was a tough, no-nonsense North Easterner who was a hard taskmaster, and, while he was never an easy man to get to know, I eventually found I got along with him very well. It was not easy to gain his respect but he became one of my staunchest supporters. Indeed, I doubt if anyone did more to encourage my development and improve my game.

I have to admit it was not difficult to get on the wrong side of Alan Brown and I managed to do exactly that not long after his arrival in Sheffield. It was in the spell when I often found myself back in the Yorkshire League team, but on this particular occasion he chose to deny me the opportunity to play even at that level!

One holiday weekend when we were scheduled to travel to face Scarborough, Ivor Seemley and I went to catch the Outer Circle bus on Hatfield House Lane. As always, we were in good time to get to Hillsborough and join up with the team coach, but, for some reason, the Corporation bus didn't turn up. By the time we started out to walk to the ground we were well aware of being in danger of arriving too late. When we got to Fir Vale, I stopped at the Post Office and asked the man there to phone the ground and explain we were about to walk the length of Herries Road. Could the coach head towards us? We had gone as far as the roundabout near the Forum Cinema at Southey when we spotted the team-bus coming towards us. To my dismay, I noticed Alan Brown sitting on the front seat. As the first-team was without a game, obviously he had decided to watch the Yorkshire League side.

I wasn't entirely surprised when both Ivor and I received a strongly-worded dressing down but I soon realised that Alan was much angrier with me than Ivor. Alan didn't want to hear my explanation and I sensed this was not the end of the story. My fears were confirmed when, in the dressing room at Scarborough, I had started to strip off, and Alan asked: 'What are you doing?' I told him I was getting changed. He said: 'But you're not playing. If you can't get to the ground in time, you can't play'.

I noticed he had not said anything to Ivor Seemley, who was changing into a number six shirt on the other side of the dressing room. I learned later that Alan had brought along a lad called Hill, whom he wanted to have a look at, and my misdemeanour had provided him with the perfect excuse to replace me.

When I got to the ground the next morning, I tried again to explain to Alan what had happened, and to emphasise that it wasn't my fault. He just gave me an icy look and said: 'I don't want to listen'.

If that incident didn't get us off on the right footing, I ended up full of admiration for Alan Brown's patience, persistence and support for me. I think he saw that, whatever shortcomings I had as a player, the one thing I didn't lack was a determination to work to improve myself. I never hesitated to volunteer for extra practice sessions, and Alan spent countless hours working with me on that modest little pitch behind the old north stand. He was brilliant with the pressure training, arranging for balls to be delivered from left and right in quick succession. The idea was for me to turn and whack the ball first time towards the goal. Frankly, it was some weeks before I got it right, and there was one day when everything that could go wrong did. I stood on the ball and fell on my backside, hit another ball over the houses and into Vere Road, and seldom seemed capable of making a half-decent connection because my eye and feet weren't synchronising. My lack of co-ordination was driving 'Brownie' potty!

Alan Brown...He showed great patience with me and was a tremendous help in my early development.

In those days, Alan invariably swore like a trooper and his vocabulary included every swear word you ever heard. He must have used every expletive he knew to describe my display that afternoon, and, when I walked back across the main pitch towards the dressing room, I felt totally dejected. I was sure 'Brownie' would lose interest in me. Suddenly, he appeared behind me, put an arm round my shoulder, and said: 'Don't worry, Derek, we'll sort it out. We all have our bad days. Let's try again tomorrow'.

I was always immensely grateful for the huge amount of time he gave me then, and later. We worked on my weaker left foot for what seemed endless hours, then Alan turned his attention to improving my heading. In the following months we also rounded off training sessions by talking about opponents and discussing how I could improve my technique in certain situations.

I think 'Brownie' liked players who showed a bit of genuine spirit and admired those youngsters who refused to be intimidated by older lads. I have never forgotten an incident involving Gerry Henry which occurred shortly after our new first-team coach arrived on the Hillsborough scene.

Gerry, a thick-set wing-half or inside-forward, was a tough product of the rugged Bradford Park Avenue school, and when Eric Taylor signed him in 1950 it was in order to add a bit of steel to the Wednesday team. It is fair to say Gerry was a past master at dishing out the stick and you much preferred having him on your side than playing against him. Unfortunately as a reserve team player I had the discomfort of facing him in practice matches against the first-team.

At corner-kicks he had a habit of coming up behind you and rattling your ankles or jabbing you in the back. When you went up to head a ball Gerry would contrive to jolt you with a knee in your back. When he first started niggling me in this way I shrugged my shoulders and accepted it, but after a while I started to feel rather fed up. I was determined to get my own back.

I waited several weeks for a situation to arise in which I could give him a taste of his own medicine. The opportunity finally came about five minutes from the end of a Tuesday practice match. At a corner kick I made sure I was ready for him when he moved in to dig me in the ribs. I think Gerry was surprised when I suddenly hit him and shoved him to the ground. At least I knew he would give me no more trouble after that, and he didn't.

However, my action had been spotted by Alan Brown, who blew his whistle and shouted at me: 'Right, I want to see you in my room after training'.

I feared the worst when 'Brownie' asked: 'What did you do that for?' and I spluttered out the story of how I had been waiting to get Gerry back for the pain he had been inflicting on me.

'I've got some advice for you' he said. 'The next time somebody treats you like that, don't wait so long to retaliate. What you did this morning, you should have done six weeks ago!'

It was gratifying to know that I had gained Alan's respect. He hadn't given up on me even though my prospects weren't looking too good in those late weeks of the 1950–51 campaign and showed little sign of improving when the 1951–52 season started.

How was I to know Alan Brown's faith and my spirit and persistence would soon start paying dividends and lead to brighter days?

Chapter Eleven

Third Time Lucky

The early post-war era was a period when most clubs staged a public practice match a week before the start of each new season. The tradition, which involved two matches for the price of one, was popular with supporters. The fans invariably turned out in force because the occasion enabled them to enjoy their first look at summer signings and to familiarise themselves with just about every player at every level on the club's books. At half-time the teams in those Stripes versus Whites fixtures were switched around with the idea of ensuring every player got a game. Many of the players, as well as the spectators, considered these events good fun.

However, anyone who attended Wednesday's public practice match in August 1951 would have struggled to believe that a red-haired twenty-one year-old called Derek Dooley figured in the club's plans for the new campaign. Fifty players were used during the afternoon, but I was not one of them. I didn't get a kick other than during the pre-match knockabout, and as I was the only full-time professional on the club's books not called into action, I didn't appear to have much of a future at Hillsborough. The sun may have been shining but for me the outlook was decidedly overcast with a forecast of rain to come!

Some months later, by which time my situation had taken a dramatic turn for the better, it was said Wednesday had me on offer at less than £1,000 in the early weeks of the 1951–52 campaign. I'm not sure how true this was but I do remember feeling very depressed, although deep down I felt more determined than ever not to fail without a fight, even though everything seemed to point to a premature end to my hopes of making the grade with Wednesday.

It spoke volumes for my prospects when I started the season unable to get a place in any of the club's teams. When the first team-sheets of the campaign were posted on the dressing room notice board, I was named as reserve for the reserves. After remaining on the sidelines in each of the first three games I decided it was time to take up the matter with Eric Taylor.

No doubt I had every intention of telling Eric exactly what I thought, and my plan probably involved spelling out in a few blunt words the injustice of my situation. Alas, not for the first time and certainly not for the last, I came out of Eric's office feeling I had been rather unfair to him by complaining about my lot. Eric agreed with everything I said and I accepted that his explanation really did sound as if he had been doing me a favour all along!

Yet Eric clearly took what I had said to heart and, when the reserves travelled to Chesterfield on the following Saturday, I was picked to play. I celebrated with both goals in a 2–1 victory. I also claimed doubles in each of the next two Central League games, against Sheffield United and Leeds, which prompted a hint that another first- team call might soon be in the offing.

On the penultimate Saturday in September, there was an unexpected extra air of excitement about the Central League trip to Bolton when we discovered secretary-manager Eric Taylor, senior coach Alan Brown, and two club directors were joining the reserves on the journey over the Pennines. Their presence was unusual and prompted speculation that some first-team places were up for grabs.

In fact, the reason so many members of the Hillsborough top-brass were making the journey was to look at Matt Gillies, the Bolton centre-half. Until recently, Matt, a Scot who had served Bolton for eight years, had been rated as one of the best defenders in the First Division. Unfortunately he had lost his place to big Malcolm Barrass, the son of an Owls' favourite of the 1920s. Wednesday had learned Matt was available for about £10,000, and they were seriously interested in pursuing a deal.

Regrettably for Matt, he did not enjoy that afternoon at Burnden Park and I was to blame. I scored four goals including three in the first thirty-five minutes. Alas, while I savoured a display which I felt sure would earn me a first-team call, Gillies was crossed off Wednesday's 'wanted' list. Later in the season he moved to Leicester City, where he not only proved a good buy but eventually went on to start his management career.

Incidentally, I think that Bolton match raised my tally of appearances for Wednesday at all levels to exactly 100 and the milestone came just a week after I completed a century of goals for the Owls! It would have been nice to have completed a treble of landmarks with a recall to the first-team. However, the step was delayed, and it was probably my own fault.

It was around this time that Wednesday signed a wing-half called George Davies from Oswestry Town and, in the midweek following the Bolton match, Eric Taylor sent an Owls' team to Shropshire to play in a friendly. The game was staged as part of the Davies deal, but I don't think many of the lads were keen on playing. I know I wasn't all that bothered and, perhaps because I wasn't 'up' for it, I didn't play well. How ironic that a poor performance in an unimportant match almost certainly cost me the chance of a first-team call. Perhaps there is a moral in that.

Following relegation back to the Second Division, Wednesday were not doing very well. They had won only three of their first ten games, and three defeats in four matches in mid-September had dented a promotion push which some people had predicted would be a formality. Just to compound Wednesday's woe, two of their most embarrassing setbacks had come against neighbours Sheffield United and Rotherham, while the Blades had hit seven goals at Bramall Lane the Millers had scored five at Hillsborough.

If those results confirmed Wednesday had problems in defence, the attack was still an area Eric Taylor wanted to strengthen and he continued to be particularly troubled by the centre-forward position. It was said Eric tried to sign Charlie Vaughan, who was then banging in the goals at Charlton, but Jimmy Seed, the Charlton manager, refused to sell him. In the meantime, Dennis Woodhead had continued as an emergency leader of the Owls' attack in the first seven matches of the season, and though he scored seven goals he was switched back to the wing and McJarrow had been recalled for a couple of games.

It was a source of some surprise when, despite my good scoring run with the reserves, Eric not only overlooked me again for the match at Cardiff but chose one of the smallest men on the staff, winger Walter Rickett, to lead the attack.

Walter, a local product who had started his career at Bramall Lane, was a one hundred per cent man and one of the pluckiest players in the game. Indeed, one of my most abiding memories of this pint-sized East Ender is a match at Coventry in April, 1952, when he played the last five minutes without a boot on his right foot. He had removed the boot because he was in pain with blisters but that didn't prevent him taking on a full-back on a run down the wing. However, as Walter readily admitted, he was no centre-forward. Not surprisingly, perhaps, some critics suggested Rickett's selection smacked of desperation.

While Wednesday were losing again at Ninian Park on the last Saturday in September, I played in the Central League side which beat Newcastle 2–1 at Hillsborough. As Newcastle had won the FA Cup the previous April and the reserve team they sent to Sheffield included seven of the men who had helped in the Wembley triumph, it was an excellent result for us. Tom Smith, the centre-half whom I faced, may not have been one of Newcastle's senior regulars at the time, but, even so, I knew I had done well in emerging with another two goals.

A tally of thirteen goals in nine Central League games suggested I had done enough to justify another first-team chance, and, to my great relief, when the team to play Barnsley at Hillsborough was picked, I was in.

The date was Saturday, October 6th, 1951, and it was certainly a red-letter day for me. I knew my third senior chance was a make or break opportunity. If I failed this time, I felt sure it would definitely signal the beginning of the end of my Hillsborough career. I so desperately wanted it to prove a turning point which would set me on course for a spell of sustained progress because I knew I had the potential to succeed. Thankfully the fates were kind and the Barnsley match marked the start of an unforgettably triumphant phase for me and the team.

Teenager Albert Quixall, who replaced Keith Thomas, was also recalled to the side for what was also only the third senior outing of his career, and the game marked a home debut for new signing George Davies, who came in at left-half for Doug Witcomb, the captain. With my pal Woodhead injured, Rickett was switched to outside-left, and when Norman Curtis cried off at the last minute with a poisoned foot it meant Keith Bannister stepped up for his first League game since February. Mick Kenny moved to left-back to accommodate Bannister on the right.

Incidentally, Keith Bannister did not know it then but, having like myself been brought in from the wilderness, he was destined to end the season in the role of captain and collect the Second Division championship shield. The campaign proved to be the pinnacle of his career and for a local lad it was a wonderful and unforgettable phase. I believe Keith was initially given the captaincy on a temporary basis because Jackie Sewell was away on England duty, but did so well he was allowed to keep it.

Whether it was by accident or design, the changes inspired the team to discover a winning formula in the sense that we lost only one of the next thirteen games and claimed nine victories which transformed us into firm promotion favourites long before the turn of the year.

I have to admit that right from the start of the Barnsley game I felt things were going to work out for me. The difference between this game and my two previous senior outings was that I seemed to get better service, the lads ensured I saw a lot more of the ball, and, well, although I missed easier chances and also hit the Barnsley crossbar, I scored twice and we won 2–1.

However, we had only been playing for about ten minutes when Barnsley scored. They had not won an away game all season but the fates appeared to be smiling on them when Gavin Smith was brought down and they were awarded a penalty which Jimmy Baxter shot past Dave McIntosh. It was just the boost Barnsley needed and, frankly, but for McIntosh's agility their confidence was such that we might have trailed by more than one goal at half-time.

After the interval, Tommy Taylor headed against the Wednesday crossbar and produced a terrific shot which nearly carried McIntosh into the net. Happily, in the meantime we had made a breakthrough when I equalised four minutes into the second half, then my joy was complete when I claimed the winner thirteen minutes from the end.

Fred Walters, sports editor of the Sheffield evening paper, the *Star*, said neither goal was a chance in the accepted sense. He suggested they were strikes many recognised centre-forwards would not have seen or considered 'on'. I don't know about that. I only remember I turned and shot both from the edge of the box with my right foot. The first followed a pass from Gannon, the second stemmed from a good ball from Sewell. The sight of the bulging net was something special and few goals I scored gave me more satisfaction. They came when I really needed them and it added to my pleasure that they sealed Wednesday's first victory in seven games.

The Sheffield *Green 'Un* celebrated my breakthrough with a front-page headline which read 'He'll Dooley Alright at Hillsborough!' I felt sure I would keep my place for at least one more game and hoped I might enjoy an extended run in the side. However, for all my elation, I knew I would have to keep scoring to be sure of staying in the team and when I failed to find the target in the next two games, against Hull and Blackburn, I must admit I started to fret.

Of course, it helped that we won both games, and one of our goals in the 2–0 defeat of Blackburn came from a Rickett penalty after Willie Kelly, the Rovers centre-half, had brought me down. Kelly, a tough Scot, was one of the most difficult defenders I ever faced and I never did manage to score against him. However, I knew my luck was in because when I won the penalty I had actually lost control of the ball and would not have been able to score anyway.

Many of the goals I went on to score in the 1951–52 season stemmed from what the papers invariably described as 'typical Dooley bursts down the middle' and the first of this type I claimed at senior level was at Queen's Park Rangers' Loftus Road ground in late October. I ran onto a Quixall through ball, beat centre-half Reg Chapman for speed, and smashed the ball past the advancing goalkeeper Harry Brown. It was a very fulfilling moment. However, the real significance of the goal was that it completed a tremendous Wednesday comeback which salvaged a 2–2 draw after we had gone two goals down in the first thirty-five minutes.

The headline in the local sports paper after I scored twice against Barnsley in October 1951

Reference to the QPR game reminds me that sometimes my speed didn't coincide with my ability to keep control of the ball. On a number of occasions I couldn't persuade the ball to move forward at the same pace as me! There was an amusing incident at QPR which illustrated the point. I set off to chase another of Quixall's through passes with two defenders in hot pursuit and, somehow, perhaps because of the uneven pitch, I contrived to accidentally step on the ball and continue speeding forward without it, taking both defenders with me.

As fortune would have it, Jackie Sewell was right behind me and he thought I had purposely stopped the ball and run clear to enable him to follow up. Jackie delivered a terrific shot which the goalkeeper did well to save. 'Good ball, Derek!' he called. I hadn't the heart to admit the ploy had been quite unintentional!

The fact that Sewell and I shared seventy goals in 1951–52 confirms we formed a good strike partnership. We suited each other very well and, while he was a top quality player with the vision and craft to create his own chances, he was always on hand to snap up the rebounds and chances stemming from the havoc I created in penalty areas.

At the end of my first month back in the team I had scored three goals in four matches but I still felt a bit unsure about my place. Fortunately, the goal at QPR marked the start of a nine-match run in which I scored in every game and bagged twenty-two goals, with November and December 1951 proving the most memorable two-month phase of my playing career.

Chapter Twelve

Singing in the Rain!

One of the most fulfilling days in my short and eventful career as a player in the Football League coincided with a very wet and unpleasant November afternoon in 1951. Obviously the golden moments in one's life and career don't always occur when the weather is bright and sunny, even if one does tend to look back on them through a haze of warm nostalgia!

You could say this was an instance when I got lucky in the rain but, anyway, I remember it as a time when I felt I had finally arrived and could start to feel my place was reasonably secure after scoring five second-half goals in a 6–0 triumph over Notts County in front of a 46,570 Hillsborough crowd.

It was not a club record, Douglas Hunt had once notched six in a Second Division game in November 1938, but my five-goal feat put me alongside Jimmy Trotter and Jimmy Dailey in the Hillsborough record books. Trotter scored five in a match twice, in December 1924 and September 1925, while Dailey's 'nap' hand had come in September 1947.

It was nice to shoot into the history books but, when I recalled how Dailey's feat had not guaranteed him long-term success with Wednesday, it served as a reminder not to rest on my laurels. All the same, it was an achievement to savour and I still treasure the memory of that afternoon. It probably sounds like pure 'Roy of the Rovers' stuff when I say a match which had seemed so ordinary in the first-half was transformed in the space of thirty-two magical second-half minutes into something akin to a piece of schoolboy fiction.

It is amusing now to reflect on a tale one of the Notts County players told my team-mate and former Meadow Lane favourite Jackie Sewell after the game. The County goalkeeper was Roy Smith, who had spent twelve years at Hillsborough and moved to Nottingham in 1948. On the journey to Sheffield, Roy's colleagues had asked him: 'Who's this lad Dooley? Is he any good?' Apparently Roy, who remembered me as a Yorkshire League player from my first season at the club, had replied: 'No, he's big, awkward and useless'. I imagine Roy took some stick in the dressing room after the game!

Notts County didn't have a bad side in those days and it is worth noting that only a fortnight earlier they had crushed Everton 5–1 at Goodison Park. Their team included the legendary former England centre-forward Tommy Lawton, and in Leon Leuty, an England 'B' centre-half, they had a man considered one of the best uncapped players in his position in the country. Leuty had cost them a £25,000 fee from Luton when that was big money.

I could, and probably should, have hit the target in the first minute of the game, but the scoreline remained blank until just before half-time when Jackie Sewell met a corner-kick from Walter Rickett and headed the ball past Smith. That goal gave us a boost at exactly the right psychological moment and we never looked back.

I always seemed to rise to the occasion when we were kicking towards the Hillsborough Kop and the Notts County match provided a classic example of my penchant for scoring at the Penistone Road end of the ground. This was one of those days when almost everything I attempted paid a dividend. I hit my first goal five minutes into the second half,

How the Green 'Un *announced my five-goal feat against Notts County in November 1951.*

claimed my fifth eight minutes from the end, and in the meantime had another effort disallowed for off-side. I almost bagged a sixth goal just before the final whistle, and it is fair to say my feet barely seemed to touch the ground as I walked off at the finish.

According to one of the newspaper reports of the game, Leon Leuty had given me up as a bad job long before the finish. He ended up trying to play me off-side which only gave me even more scope because I was faster than him and there was nothing I liked better than a chase. The conditions may have been far from ideal for defenders but they gave me the opportunity to emphasise my strength and speed. I revelled in turning my marker and outpacing him as I set off down the middle with only one thought in my mind, to shoot for goal. I scored with three shots on the run, notched one goal when the ball went in off my chest, and also beat goalkeeper Smith with a header.

In those days I was living at Firth Park and travelled to and from Hillsborough by bus, and an amusing incident occurred on the journey home after the Notts County match. Of course, there were no such things as sponsored man-of-the-match awards and suchlike then and, with nothing to delay me, I got away from the ground fairly promptly. My girlfriend Sylvia was waiting for me and we caught the Outer Circle bus in Leppings Lane.

When we reached the Five Arches on Herries Road a middle-aged Wednesdayite boarded the bus. It would be an understatement to say he was soaked to the skin. The poor chap wore neither a hat nor an overcoat and such was the state of his navy blue suit he looked as if he had been swimming in it.

The conductress exclaimed: 'What the devil have you been doing? Did you fall in the Don?'

He laughed: 'Nay, lass, I've been t' football match. I've been standing on yon ruddy Kop an' it's rained cats and dogs all afternoon. About five times in t' second half I decided I was going to come out, but every time I got t' top o' Kop that begger Dooley scored, so I went back.'

Sylvia and I were chuckling as we watched this exchange between the man and the conductress. I often wonder what the man would have said had he known I was sitting just a few feet from where he stood.

'Wait 'till you get home, you'll get some stick from your missis', the conductress said.

'Eeh, I'm not bothered about her, lass' he replied. 'I can't wait till I get to work on Monday morning and give them Unitedites at the factory what for. They'll be sick of hearing about Dooley when I've done.'

As I mentioned earlier, this was the day when, probably for the first time in all the years he had followed my progress in football, my father

Mum and Dad, seen here with me and Sylvia, always took pride in reading about my success in the newspapers, but Dad made sure I kept my feet on the ground!

forgot his normal reluctance to praise my performances. His first words when I walked into our house were 'Well done, son'. As my mother was quick to remark, I must have played well and, if I'm honest, that plaudit from the old man put the top on a day I have always remembered with extra pride.

I have never forgotten, either, that, on the following Friday at the ground, I broke a habit. Until then whenever the team sheets were posted in the dressing room, I had always looked first at the reserves' line-up. Now I went straight to the senior team and I would have been very shocked had my name not been there!

Chapter Thirteen

Goal Rush

The transformation in my playing fortunes in the last three months of 1951 was truly remarkable, the contrast between the depression I had experienced at the start of the season and the elation I felt by the end of December could hardly have been greater. It was all rather flattering to discover myself enjoying a taste of fame and being dubbed a local hero.

By the final Saturday of the year I had claimed twenty-seven goals in fifteen games, and the newspapers were describing me as 'the scoring sensation of the post-war era'. Fred Walters, perhaps the best-known local football pundit of the period, hailed me in the *Star* as a serious candidate for an England call-up, while the *Sheffield Telegraph* went so far as to suggest I had become a more famous symbol of Sheffield than Vulcan. They even used a touch of artistic licence to create a photograph in which I replaced the statue of the god of fire and patron of metalworkers atop the Town Hall!

Meanwhile, Wednesday fans had adapted a Guy Mitchell song which was then all the rage changing the title from 'Truly Truly Fair' to 'Dooley Dooley Fair', and, at Christmas when 'Rudolf the Red-Nosed Reindeer' was the number one song in the hit parade, someone produced new words to the same tune and it became 'Dooley the Centre Forward'.

I doubt if there was any real danger of all this going to my head, but it is amusing now to recall how keen the management at Sheffield Wednesday were to ensure I kept my feet on the ground. For instance, in early December, at the time my goal tally totalled fourteen in eight matches, they put the following official comment in the match programme:

His is a very good record and he is complimented on it. Let us give him credit, but we must give credit to his colleagues who have given him as much support as possible. Without the help of colleagues Dooley, indeed no man, no matter how brilliant, could be a success. Football is a team game. Players must pull together, and there must be no lauding of one player without just recognition of the work of others. It does not matter who scores the goals as long as they are scored. To single out individuals for special mention at every end and turn is a mistake.

I suppose even then I agreed with the philosophy expressed in those words, but viewing it from a distance of nearly fifty years and in the context of modern times it does have a slightly Victorian ring!

Of course, there were people who said it was all a flash in the pan and contended that my success would not last. My style was described by some critics as ungainly, awkward and based solely on speed and sheer physical strength. Nobody was more aware than me that I lacked finesse and still had a great deal to learn in terms of pure football skills, but I just wanted to make the best use of my assets and what abilities I had. However, right from the start, some people tended to suggest I was over-physical and even a dirty player, but I always played within the rules while accepting that taking and giving the knocks was part and parcel of the game.

In those days you could charge goalkeepers, so long as they had the ball and their feet were on the ground. If you didn't do what all centre-forwards were expected to do and keep the man in the green jersey under pressure you weren't doing your job. For instance, whenever there was a corner-kick, I always made sure the goalkeeper was aware of my presence—and there was no way I was going to let him catch a ball unchallenged.

Early in a game against Everton I went for an Alan Finney cross with Jimmy O'Neill and the goalkeeper ended up in the net. Afterwards my girlfriend, Sylvia, said: 'What did you charge him for? He's only a little chap'. I explained: 'That was for later, to let him know I was there. Did you notice he didn't come for any more crosses after that?'

There was one game, against Sheffield United at Hillsborough, when Arthur Ellis, the referee, made sure I never got to grips with Ted Burgin, the Blades' goalkeeper, in the way I planned. Burgin and I had a bit of a confrontation and he provoked me by collecting the ball and looking at me as if to say 'Are you coming then?' Later, at the Kop end, Burgin caught a cross and I was all set to knock him and the ball into the net. I had barely moved when the referee blew his whistle, I asked: 'What's that for, ref?' He said: 'You were going to charge the goalkeeper'. I replied: 'For all you know, I might have been going for a run up the Kop'. Ellis said: 'If you give me any more cheek, son, you'll be running up that tunnel'. You didn't mess about with Arthur.

The irony was that when a goalkeeper came out for a high ball it was not uncommon for the challenging forward to receive a knee in his back

I look on with pleasure as Sam Powell, a member of a great backroom team at Hillsborough in my playing days, puts some new studs in my size 12 boots.

or a punch on the head. I felt the full force of countless blows but I accepted them and soon learned it did not pay to give an opponent the pleasure of knowing how much pain he had inflicted. If they saw they had hurt or upset you, they were sure to repeat the punishment without delay!

An amusing incident occurred at West Ham when we beat them 6–0 in early December. I was up against Malcolm Allison and the hat-trick I scored took my tally to nineteen and made me the Football League's joint leading marksman along with Jack Shaw of Rotherham. Curiously, the goal I remember best was our fifth, notched by Albert Quixall five minutes from the end, because it had long-term implications. Ernie Gregory, the home goalkeeper, and myself both went for a high cross from wing, and somehow we ended up in a tangle on the ground. The ball fell loose but was just within Gregory's reach if he stretched. However, I deliberately laid back to ensure he couldn't raise his body, and 'Quickie' nipped in to place the ball in the net. I think it was Albert's first goal of the season and only his second for Wednesday in the Football League, and I have never forgotten how he celebrated with the kind of wild joy one normally associates with someone who has just bagged the winner at Wembley. Gregory, meanwhile, was venting his anger over the way I had kept him pinned down and I dare not repeat the few choice names he called me!

In the following April when West Ham came to Sheffield, Gregory got his own back. Before the game he came up to me and said: 'I've not forgotten Upton Park'. I had been warned. He waited until I was right through with only the goalkeeper to beat. Gregory advanced and kept advancing. I lobbed the ball over him, saw it drop just over the bar, then there was a collision. I ended up with five or six stud marks across my chest and my shirt was so badly ripped I had to replace it.

Goram, the Bury goalkeeper, beats me to a cross.

Another high duel with Goram in the Bury match of 1951.

*I scored twice against Bury that day, but Goram did his best to frustrate me,
and here he is tipping an effort over the bar.*

Most of the goalkeepers of that era certainly knew a few tricks—and so did the majority of defenders. In one of my early games, I remember having the skin ripped off my nose in a clash with Luton's Syd Owen, but I saw it as just another battle scar. By the same token, the following week when Bury's veteran centre-half Les Hart and I finished up in the back of the net when I barged him and the ball across the line, he had no complaints.

When Coventry came to Hillsborough in early December I faced a tough old campaigner called George Mason, and there was one incident when we clashed and he ended up in the back of the goal with his boots caught in the netting. George, who was then aged thirty-eight and in his fifteenth year as Coventry's captain, was never a man to mince his words. He turned and swore, telling me exactly what he was going to do with me. If he had carried out his threat I might not have been able to walk off the field at the end of the game. However, when the final whistle blew he put an arm round my shoulder and said with a smile: 'Well done, kid'.

I revelled in the sheer joy of being a first-team regular, and my only fear was I might miss a game through injury and find I couldn't get back into the side.

I had only been in the team about six weeks when I badly twisted my left knee. Daft as it might seem, the accident didn't happen in the heat of a match but in a harmless, impromptu table tennis tournament at an hotel in Porthcawl. We had gone there two days ahead of a Saturday fixture at Swansea and, because the weather was too bad for normal training, it was decided we should while away the time with some indoor games.

Such was the damage to my knee I was unable to bend it and my prospects of recovering within less than forty-eight hours did not appear promising. I was given the hot and cold towel treatment, but even when we were travelling to the ground on that wet and miserable Saturday I still felt stiff and uncomfortable. Frankly, when we passed a succession of flooded fields on the journey, I hoped the game might be postponed. Once at the Vetch Field, we found the recent heavy rain had left pools of water all over the pitch and, as Swansea's officials had not yet opened the gates for spectators, we felt sure the ground would be declared unfit. Alas, even though no player on either side considered the pitch playable the referee decided the match should go ahead.

Eric Taylor and Alan Brown both wanted me to play and, despite my discomfort, so did I. By now it was more a case of not wanting to let the lads down, although I did worry about what might happen if I ended up being little more than a passenger. In modern times when we take substitutes for granted the situation would not have had quite the same implications.

In the first ten minutes, I felt a sharp twinge, then the knee stung every time I tried to run. I suppose it was frustration that induced me to take the make-or-break decision which, to my astonishment, turned an apparent invalid into a perfectly fit young man. I thought: 'Right, the next time Albert Quixall hits a through ball, I'm going to chase it with everything I've got. I'll grit my teeth, give it a go, and if I end up being carried off, so be it'. Remarkably, when the moment came and I started running, albeit more half-heartedly than I had intended, suddenly something in my knee clicked and the pain completely disappeared.

The pitch was a quagmire, but with my confidence restored I revelled in the conditions and certainly gave the home centre-half, an experienced guy called Don Weston, a run for his money. After about half-an-hour one of my bursts down the middle brought the first goal and late in the second half I grabbed what proved to be the winner. Swansea had hauled themselves level soon after half-time but I had a hunch it was going to be our day when they missed a penalty. Ivor Allchurch, a legendary figure in Welsh football and Swansea's star player, had converted eight successive spot-kicks prior to this game, but now he contrived to shoot the wrong side of a post.

Intriguingly, when I came out of the bath after the game, my knee went again and it did rather look as if I might be in for a bout of cartilage trouble. Happily, within a few days the pain again suddenly disappeared and I had no more trouble with it.

Curiously, the only match I missed in a run of thirty-two games in 1951–52 just happened to be on our next trip to Wales in February. I was unable to travel to Cardiff owing to a pulled muscle, and when the lads emerged with a 4–2 victory after trailing by two goals I was worried I might not get back into the team. This win came after three games without a victory and I knew some people felt you shouldn't change a winning team. All our four goals at Cardiff had been scored by Jackie Sewell. My place in the team was taken by Clarrie Jordan and by all accounts he had done well. It was Clarrie's first senior outing for nearly two years and he knew better than anybody what it was like to lose one's place through injury and then find it impossible to get back.

At his peak Jordan was considered an outstanding centre-forward. He was popular with the other players because on the field he was the essential professional and he was also a good influence in the dressing room. Clarrie always had a lot of time for younger players, he invariably talked a lot of

*Not a case of 'heads I win' on this occasion at Doncaster, for I saw my
effort scrape the wrong side of a post.*

common sense while lacing his comments with humour typical of his
background as a South Yorkshire miner.

Unfortunately, he had a lot of bad luck with knee trouble, and when
he was fit again the fact that I was keeping him out must have been a
source of considerable frustration. Yet he was so often the first man to
pop into the dressing room to wish me well and he never once showed
any malice or jealousy. Indeed, when I mentioned to him that it might
now be his turn to keep me out of the side, he said: 'Nay, Derek, tha'll
be back next Saturday'. Typically, when his prediction proved correct,
he made a point of wishing me well.

Later in his life Clarrie suffered the cruellest of fates when both his legs
were amputated, but, in circumstances which would have broken a lesser
man, he always retained a lively sense of humour.

December was an especially rewarding month. I claimed the mantle of
leading marksman in the entire Football League, my tally of goals establishing
a post-war record with the season barely past the halfway mark. More
importantly, Wednesday went top of the table for the first time that season
exactly three days before Christmas when we beat Everton 4–0 at
Hillsborough.

This match sticks in my memory not simply because I scored all our goals but also by virtue of the fact that my experience that day serves as a reminder of just how much I still had to learn. It was also another occasion which shows how much I owed to the encouragement and patience of Alan Brown.

All four goals came in the second half but, typically, I had wasted two excellent chances in the first period when we were attacking the Leppings Lane end. Both were one-on-one situations stemming from breakaways, but twice I was thwarted by my own inexperience and the wisdom of Everton's Eire international goalkeeper Jimmy O'Neill. Once you have burst clear and have only the man in the green jersey to beat, the act of placing the ball into the net might seem such a simple task to the spectator. From the terraces my first miss, as early as the second minute, must have looked like a laughable error of judgement. When the goalkeeper advanced from his line and narrowed my angle, I decided I was going to chip the ball over him. Alas, I only succeeded in chipping it into his hands.

Just before the interval, an identical situation arose. Naturally my earlier miss was still on my mind as I pounded down the middle pursued by two defenders. This time there was no way I was going to chip the ball and, as O'Neill again came off his line, I decided I was going to hit the ball and 'paralyse' the goalkeeper. O'Neill had left me with just enough of the goal to his left to shoot at. I aimed at this gap with a fierce right-foot shot. Alas the ball flashed several yards wide of the post and was more likely to hit a spectator than the net.

When we went off at half-time my confidence could not have been lower, but Alan Brown, rather than criticising my misses, insisted they had been difficult chances. He said the next time the situation arose I needed to touch the ball to the right or left of the advancing goalkeeper and this would create a better angle to shoot at. He was stating the obvious, but sometimes the obvious doesn't occur to a young player in the heat of a tense moment in a game.

Four times in the second half I had the chance to prove the merit of Brown's advice. The first opportunity came within six minutes of the restart and while the fans on the Kop were still cheering our opening goal I turned to the trainer's box and nodded to our coach: 'You were right, boss'.

In the following weeks I spent a lot of time on the training pitch with Alan Brown and we concentrated solely on developing my ability to exploit one-on-one situations against an advancing goalkeeper. I was delighted to discover how to convert a gap reduced to one yard into four or five yards and, on the practice pitch, I found myself hitting the target nine times out of ten.

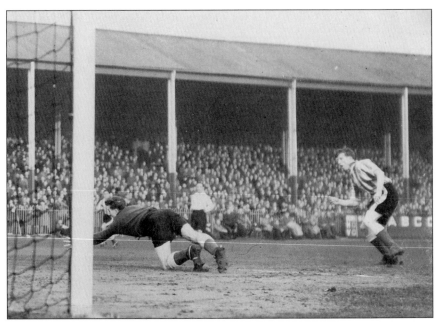

Almost but not quite there in the first half of the game against Everton in December 1951.

*This picture of a goalmouth battle at the Leppings Lane end reminds me that
I gave the Everton goalkeeper a hard time all through the 90 minutes, but I had to wait until
the second half before I managed to put four goals past him.*

In fact, within a week of the Everton game, we went to Southampton where we won 4–1 on a very muddy pitch. I scored two first-half goals which illustrated the benefits of the work we had done in training—it was Southampton's heaviest home defeat since before the war.

I could hardly have wished for a happier end to 1951, though I ought to mention that this was the year when Nottingham Forest rather took the edge off our Christmas celebrations. We met them twice over the holiday and had to settle for just a single point.

The Forest game at Hillsborough on Christmas Day earned a place in club history because the 61,187 crowd was the biggest for a Wednesday home match for more than ten years and constituted a post-war attendance record for the Second Division. As the match had a morning kick-off and public transport did not start running until 11 am, I wondered how so many people had managed to get to the ground. Even I had to walk from Firth Park, and while this was no hardship I was staggered to learn many fans had walked twice as far as me. Incredibly, the gates were closed long before the 11.15 start with thousands locked out.

The only thing that spoiled the occasion was I failed to score for the first time in nine games. The fact I had insisted on being in bed by half-

There was a 65,000 crowd at Hillsborough on Christmas morning 1951, but I couldn't find the target, and this was an instance when I shot the wrong side of the post at the Kop end.

past nine on Christmas Eve didn't prevent me from producing a tired, below-par performance. Although Walter Rickett notched our goal with a penalty after I had been brought down in the box, Forest grabbed a late equaliser.

The following day we travelled to the City Ground and lost 2–1 in front of a 39,380 crowd which was a post-war record for Forest. Our lone consolation was a late header with which I resumed my scoring habit and, while this was a day when my bustling tactics failed to unsettle the wily Forest centre-half Horace Gager, they ensured the home fans did not show me any festive spirit.

At least the Wednesday fans were in good voice as they sang the new Hillsborough 'carol', which had the following words:

> *Dooley the centre-forward*
> *Has a very awkward style,*
> *And if you ever saw it,*
> *You'd say it stuck out a mile.*
>
> *All of the other players*
> *Used to laugh and call him names,*
> *They wouldn't let poor Dooley*
> *Play in any first-team games.*
>
> *Then one Saturday afternoon,*
> *Taylor came to say,*
> *Dooley with your hair of flame*
> *Won't you play in the Barnsley game?*
>
> *Then how the supporters loved him,*
> *And they shouted out with glee,*
> *Dooley the centre-forward*
> *You'll go down in history!*

Chapter Fourteen

Just Champion!

In that unforgettable 1951–52 campaign the Owls notched a century of Football League goals of which I had the satisfaction of scoring forty-six to claim a club individual record which survives almost fifty years later. On our day we certainly had the look of champions, yet the race for a place in the top-grade was never a formality and such rivals as Cardiff and Birmingham dogged our heels all the way. We finally sealed promotion, plus the Second Division title, with two points to spare. Moreover, to our relief, the issue was settled a week before the end of the season.

After moving into top spot just before Christmas, we always looked a good bet to finish in the top two but, as often happens when the chase is tight and tense, we had a few inhibited spells when things did not go quite as we wanted. For instance we started 1952 with just one victory in five League games and also crashed out of the FA Cup against Bradford Park Avenue of the Third Division North.

It was not without irony that the only game Wednesday won in this spell, at Cardiff in early February, coincided with my enforced absence owing to a pulled muscle. All the same a 4–2 success against one of our main promotion rivals proved particularly significant in the context of the final table. I was delighted my pal Jackie Sewell grabbed four goals at Ninian Park as the lads came from 0–2 down to regain top spot. As I mentioned earlier, at the time I feared I might not get back into the team.

January was a dismal month which began with an unexpected home defeat against Sheffield United. The Blades were actually just three points behind us but, having won only two of their previous twelve games and slipped to fifth in the table, they were not considered likely to halt our progress.

Indeed, Harry Heap, the famous local cartoonist, summed up the optimism of most Wednesdayites when he featured the Bramall Lane cricket scoreboard in his Friday cartoon in the *Star* and had a pipe-smoking character called Alf suggesting United ought to take it to Hillsborough to keep count of the goals I was going to put past them on the following day.

Of course we all know Sheffield derby games seldom go according to the form-book and United have invariably had a knack of confounding the pundits whenever they are rated underdogs on these occasions. The match attracted a crowd of 65,384, the biggest Hillsborough gate for eighteen years, and it was the Blades fans who went away with a smile on their faces. Incidentally, the game marked the senior debut of a teenager called Graham Shaw, who was destined to become one of the finest full-backs to wear a Blades shirt.

Alf Ringstead, United's Irish winger, scored twice. His first came after twenty minutes and his second nine minutes into the second half, then George Hutchinson sealed the points ten minutes from the end. We knew it was not our day when Ted Burgin saved a Redfern Froggatt penalty shortly before Hutchinson's goal.

Eight Owls on the run during special training ahead of the January 1952 derby with Sheffield United. The line up is (left to right) Eddie Gannon, George Davies, Derek Dooley, Dave McIntosh, Keith Bannister, 'Mick' Kenny, Redfern Froggatt and Jackie Sewell.

We lost 3–1, my lone consolation was to score our goal when we equalised in the first-half. It was the only time in the match when I managed to escape from United's burly centre-half, Harry Latham, who stuck so close to me throughout the ninety minutes I began the believe he was inside my shorts!

Harry, four days short of his thirty-first birthday, was at the veteran stage of his career. As he was carrying a few extra pounds I felt sure I was going to have a beano because I knew I was much faster and fitter than him. If it came to a running match there would only be one winner. Unfortunately he proved there is no substitute for experience and used every ounce of his knowledge and guile to keep me in check.

Harry may not have been the best centre-half in the business and he never claimed to be anything but an out-and-out stopper. Yet by playing to his strengths and marking me tightly he denied me the chance to exploit my speed. If I tried to turn him he just stood his ground. Harry was hard but fair and his great asset was an awareness of his limitations combined with the common sense to stick to what he did best.

It is worthy of mention that Harry was typical of the abundant crop of local players United produced over the years. In United's team of 1952, for instance, there was Fred Furniss, Graham Shaw, Joe Shaw and Harold Brook as well as Latham. Like many others before and after him who progressed through the ranks and made a mark in the first-team, Harry was dependable and wonderfully loyal. Although never a star he proved a great servant to the club, first as a player and later as a member of the training staff. He was, too, a happy and likeable man, but he was deadly serious about his football.

For all that old Harry gave me a tough time, playing against him was a pleasure compared with the centre-half I faced the following Saturday when we travelled to Bradford in the FA Cup. A week before the game, Len Horsman was issuing warnings and vowing to stop me at any price. In those days verbal threats never troubled me. Indeed, I thought I could take on the heavyweight champion of the world and beat him. Yet, if I wasn't frightened by Horsman's words and was looking forward to the challenge, I knew I could expect some rough treatment when we met.

The game had barely started when he was coming at me like a torpedo, flying into furious tackles with no holds barred. I didn't exactly help my own cause when I shot us into an early lead because it simply proved the signal for Bradford to step up the aggravation.

It is amusing now to recall that their manager at the time was none other than Vic Buckingham, who will always be remembered as one of football's great purists. However, on that January afternoon in 1952, Vic fielded a team which lived up to the Park Avenue tradition for uncompromising physical football sure to intimidate all but the stoutest hearted.

The referee, Alf Bond, was reputed to be one of the best in the business but he turned a blind eye to Bradford's tactics. Horsman took every opportunity to thump me in the back and some punches were so low he would have been disqualified if they had been delivered in a boxing ring. Poor Alan Finney was also taking some terrible stick from the Bradford left-back, Frank Hindle, but our complaints were ignored by the match officials.

The game was supposed to be a one-horse race and we set off as if Bradford's presence on the field was purely incidental. For about twenty minutes we footballed them to death, but my goal seemed to ignite the home team's passion. They started throwing everything at us—and I mean everything! Phil Turner equalised after twenty-four minutes and the same man put them in front two minutes after half-time, so we ended up on the wrong end of one of the shock results of the third round.

My only pleasing memory of our trip to Bradford was an evening visit to Odsal Stadium where, as guests of Bradford Northern, we watched a Rugby League game and enjoyed the novelty of floodlit football. Within a few years, of course, floodlights became an essential part of the sporting scene, but in those days the average football fan had little idea of how the development was destined to catch on and eventually influence major changes in the game.

Our exit from the FA Cup left us voicing the old cliché about being able to concentrate on our promotion push. Unfortunately, when we resumed our Second Division programme against Leeds United we suffered our third successive defeat and our second on the trot at home. Once again I had the consolation of scoring but I didn't manage to find the net until three minutes from the end. By then Ray Iggleden had put Leeds 2–0 in front.

The occasion gave me my first sight of John Charles and I knew I had faced a centre-half who was destined for greatness. Charles was then just twenty years old but already the big Welshman had a touch of sheer class and the poise of a much older and more experienced player. To describe this gentle giant as a colossus is almost an understatement. He seemed to have so much time and was so naturally gifted that he never needed to resort to physical force. There were no verbal threats from Charles. If he intimidated you it was simply by his mere presence. Later, of course, he moved to centre-forward and topped 150 goals for Leeds.

The man in the number five shirt heading clear, while a number nine called Derek Dooley can only look on, is none other than the legendary Leeds and Wales centre-half John Charles.

It is curious now to look back and note that our modest run in the first two months of 1952 coincided with so many Yorkshire derbies. I have not forgotten the frustration we felt during this phase when we had to settle for a draw at Rotherham after leading 3–1 in front of a record Millmoor crowd and then lost a nine-goal thriller at Barnsley.

The match at Oakwell was a magnificent duel with a dramatic climax in which I was denied what I felt was a perfect goal and our dismay was compounded when Barnsley grabbed a last-gasp winner. We came from behind to lead 2–1 after only twenty-three minutes but by the same stage in the second half we were trailing 2–4. Then I bagged a goal and Redfern Froggatt scored to haul us level at 4–4 with about fifteen minutes left.

It was towards the end that I thought I had made it 5–4, only to have the effort disallowed because the referee decided to award us a free-kick for a foul on our goalkeeper Dave McIntosh at the start of the move. It seemed a harsh decision when one of the best goals I ever scored was not allowed to count.

McIntosh had collected a cross under pressure, gone to the edge of the penalty box and cleared the ball downfield despite the attentions of a home forward. It reached me just inside our half. Even though I was being

Poor John Quairney, the Rotherham goalkeeper, is flat out in the Millmoor snow and unable to prevent me from scoring our second goal in a 3–3 draw.

challenged and pulled all over the place by two defenders, I managed to stay on my feet and pound my way through the middle until I was left with only goalkeeper Harry Hough to beat. As Hough advanced I made sure I gave myself a decent sight of the goal and hit a shot which found the target.

Wednesday fans in the Oakwell ground roared their approval, my team-mates shook my hand and showered me with congratulations, and it was only when we had walked back to the centre circle that we realised the goal had been disallowed. As I had picked the ball up in my own half, I knew I could not have been off-side. The referee explained he was giving us a free-kick on the edge of our own box and was doing so because a linesman had spotted an infringement and insisted on keeping his flag up even after we had gone on to put the ball in the net at the other end. We were punished for a foul committed by the opposition!

The match was a typically passionate South Yorkshire derby in which the fact that we were top of the table while Barnsley were battling against relegation lent an added touch of spice to the occasion. It was played in a hard but sporting spirit. Unfortunately a couple of home players were injured and I was viewed as the villain of the piece by some Oakwell regulars.

Harry Hough, who had just been selected for his England 'B' debut against Holland, had the misfortune to break a bone in his forearm. As he said afterwards it was a pure accident and he didn't blame me. We both went for a loose ball in the goalmouth and I kicked it against his arm. Harry stayed on the field after treatment and the extent of his injury was not discovered until later.

Matt McNeil, the Barnsley centre-half, suffered a knock which did not prevent him from playing the following week. However, at the time it reduced him to the role of a passenger playing up front and the veteran Tim Ward was switched from wing-half to the middle of the defence. The irony of McNeil's injury was that he was the man who headed the winning goal two minutes from the end. We made the mistake of leaving him unmarked and a sudden home breakaway found him in just the right position to score what proved to be the only goal of his entire playing career.

Eddie Gannon (left) a regular in the Eire team in the early 1950s, is showing 'Mick' Kenny, Keith Bannister, Dave McIntosh and me one of his international caps.

Happily, our defeat at Oakwell was the last we suffered that season. We won seven of our last eleven games and dropped only four points. I added another fifteen goals to my tally, and Jack Sewell and I shared twenty-one of the twenty-six we scored in this spell. As a pair we ended the season with seventy goals between us.

The first day in March marked the start of our revival with a 6–0 defeat of Raich Carter's Hull City, a match I seldom think of without recalling a conversation I had with Doug Witcomb in the dressing room before the game.

This was Doug's first senior game for four months because he had been unable to reclaim his first-team place after missing one match with a minor injury. Ahead of the kick-off he said: 'Get your finger out today, Derek, and make sure we win because I don't want to go back into the reserves'. I obliged him with four goals and, happily, Doug remained in the side for the rest of the season.

It was Witcomb who spotted my tendency to get very nervous before a match. Such was his concern I thought he was going to offer me a magic cure as we started discussing the subject. In fact, he simply admitted that he, too, was a victim of pre-match nerves despite his long years in the game. Doug said if I ever stopped feeling nervous ahead of the kick-off I would know it was time to hang up my boots!

Scoring the first of my four goals against Hull City with a left-foot shot.

A couple of weeks after the Hull game we played the return fixture with Notts County at Meadow Lane, and when a rather robust veteran called Bill Baxter was charged with the task of marking me it was obvious they were keen to prevent a repeat of my five-goal performance of the previous October. Leon Leuty, who had faced me at Hillsborough, was still at centre-half, but he was left to mark Sewell while Baxter announced that he was going to 'look after' me. Even before the kick-off he was threatening what he was going to do. In the event he failed to prevent me from shooting us in front twice but I suppose he felt he hadn't done too badly when County recovered to salvage a draw.

My second against Hull was a header—in true Tommy Lawton style!

As I mentioned earlier, in 1952 there were no such things as floodlights and it is interesting now to reflect that when a rare midweek game was staged at Hillsborough in early April the kick-off was fixed for 2.30 pm. Because a lot of fans could not get time off work the gate was only 25,848 compared with 41,700 at our previous Saturday fixture.

The match, in which we beat Luton 4–0, was notable in that the victory put us back on top of the table, but what made it especially significant for me was that my two goals raised my tally in League and Cup to thirty-nine. This equalled the club's individual record aggregate for a season held by Jack Allen and Jimmy Trotter, and my thirty-eight in the Second Division meant I had passed Trotter's 1926–27 League record of thirty-seven.

It had taken Trotter forty-one games to score his goals and here I was having managed it in just twenty-four outings. When I realised the implications of what I had achieved I felt as if all my birthdays had come at once. However, at the precise moment when I claimed the record I don't think I was conscious of it. It is amusing now to reflect that the record-breaking goal, which came on fifty-five minutes and made the score 4–0, actually went in off my shin after Rickett had taken a pot shot.

Afterwards I don't think anyone remarked on the record in the dressing room and there were no queues of reporters seeking a 'quote' when I left the ground. The implications of my double didn't dawn on me until I read the *Sheffield Telegraph* the following morning.

I might have made a bit of club history, but as I proved at Gigg Lane a few days later I could still miss the easiest of chances. At least now I was established in the team and scoring freely, so it was easier to see the funny side when I missed a 'sitter'. Moreover, it did help when I saw my team-mates could occasionally prove just as wasteful. I think we won 2–1 at Bury but it ought to have been 4–1, for, like me, Albert Quixall failed to hit the target when it seemed impossible not to. The irony was I forsook the chance to score myself and rolled the ball to Albert, I couldn't believe it when he blasted it over the crossbar. 'I could have done that!' I told him.

Albert was a great lad. A local product from Parson Cross who had gained international honours as a schoolboy, like me he never wanted to play professionally for anyone but Sheffield Wednesday. We had played together in the Yorkshire League and Central League teams and from his earliest days he boasted wonderful natural ball skills. My girlfriend Sylvia often reminded me she had seen Albert play long before she ever watched me, she was a great fan of his.

Scoring at the Kop end against Luton in April 1952.

On target again in the 1952 game with Luton and I learned later that this goal meant I had overtaken Jimmy Trotter's club record.

Albert ought to have gained more than the five caps he collected between 1953 and 1955. His talents were such that in 1958 he became Britain's most expensive footballer when Matt Busby, in the Manchester United manager's first deal after the Munich disaster, took him to Old Trafford for a then staggering £45,000 fee.

'Quickie' was also blessed with an impish sense of fun and it was quite an experience to be in his company when we travelled to away games. I was often his room-mate on trips but it was Albert and his pal, Alan Finney, who were invariably the architects of most of the mischievous fun that occurred. They just could not resist playing pranks on the older players, or, indeed, anyone who was likely to prove their innocent victim.

I have never forgotten one incident at a theatre in Manchester when they dropped sneezing powder from the balcony during the performance. At the interval the people in the stalls were totally mystified by the white spots on their shoulders!

Eric Taylor and Alan Brown were always tolerant of their humorous escapades. Eric dubbed the boys 'Null' and 'Void' and I think he enjoyed witnessing their mirth. However, I don't believe he, or Alan Brown, appreciated the joke on one occasion when the pair missed the train from London to Luton ahead of a match in the autumn of 1951. 'Brownie' was not too pleased about having to remain behind to search for the missing 'twins' and organise a taxi to follow us to Kenilworth Road. I feel sure that had we not been limited to twelve players in the travelling party, Alan would have gladly left them out of the side.

The only time when Albert didn't exactly see the funny side of things was on Good Friday in 1952. A commissionaire on the gate at Brentford would not believe the baby-faced Quixall was a player and refused to let him into the ground! Albert had already been in the dressing room but had popped out again to give some complimentary tickets to a pal. When the man in the uniform blocked his path back he was starting to panic. Fortunately, when he did not appear, I went looking for him. When I told the commissionaire Albert was a player, he said: 'Aye, pull the other one'. It was several minutes before the guy was convinced.

As it happened, Albert had a part in the two goals I scored in the opening twelve minutes of the match. He nodded on a corner-kick for me to head the first, and two minutes later I pounced when the goalkeeper fumbled an effort from 'Quickie'.

I managed a third goal after half-time and it was satisfying to have done so well against a centre-half of the calibre of Ron Greenwood. Ron, who later managed West Ham for many years and subsequently had a spell as manager of the England team, boasted one of the most astute football brains in the game, but on that afternoon at Griffin Park he made the elementary mistake of allowing me far too much room to play in.

The legendary, Tommy Lawton, who had been in the Notts County side on the day I scored five, now saw me raise my tally to eight in two games against him. Lawton, who had moved to Brentford for £15,000 in early March, suffered the frustration of having an effort disallowed in the match at Griffin Park and it is intriguing to reflect that while we were on opposing sides three times during the 1951–52 campaign I had a beano and the former England centre-forward did not manage a single goal.

In fact, when we played the return with Brentford at Hillsborough on Easter Monday, like Lawton I failed to find the target. This was partly because Brentford's double-marking made certain I was not given as much space as had happened a few days earlier. However, the opposition's preoccupation with me enabled my colleagues to benefit from the freedom they were allowed, and we won 2–0. Alan Brown, well aware of the tactics Brentford might use, told Jackie Sewell to play down the middle and instructed me to take my markers for a walk!

Reg Newton, the Brentford goalkeeper, punches the ball away while me and Froggatt try to put him under pressure.

With Reg Newton needing a touch of 'magic sponge' attention from the Brentford trainer, I find myself receiving a few words from the referee, who insists I have been a bit too hard on the goalkeeper!

The goal with which Sewell gave us the lead on the half-hour is worthy of a special mention and I cannot do better than to quote the description offered by Monty Marston in the *Sheffield Telegraph*. Monty is largely forgotten now but he was a very accomplished writer who deserves to be remembered. He wrote: 'The goal ranks among the finest scored at Hillsborough. It began with a forward pass from Dooley to Sewell, who was well out on the right. Without waiting to kill the ball Sewell leapt straight at it and hit it magnificently while in the middle of his jump and at least two feet in the air'.

Promotion was now almost within our grasp, we finally clinched it the weekend after Easter with a 2–0 victory at Coventry. I always remember Eric Taylor coming into the dressing room before the game at Highfield Road saying we needed an early goal. I think he was quite pleased when I obliged with one in the first minute! Then I managed a second goal just before the final whistle, and, because Cardiff failed to beat Luton on the same afternoon, we not only sealed promotion but ensured we would go up as champions.

We learned of our title triumph in a humorous little incident in the dressing room a few minutes after the end of the game. Cyril Hemmingfield, a director, burst through the door exclaiming 'We've won, we've won', we thought the poor chap had gone off his head.

'Of course, we've won' one of the lads said. 'The score was 2–0.'

Cyril replied: 'No, in my excitement I forget to say it's the championship we've won!'

On the way home we stopped for a meal at the George Hotel in Lichfield and I savoured the taste of the champagne with which we toasted our triumph.

Curiously, our final League game, at home to West Ham, was a bit of an anti-climax, although when I scored in the last minute to salvage a 2–2 draw it raised our tally of goals in the Second Division to exactly one hundred. After the final whistle we witnessed some wonderful celebration scenes in the ground and I suppose that was the point when I really began to appreciate the full extent of the transformation in my fortunes in the space of a few months. If someone had used the story in a novel it would have been dismissed as a piece of schoolboy fiction, more fairy-tale than fact!

It is strange the trivial moments one remembers. In the context of the West Ham game, I have never forgotten how keen I was to ensure I did not miss a match I knew would be a very special occasion no matter what the result. When we held our customary midweek practice match I decided I was not going to risk getting injured, and there was one instance when, unusually for me, I pulled out of a challenge on Dave McIntosh. Unfortunately, I didn't get out of Dave's way quickly enough and he caught me on the leg. I nursed a cut calf for the rest of the week and I was still not fully fit when we took to the field.

Frankly, in the first half, the entire team seemed to be simply going through the motions. Just before the break, West Ham scored twice in two minutes—Alan Brown gave us a rare old rollicking when we returned to the dressing room. Eric Taylor made the point that the 44,000 fans in the ground had come expecting to see the Second Division champions and not a bunch of strolling players.

One of our rewards for bouncing back to the top grade at the first attempt was a trip to the FA Cup final of 1952 in which we saw Newcastle beat Arsenal 1–0 with a goal from George Robledo. The club formally celebrated the success with a splendid banquet at the old Grand Hotel, and Eric Taylor also bought each of the players a pair of sterling silver cuff-links. With typical humour Eric had had these inscribed with the letters SWFC on one side and EWT on the other. It was a gesture the lads appreciated, though, frankly, few of us boasted the kind of shirts on which one used cuff-links!

Goalkeepers knew how to look after themselves, and here West Ham's Ernie Gregory comes
out with his foot up, which certainly made an impression on my chest!
The West Ham defender looking on is Malcolm Allison.

An exciting moment in the West Ham game of 1952 as I witness Ernie Gregory
turning to see a shot from Redfern Froggatt going over the bar.

In financial terms, our share of the prize money awarded for winning the Second Division title was based on individual appearances. Naturally, as I boasted only thirty outings, my share was less than such colleagues as Dave McIntosh, Jack Sewell, Keith Bannister and Eddie Gannon, who had all played more games. I think I got £68, and, as this added up to nearly six weeks' wages, it was a bonus for which I was grateful, all the more so as Sylvia and I were getting married in the summer.

Wednesday with the Second Division championship shield in 1952.
Back row: Witcomb, Gannon, Davies, Dooley, McIntosh, Turton, Kenny, Woodhead, Curtis.
Front row: Alan Brown (coach), Finney, Froggatt, Bannister, Sewell, Quixall,
Rickett, Eric Taylor (secretary-manager).

Chapter Fifteen

Wedding Bells

In the first six or seven weeks after the end of the 1951–52 season I doubt if there was a happier young man in the whole of Sheffield than a lucky twenty-two year-old called Derek Dooley. The remarkable transformation in my football fortunes had raised my stock and spirits, while on a personal level my world could not have been rosier. With my career now firmly on course I enjoyed my first foreign tour, and a few weeks later my happiness was complete when Sylvia and I were married.

At the time of our wedding, Sylvia was three months short of her twentieth birthday and we had been courting since 1948. In fact, Sylvia's first sight of me had come much earlier than this, her earliest memory being of seeing me play for the YMCA against Oaks Fold. The daughter of Hives and Beatrice Barber and the youngest of three children, she lived in Fife Street, Wincobank, and was a regular at Oaks Fold matches in Concord Park.

Sylvia has often reminded me that her first impression was of a lanky, awkward and big-headed kid. Later, when she saw me in and around the Firth Park area, I don't think I did much to improve her opinion—she was certainly not impressed on one occasion in the park when I pushed her then boyfriend through a hedge!

I have often said that marrying Sylvia was the best decision I ever made, the second best was deciding to ask her out in the first place. She was then not quite sixteen and neither of us knew what a momentous step we were taking. However, it was one we never had cause to regret. Our children Martyn, born in early September 1955, and Suzanne, born in late September 1964, are both now grown up and have children of their own, so, when we gather as a family and enjoy the company of our grandsons Del and Ben and our granddaughter Georgie, we reflect with pride and happiness on our good fortune.

It is amusing now to recall that on our first date, when we went to the Roxy Cinema and saw a film called 'Hornblower RN' starring Gregory Peck, Sylvia insisted on taking along a pal called Doreen Bishop. Three may have been a crowd on that occasion but happily Sylvia preferred just my company on subsequent dates!

Yours truly in reflective mood.

It is fair to describe 1952 as a vintage year in my life. Certainly it is one I remember with great affection because it was a special time when so many good things were happening. It was wonderful just to be alive and able to enjoy them.

This was a period when I first began to appreciate the benefits of being a professional footballer. One benefit I always found particularly rewarding was the chance to broaden my horizons. The game has given me an opportunity to travel far and wide, and now, at the age of seventy, I suppose I am a seasoned traveller who takes flying to distant places in his stride. Of course, I still get a kick out of making a foreign trip but nothing can quite match the thrill of that first venture abroad.

It is difficult now to imagine there was a time when I had never travelled further than Blackpool on our annual family holidays. In fact, I was twenty-one before I paid my first visit to London on the weekend on which I made my second senior appearance for Wednesday in 1951, and I have never forgotten the novelty of the experience, and the sense of awe I felt.

My goal scoring successes meant I often found myself in exalted company at public functions, and here, at a Wadsley House Social Club dinner, I am a member of a group which includes Reg Freeman, the Sheffield United manager, Stanley Royle, who ran Hillsborough Boys' Club, Mark Hooper, the old Wednesday winger (all on the back row) and Jimmy Hagan, the legendary Bramall Lane idol, on the extreme right of the front row.

In retrospect the memory might suggest I was a bit naïve and unworldly, but it serves to confirm how different things were in those days. I am not saying things were better then, but it was a time when you didn't expect a lot and, when you got more, it was a bonus you really enjoyed.

Once I got a regular place in the Owls' team I found myself visiting towns and cities that were all new to me and I must admit until then I had never thought geography could be so interesting! For instance, I have not forgotten how, when we were preparing for the trip to Southampton, the place seemed a million miles away. Of course, there were no such things as motorways then and it was a great education to pass through so many towns and villages which had previously been mere names on a map. To be honest, I didn't know most of those places existed until I saw them from the team-bus or the train.

There was, too, the additional novelty of staying overnight in big hotels in London and other places, and it is not easy now to recapture the sense of wonder and fascination the experience inspired in me. It was like being in another world and I did rather feel the kid from Pitsmoor had come a long way!

The chance to travel around England was rewarding enough in itself, but the prospect of going abroad for the first time was tremendously exciting. Indeed, the entire build-up to our two-week trip to Switzerland was an adventure I have never forgotten. Nowadays when we tend to take so many things for granted, the way players of my generation and background reacted to their first foreign tour might seem unsophisticated, but I wouldn't swap those memories for anything.

Even a simple thing like getting a passport was an event touched with magic, and I shall never forget the pride with which I wore the new club blazer and flannels with which, like the rest of the players, I was equipped for the tour. Just turning up with the other lads at Stewart & Stewart's shop in Pinstone Street to be measured for the new outfits was an occasion to relish. When I saw the badge on the blazer it seemed to symbolise my elevation to the elite membership of a very select group of players, and that was definitely the best outfit I ever had!

In terms of results, the tour was not exactly a great success for we won only one of our five games, although I must stress that there were one or two occasions when we faced opposition of international standards. However, the exercise as a whole was a tremendous adventure for a young man because to me everything we saw and did appeared so different from anything I had known before.

I felt privileged to be able to travel through the Swiss countryside, to explore the mountains and see such places as Berne, Geneva, Zurich, Lucerne and, when we crossed the Austrian border, Vienna. Eric Taylor was a past master at ensuring we not only saw all the sights every tourist might expect to visit but many that were seldom on the average visitor's itinerary.

The football, too, offered an insight into attitudes that were different from those at home. This was novel because, unlike in modern times, we didn't have the advantage of having watched Continental matches on television. Indeed, in those days, most of us didn't even boast the luxury of a television set. Incidentally, it might sound trivial now, but I have not forgotten how intrigued we all were when, in a game at St Gallen, near the Austrian border, we had the chance to try out some lightweight Continental boots such as we were unlikely to find in Jack Archer's sports outfitters shop in Sheffield. Those boots were obviously very comfortable for we won the game 5–1!

Our opening fixture, in which we drew 2–2 with Bellinzona, was interesting on two counts. If I say it made history as the first floodlit match in which Wednesday ever played, I must stress that the floodlights were nothing like you might imagine. In fact, they were very basic fittings hoisted on four trucks, one at each corner of the ground. Of much greater interest to me than the lights was the reaction of the home goalkeeper on one occasion when I challenged him.

The poor fellow went down as if he had been poleaxed and he must have rolled all of eighteen yards. His roll was so dramatic and he appeared in such agony, I feared I must have murdered him. The crowd certainly made it plain they saw me as the villain of the piece! Jackie Sewell, who had some experience of Continental football and was familiar with the theatrical posturing of foreign goalkeepers, told me not to worry. He was quite right when he said: 'He'll be up in a minute, Derek, there's nothing wrong with him'.

Our third game, against Inter-Milan in Geneva, was notable in that Norman Curtis, our left-back, was sent off in mysterious circumstances which also illustrated the difference between English and Continental attitudes to the physical side of football. Norman made a sliding tackle on an Italian winger and took the ball clean as a whistle, but the winger went down and, to our astonishment, the referee gave Curtis his marching orders. We didn't think there was anything wrong with the tackle and the Italian didn't even require the services of the trainer. Discussing the incident afterwards we came to the conclusion that the referee had been influenced by what he had read about us in the local newspaper. In our previous match, in Berne, Norman had been involved in an incident which had prompted one Swiss journalist to describe Wednesday as the most brutal team he had seen. We knew this was pure fiction but, of course, some people believed it to be fact.

Older Wednesdayites will not need reminding that Norman Curtis, while he was the mildest man you were ever likely to meet off the pitch, had an absolutely fearless style of playing the game. Like so many defenders of that era he was totally uncompromising, invariably hard in the tackle but always fair. He was the kind of player you liked having in your own side but never relished facing as an opponent. The other team's supporters seldom appreciated Norman's qualities.

On this occasion, when Norman brought one of the home lads down, a spectator promptly climbed over the ropes on the perimeter of the pitch and ran to confront him. When two or three other fans also invaded the field some of the Wednesday players, including me, felt we ought to go to Norman's aid. I don't know what this chap had said or done, but I had just got to within a few feet of Norman when he smacked the man, causing him to stagger back. Happily, the upshot was an instant end to the problem, the man walked away and the match continued without any more trouble.

However, when we returned to the dressing room at the end of the game, someone noticed Norman was missing. We feared a section of the crowd, who had been giving him continuous verbal stick, might have ambushed him! In the event, just as one or two of us were going back out to investigate, a smiling Norman appeared. He explained he had simply stayed behind to seek out the man and apologise for hitting him. They had shaken hands and parted good friends!

One of the highlights of the tour came almost at the end when we travelled to Vienna to see England face Austria. Our own Jackie Sewell was in action that day and he celebrated his second international cap by scoring in a 3–2 England victory. Of course, the game has passed into the records as the occasion on which Nat Lofthouse, the Bolton centre-forward, bagged two goals and produced a famous battling performance which earned him a place in football folklore as 'the Lion of Vienna'.

An amusing footnote to the tour came in Zurich where we bumped into a party of Arsenal players. Talking to Alex Forbes and Joe Mercer we learned the boys from Highbury were getting a lot more spending money than us. Consequently Keith Bannister, our captain, led a deputation to ask Eric Taylor for an increase in our £2 a day allowance. Needless to say we didn't get it. Typically, Eric made such a good job of convincing us we already had more than enough money with which to enjoy ourselves, that some of the lads came away feeling guilty about asking for a rise!

It might have been nice to have had a bit extra but, frankly, I don't think I would have wanted to have missed that trip even if I had been told I must provide my own spending money.

The crowds gather outside the church at Wincobank to watch Sylvia arrive for our wedding in June 1952.

We were staggered by the huge turn-out of friends, neighbours and football fans at our wedding, this picture shows the crowds watching as Sylvia and I emerge from the church.

My brother Alan is on the right as local youngsters watch the new Mr & Mrs Dooley pose for the camera.

A Sheffield United fan presents Sylvia with a rolling pin.

Of course, for all that I enjoyed every minute of the Swiss trip, I was glad to be home again. Within barely two weeks of returning to Sheffield I had the most important date of my life at St Thomas' Church, Wincobank, where, on the 14th of June, Sylvia and I were married.

There must have been well over four hundred people at the wedding, for as well as about three hundred packing the church another one hundred well-wishers waited outside. Those figures might not sound a lot, but we were staggered by the size of the turn-out and the scenes when we emerged from the church were remarkable. Indeed, the situation was so unexpectedly chaotic that our official photographer was unable to get near enough to organise the traditional pictures and, as a consequence, we never had the customary wedding album. Fortunately a lot of friends and supporters who were present took snaps and over the years we have collected some of these as treasured souvenirs of an unforgettable day.

Following our honeymoon in the Isle of Man, where we stayed in a boarding house run by a friendly Lancashire couple called Evans, Sylvia and I began our married life sharing the home of my parents at Addison Road. We were comfortable and happy there but, naturally, like many other couples in those days, we would have preferred to have started out in a place of our own. Unfortunately, as a footballer only recently starting to earn £12 a week in the winter and £10 a week in the summer, I had not managed to save much and the means of buying a house were beyond my resources.

We did always hope for a club house and my name went on the waiting list. For a time we thought we were in line to rent a club property in Crofton Avenue, off Middlewood Road, but nothing came of this and, curious as it might seem from a distance of nearly fifty years, I was not unduly troubled when my frequent enquiries at Hillsborough failed to produce results. Expectations were not so high in those days and most players in my situation, even those who had just claimed a club scoring record, would have considered themselves very well off and held in especially high esteem if they were allowed to rent a club house as soon as they were married. Sylvia and I were content to be patient and I felt sure that, all in good time, our turn would come.

Of course, I was not then aware that my playing days would be over before the end of the following season, and I didn't know that the accident which finished my career would mean we lost our place on the waiting list.

Cutting the cake at the wedding reception.

Chapter Sixteen

Dropped!

With Wednesday back in the top grade and optimism at a peak, I had plenty of reasons to look forward to the 1952–53 campaign with eager anticipation. The prospect of playing against many of the biggest clubs in the country and facing some of the best defenders in the game left me excited rather than intimidated. I knew I might not prove as prolific as in the previous season but felt confident the goals would come. Nobody knew better than me that there was still so much to learn and plenty of room for improving my skills, but I could hardly wait to get started on the challenge of proving I could make my mark in the First Division.

Unfortunately, the season kicked off under a cloud of anti-climax for Wednesday as well as myself. We collected only one point from our first five games, I suffered the indignity of being dropped, and my first goal did not arrive until mid-September. My long wait to hit the target ended in my sixth senior outing. If, in retrospect, that hardly seems a painful statistic, the spell when the scoring stopped proved a chastening experience, and it is fair to say I learned a lot the hard way.

Pre-season training that year followed the traditional pattern in that we were not allowed to touch a ball in the first two weeks after our return from the summer break. Getting fit was the top priority, and that meant running and more running. If within a couple of days you didn't need treatment for foot blisters it meant you weren't working hard enough on what seemed like a daily marathon!

Our regular route took us up through Woolley Wood, past Middlewood Hospital as far as a bridge at Oughtibridge. We then headed back via the woods, Middlewood Road and Leppings Lane. As if that was not enough, the run was invariably topped up with a few laps of the running track around the main pitch.

Some of us might try to shorten the route by wading across the Don on the way, but the state of the river bed in some parts was such that we learned to err on the side of caution after one of the lads picked up an infection in his blistered foot.

There was one occasion when a group of us thought we had found the ideal way of reducing the running distance. We begged a lift on a passing Tizer lorry! Unfortunately, when we dropped off the vehicle outside the Park Cinema, round the corner from the ground, Alan Brown just happened to be passing. Our punishment was so many extra laps of the Hillsborough pitch that we started to wonder if the coach had forgotten to call us in!

Because of my contribution to our Second Division title triumph, I was the focus of considerable media attention as the new season approached. Of course this was not as extensive or intrusive as often tends to be the case these days, but I had my first lesson in the way television can sometimes alter reality for the convenience of a good camera shot. Ahead of our opening game, against Newcastle United at Hillsborough, the BBC wanted

Portrait of a young man with a bright future, summer 1952.

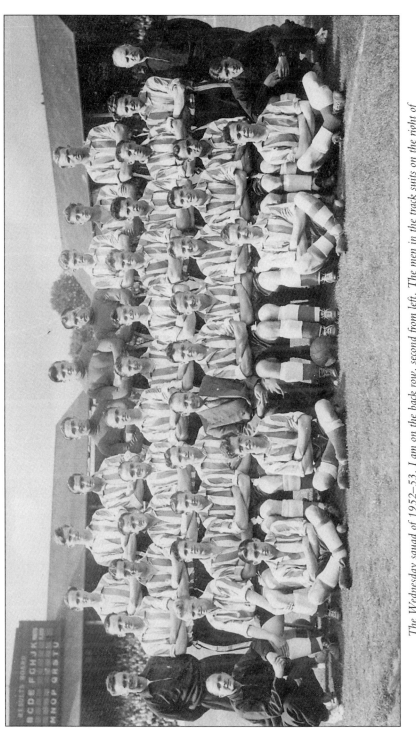

The Wednesday squad of 1952–53. I am on the back row, second from left. The men in the track suits on the right of the group are Tommy Walker (standing) and Johnny Logan, key figures in my early development.

to film me catching a tram at the foot of Addison Road, supposedly setting out for the match. They decided it was easier to do this on the upward route, which meant I boarded a tram bound for Firth Park. Then, out of sight of the cameras I crossed the road and caught the tram I really needed, one going in the opposite direction and taking me to our meeting place at the Athol Hotel in town!

I wished the cameras could have produced an 'improved' version on our match with Newcastle, which attracted a crowd of over 55,000 but proved a disappointment for our fans. Thanks to goals in the last five minutes from Jackie Sewell and Redfern Froggatt we salvaged a 2–2 draw after the FA Cup holders had led 2–0 within less than half-an-hour of the kick-off.

To my dismay I endured a miserable afternoon against big Frank Brennan. On and off the field Frank, a Scottish international centre-half, was a gentleman but he was such a competent and experienced defender that he not only had me well and truly tied up but coped with the entire Wednesday forward line on his own.

We lost our next three games and failed to score in all of them. The critics were already saying our results suggested we were proving yet again

Frank Brennan makes sure I don't get to the ball first during the game with Newcastle, August 1952.

that we were too good for the Second Division and not good enough for the First, but we felt the fates were as much to blame as our form for the defeats we suffered in two midweek matches with Liverpool.

We lost at Anfield to a goal scored by Kevin Baron just two minutes from the end, and it summed up our lack of luck that Baron's header was inadvertently deflected past Dave McIntosh off Cyril Turton's chest. However, what really hurt was being denied a penalty moments before Liverpool's winner. My wait for my first goal would have been over if Ronnie Moran had not dived and punched a shot of mine off the line. We could not believe our eyes when referee Gavin Black didn't even award us a corner. He gave Liverpool a goal-kick with which goalkeeper Ashcroft found Billy Liddell, and it was the Scot's cross which led to Baron's goal.

When Liverpool came to Hillsborough a week later, Baron again gave them the lead. This time he struck just before half-time. Unfortunately, a few minutes earlier he had gone for a high ball with McIntosh and our goalkeeper ended up with a fractured arm. 'Mac' stayed on the field until the interval but then Norman Curtis, our left-back, took over in the green

We beat the Newcastle goalkeeper, Ronnie Simpson, twice that day, but I had to settle for watching Jack Sewell and Redfern Froggatt notch the late goals that earned us a 2–2 draw.

Goalmouth action in the home game with Liverpool.

Tom McAnearney (left) was a new boy in the first team, and here he watches as Redfern Froggatt conducts a mock interview with me in the dressing room.

jersey. Norman had a reputation as an excellent emergency goalkeeper but for all his heroics on this occasion he was unable to prevent Liddell from sealing a 2–0 victory for the Merseysiders.

This was the game in which I was cautioned for the only time in my career, the irony was that referee R.P. Hartley took my name for alleged dangerous play when all that happened was I fell over someone's legs and onto the goalkeeper—even the Liverpool players pleaded my innocence!

It simply added to my frustration that we missed a penalty ten minutes from the end. I was brought down in the box and, being desperate to end my goal-drought, would have loved to have taken the spot-kick myself. However, Walter Rickett, for whom this proved the penultimate game of his Wednesday career, was given the job and his shot was fisted away by Ashcroft.

In between the games with Liverpool we travelled to Cardiff and the team that had been promoted with us a few months earlier enjoyed a comfortable 4–0 victory to celebrate the first Division One game staged at Ninian Park since 1929.

Considering the Cardiff fans had waited since six months before I was born to see their favourites return to the top grade, no doubt they had every reason to enjoy the occasion. Alas, it was not one I had cause to remember with any affection. Stan Montgomery, the home centre-half, did rather more than give me a hard time and this was another day when we were denied a penalty.

We were only one-goal down when Montgomery hit me with something and knocked me out cold. A chill dose of the magic sponge soon brought me round. However, I learned the referee had awarded us a penalty for Montgomery's foul but then been persuaded to change his mind. To the dismay of the Wednesday lads he insisted on re-starting the game with a bounce up!

Montgomery was not the only opposing defender to give me some stick. In this period there was a lot of talk in the Press about the treatment I was getting from many defenders and several pundits noted the pleasure it seemed to give some opposition supporters when I was floored by foul, as well as fair, means. Writing of the Cardiff match in the *Daily Mail*, J.L. Manning said: 'Because Dooley is so big, players and spectators think he can be tackled without regard to the rules of fairness observed for smaller men'. A few days later R.A. Sparling, commenting in the *Sheffield Telegraph* after the second Liverpool match, noted: 'Dooley's record last season has made defenders determined he will not pass and the methods of stopping him are not always within the rules'.

Frankly, while I did not enjoy some of the tactics used against me and if I was bitterly disappointed not to have compensated for the rough treatment with a few goals, I accepted that taking the knocks was part and parcel of the game. I only wanted to battle on and felt sure my fortunes would improve. Unfortunately, our secretary-manager, Eric Taylor, believed the moment had come when the right thing was to rest me.

When Eric confirmed he was dropping me for the home match with Charlton he told the *Sheffield Telegraph*: 'We are doing this to give Dooley a chance. We think he has not had fair treatment in the First Division and do not wish to break his heart. I am giving him a chance to regain his spirit. He has been a marked man. I have twice seen him knocked out by a fist without the referee even penalising the opposition'.

There was nothing I could do about being dropped, but when Eric Taylor called me into his office and announced I was being rested I could not resist disagreeing with his decision to make me twelfth man to the first-team. It is amusing now to recall that during our meeting Eric handed me a benefit cheque to which I was due. I imagine he thought the money, totalling £500 less tax, might temper my dismay at being dropped. In the event I was so disappointed I completely forgot to look at the figure on the cheque.

I was too busy telling Eric that standing on the sidelines was no way of getting myself back onto the goal-standard. I said I needed to keep playing and insisted I would much prefer a run with the reserves, or even the third team, to watching the Charlton match from the players' pen.

By one of those curious coincidences which football frequently throws up, the next reserve fixture was against Sheffield United at Bramall Lane. Eric had already posted the team sheet on the dressing room notice board but he readily altered the line-up to accommodate me. In later years I think he was able to make a joke about the fact that my presence at Bramall Lane prompted some Wednesday fans to support the reserves and boost Sheffield United's income by so doing!

While the first-team's game with Charlton attracted a 35,000 crowd, six thousand down on the previous home match, the Central League fixture between the Blades and the Owls was witnessed by more than 8,500 spectators. Happily I was able to reward the Wednesday fans present by scoring for the first time that season. I had to wait until ten minutes from the end before I hit the target, but I then did it twice in the space of a minute and we won 3–1 while the first-team were going down 3–0 over at Hillsborough.

Action during the Central League game at Bramall Lane after I was dropped in September 1952.

Shooting for goal in the match against Sheffield United reserves, the day when deciding to revert to my faithful old boots paid a two-goal dividend.

It is often said that psychology plays an important role in sport and this Central League game provided a personal example of how something apparently trivial had the effect of putting me at ease ahead of the kick-off. All I did was change my boots but for the first time in weeks I suddenly felt good.

In those days getting a new pair of boots was nearly as difficult as winning the pools but, as the ones with which I had broken the club's scoring record were falling apart, I was allowed to replace them. The new boots were fine but somehow they never seemed as comfortable as the old ones. I couldn't really blame them for my lack of success but now I decided to throw them aside and reached for the faithful battered old pair which felt just like carpet slippers when I put them on. Naturally, now I was back on the goal-trail there was no way I was going to part with those boots again.

One small incident which occurred after this match is worthy of noting. When I left the ground intending to catch a Firth Park tram at the bottom of the Moor, I found a Wednesdayite waiting outside in his car. I did not know the man and never knew his name, but he offered to run me home to Addison Road. He spent the journey explaining why he thought Wednesday had been wrong to drop me and why he had preferred watching me play in the reserves to taking his usual seat at Hillsborough.

No doubt the man was in the 8,000 crowd for the home Central League match against Liverpool reserves the following Wednesday, and I'm sure that, like me, he was delighted when I finished with a hat-trick. Happily he did not have to miss the next first-team game at Hillsborough three days later, for five goals in two matches earned me a senior recall.

I did not score on my return against Tottenham but felt I made a useful contribution to a 2–0 success which marked our first win in six games. More importantly, the victory signalled the start of a ten-match unbeaten run which hauled us off the bottom and launched a welcome climb up the table. In fact, against Spurs we didn't break the deadlock until halfway through the second half when Sewell converted a Woodhead cross, but Alan Finney completed a happy afternoon with a wonderful late goal when he ran forty yards and dribbled the ball round goalkeeper Ted Ditchburn before plonking it in the net.

Alan did all the hard work after collecting a pass, but I was grateful to earn a share of the praise for having taken the ball off defender Arthur Willis before feeding Finney.

Heading the first of my three goals against Liverpool reserves in September 1952.

That elusive first senior goal in the top-grade finally came on the following Wednesday evening when we beat Middlesbrough 2–0. The game kicked off at a quarter to six and anyone who passed within five miles of the Hillsborough ground at about five minutes past seven must have heard the roar as the 41,000 crowd greeted the moment when I poked the ball into the net. I have never witnessed anything quite like it.

I know it sounds corny but the only way to describe the atmosphere is to say the crowd went mad. Hats flew into the air, the cheers were as loud and long as any I have ever experienced, and every Wednesday player ran up to shake my hand. I think the scenes of unrestrained joy confirmed that everyone present shared my sense of relief. For myself I just felt as if a huge weight was suddenly lifted off my head.

I suppose it was what people would call a typical Dooley goal. We were attacking the Kop end and when I headed a ball forward in midfield I set off to chase it. Bill Whitaker, the Middlesbrough centre-half, was coming for it in the opposite direction but I got there first and pushed the ball wide of goalkeeper Rolando Ugolini and into the net.

Earlier in the game I had played a part in the goal with which Jackie Sewell had given us the lead. I had also missed a 'sitter' from five yards. According to match reports, this gilt-edged chance was gifted me by Jackie when he could have scored himself, but I have my doubts about the truth of that statement. Jackie was as keen as anyone to see me get my first goal but I don't remember ever seeing him pass up a scoring opportunity. He must have thought I was better placed, and I'll bet he wasn't impressed when I missed the target!

In the end the only thing that mattered was I had got off the mark at last. In the next twenty-three games I would add another fifteen goals to my tally in an eventful spell which seldom lacked incident and was often sweet and sometimes sour.

Recalled to the first team against Spurs, I went near with this header.

A tussle with Ted Ditchburn, the Spurs goalkeeper.

Spurs defenders Willis and Wetton combine to frustrate my attempts to find the net.

*My team-mate Dennis Woodhead and referee Arthur Ellis look on as
Walton clears for Preston while I just fail to reach the ball.*

No joy for me either in this aerial attack on the Preston goal.

Chapter Seventeen

Back in the Old Routine

What particularly pleased me about the period between mid–September 1952 and the first week in February 1953 was something much more than simply being back in the business of doing what I was paid for and scoring goals. By early in 1953 it was a welcome bonus to find my tally of sixteen put me second to Nat Lofthouse in the list of the country's leading marksmen, but what really boosted my morale was knowing my voluntary extra practice sessions and the experience of playing in the top grade were stimulating an improvement in my all-round game. I knew I was getting better and felt sure the best was yet to come.

It helped, too, that some of my critics were starting to remark on my progress. As early as the first week in October when I scored twice in a 3–1 win at Stoke, a respected Sunday newspaper writer called Edgar Turner really made my day when he drew attention to my development. He wrote: 'Dooley is improving his technique. He is waiting less for the ball. He is using the field more and has a more ready appreciation of open space'. Others, mostly people in the game, also made similar comments.

Alan Brown, our coach, was brilliant in that he not only continued to show great patience with me on the practice pitch but was always there with the right word on match days. Alan was a great motivator and a half-time pep talk from him could do wonders for one's self-belief. I always felt I wanted to do well as much for 'Brownie' as myself. He was always telling me not to worry when I didn't score and stressed that so long as I was contributing to the team effort there would be no complaints from him.

There was one spell in October and early November which illustrated the point. I managed only a single goal in six games but as we won three and lost just one nobody could say I didn't make a substantial contribution.

I knew I was capable of making my presence felt and my team-mates could profit when the opposition became too preoccupied with stopping me. Moreover, I didn't need telling how it often paid to chase lost causes.

When we went to Arsenal and earned a deserved 2–2 draw, I didn't score but had a hand in both our goals. 'Brownie' told me before the game to keep Ray Daniel, the home centre-half, under constant pressure. He said: 'Daniel likes to play football and he's the kind of player who will make a mug of you five times out of six. But the sixth time he'll make a mistake'. My persistence enabled me to profit from the Welsh international's over-confidence not once but twice and the upshot was I won possession and set up goals for Froggatt and Woodhead.

Of course, I was still getting rough treatment from some defenders and there were a couple of home games in the autumn of 1952, against Derby and Portsmouth, when I won two penalties in each match. Frankly, if the referee had done his job when we faced Derby we should have had five penalties instead of two because I spent more time flat on my back than standing on my feet. I was up against a giant South African called Norman Neilson who was hellbent on stopping me at all costs.

In both games the penalties were converted by Norman Curtis in his inimitable 'cannonball' style. As I have mentioned, Norman was quite a character and one of the things older fans will always remember him for is his penalty technique. Someone would place the ball on the spot, then Norman would steam in from his left-back position and slam it into the net without stopping. So long as he was on target he could not fail to score because such was the power of his shot no goalkeeper who got in the way could avoid being carried into the net with the ball. We feared if Norman ever put the ball the wrong side of the post he might decapitate three spectators in the crowd behind the goal!

Reference to Norman reminds me that it was during this spell that we won 1–0 at Blackpool and Curtis was one of our heroes in that he completely snuffed out the threat of the legendary Stanley Matthews. Before the game Alan Brown had told Norman to follow Matthews everywhere he went. Norman took the instruction so literally I think he might have followed the winger to the toilet if Stan had chosen to 'pay a call' during the match! Norman was never less than six inches from Matthews throughout the ninety minutes and the England wizard could not shake him off.

It summed up the humorous side of the situation when, at one stage, Matthews and Curtis were standing together in the home penalty area while all the remaining outfield players were engaged in the other goalmouth. Naturally, the Blackpool fans were frustrated, and as we left

I took some 'stick' from Neilson in the game with Derby, but won two penalties and here we both end up on the ground.

Derby goalkeeper Ray Middleton is explaining the trouble between me and Neilson to the referee.

As Ray Middleton blocks my shot I am ready to pounce on the rebound, but Neilson (right) challenged me and conceded a penalty kick for the second time in the game.

More conventional action as I fire in a shot at the Kop end.

the field at half-time a member of the brass band waiting to entertain the crowd could not resist telling Norman it was about time he left Matthews alone. Norman responded: 'You play the big drum, mate, and leave me to play Matthews!'

Curtis was not on his own among the Wednesday lads in seldom lacking a sharp turn of wit. A past master when it came to seeing the funny side of things was my pal Dennis Woodhead. He got the winner at Blackpool and it was one of the softest goals he ever scored. George Farm, the home goalkeeper, played a blinder that day and there was one instance when a save he made from me was so stunning I could not resist applauding him.

Ray Middleton, the Derby goalkeeper, plucks the ball off my toes.

Subsequently all his hard work was undone in a crazy moment when Woodhead somehow managed to squeeze the ball between Farm's legs and into the net. I don't say it was a fluke but certainly fortune was on our side. 'That's the way to do it, Derek' said Dennis, 'the secret is to trick him!'

Dennis, the grandson of Billy Betts, a famous old Wednesday man of the 1890s, was an outstanding player who scored seventy-six goals in 213 games for Wednesday between 1947 and 1955. There were few greater characters in the Hillsborough dressing room in my time, both on and off the field he was always the kind of guy who invariably gave you a lift. He was popular because he made us laugh with his down-to-earth sense of humour, although I must admit some of the lads failed to see the funny side one day when Dennis chose to bring a couple of ferrets into the dressing room and set them loose.

The stars in our forward line in those days were Sewell, Quixall and Froggatt, and when they followed each other into the England team, Dennis joked: 'Us two must be crap, Derek. Tha's scored all them goals and I've provided them all, but it's yon lot who've been picked for England. What are we doing wrong?'

One goal I have never forgotten scoring, because of Dennis's reaction when the home players complained I was off-side, that earned us a 1–1 draw at Manchester United. The United lads were still chuntering when they were preparing to re-start the game. 'It wasn't a goal' someone said, to which Dennis replied: 'Thee look in tonight's *Green 'Un* and tha'll see it says Dooley scored after half-an-hour, and what's in black and green can't lie!'

Dennis was unfortunate in being hampered by injuries, and the fact that he was never the physical type of player lent added humour to a comment he made during a game at Bolton. He went into a challenge with big Matt Barrass, a tough centre-half of the old school and, ironically, Barrass ended up hobbling off the pitch. Dennis looked across at me with a grin and said: 'There, I've got shut of him for thee, Derek!'

One of the most remarkable wins we managed in the autumn of 1952 was a 5–1 triumph at Newcastle, and I never think of this game without remembering Dennis. I shot us in front after only six minutes when a quick upfield break ended with Woodhead having a fierce effort turned onto the bar by goalkeeper Ronnie Simpson. The ball rebounded out as far as just beyond the penalty spot where I happened to be standing. I volleyed the ball into the net with such force it bounced back into play off a rear stanchion. 'That's it' said Dennis. 'Place 'em, Derek, don't hit 'em. I knew I'd find you at the edge of the box and just thought I'd do it with an in-off off the bar!'

Dennis and I shared a great passion for fishing and over the years we spent countless hours together on many river banks. In our playing days Monday was our regular day off and we seldom wasted the opportunity to go fishing. If Dennis saw me limping at the end of a Saturday game he would tell me to stop looking as if I was injured because he knew it would mean having to report for treatment on Monday just when we were scheduled to pack our tackle in his van and take a trip into Lincolnshire or some other angling venue.

Dennis was especially keen to get me back fishing as soon as possible after the accident which ended my playing days, and I always remember he took me and Ivor Seemley with him when I was still on crutches. My wife Sylvia was not too keen on the venture and she asked Dennis: 'You will look after him won't you?' He promised he would. We went to a place near Ely and, sure enough, Dennis made certain I was comfortably entrenched close to the water's edge. Unfortunately when a barge sailed past and the water suddenly rose, I found myself in great difficulties because I couldn't lift myself up to escape. Dennis, spotting my discomfort at the prospect of being submerged by the water, simply said: 'Derek, if tha drowns, can I have thee sandwiches?'

When Dennis died at the age of seventy a few years ago I lost a great friend and the loss was all the more poignant because I didn't learn that he was ill until a few hours before I went off on a trip. I vowed to visit him as soon as I returned home but, unfortunately, in the meantime he lost his battle with cancer.

As I started to adjust to life in the top-grade and began to feel comfortable facing some of English football's biggest names, it was probably inevitable that my robust style continued to provoke criticism and controversy. However, I think most people in the game accepted and applauded the fact that I was simply making the best use of my strengths. They knew I played hard but fair and within the rules. Unfortunately, a few spectators didn't take the same viewpoint.

I could run, I was fast and, once I was on my way, if a defender stood there I would knock him down. I felt I was wasting my time going round him! Most players accepted that giving and taking knocks was part and parcel of the game but if I never held back from a challenge I can honestly say I never attempted to deliberately injure an opponent. I never worried about the crowd's reaction but I was concerned if I thought I had injured someone.

Naturally, I took a lot of verbal stick from opposition supporters at away grounds. The irony was that the same fans would have been cheering

Dooley in action in 1952.

if I had worn a home shirt and, frankly, I always felt that overall the majority of spectators were good to me and accepted me for what I was. Such incidents as the day at Tottenham, in January 1953, when a spectator jumped onto the running track and made a beeline for me, only being prevented from reaching me thanks to a flying rugby tackle by a policeman, were the exception rather than the rule. Most of my terrace critics were content to express their views by booing me!

The press reports of the Tottenham match made the point that some of the home fans were too busy booing me to enjoy the pleasures of a Spurs victory, and this kind of preoccupation with criticising me was not unusual. A few weeks earlier J.L. Manning, writing in the *Daily Mail* about our match at Old Trafford, had noted that some Manchester fans had jumped to their feet and applauded every time I was tripped by a home man. I was told that at the same match one Wednesday fan was ejected from the ground because he had told a home supporter it was not good sportsmanship to cheer when an opponent was knocked to the floor!

I appreciated a comment which Alan Hoby made in the *Sunday Express* following a game at Charlton, where I was again the target of the boo-boys. He wrote: 'There are some people who think Dooley is a dirty player. All I can say is those folk must be blind or crazy. If I may dredge up a cliché, Britain's most talked-about centre-forward is more sinned against than the sinner'.

After the same match, Jimmy Seed, the Charlton manager, said: 'I'd rather have Dooley on my side than against me. He is one of the most dangerous centre-forwards in the country and he'll get better'.

Of course I was conscious of the jeers and boos but the crowd's reaction never hurt me. The more they booed and called me, the more I thought well, if I'm worrying these blokes and they're only standing on the terraces, I must be worrying the blokes I'm playing against.

The Tottenham game mentioned earlier is notable in retrospect because this was when I scored the last goal of my career. However, at the time I was rather more conscious of an incident involving goalkeeper Ted Ditchburn.

During the match Ditchburn called me a yellow so-and-so. Subsequently when we won a corner I reminded him of what he had said and added: 'Get ready, I'm coming'. The upshot was that when the ball came into the goalmouth Ditchburn and his colleagues, Ronnie Burgess and Harry Clarke, ended up alongside me in the back of the net. The referee whistled and after I had untangled myself I said: 'Sorry, ref, I missed the ball'. I accepted I had committed a foul but I was just making the point to the goalkeeper that I certainly wasn't yellow.

Ditchburn now threatened: 'I'll see you after the match'. That was okay by me. Indeed, instead of following my normal habit and being the last Wednesday man out of the bath after the game, I was the first. I was all wound up ready to accept Ditchburn's invitation—and it didn't matter to me that he was a former army boxing champion reputed to be pretty

Action during our game at Tottenham in late January 1953.

My challenges on Ted Ditchburn did not exactly please the Tottenham goalkeeper.

good with his fists. Unfortunately, when I made to leave the dressing room in search of the goalkeeper, Alan Brown asked: 'What are you doing?' I told him and he said: 'Sit down there and don't move'.

On the train journey back to Sheffield, Alan asked: 'What were you going to do?' I admitted I didn't think I knew and it may well be that, had there been a confrontation, Ditchburn and I would have ended up simply shaking hands. As I told 'Brownie', I was now more concerned that because I hadn't turned up Ditchburn might think I really was a coward. 'Well, he'll find out you're not the next time he comes to Hillsborough, won't he?' said the coach.

Alas, within three weeks, circumstances would conspire to ensure I would never get the chance to face Ditchburn—or any other goalkeeper again.

It is worthy of note that after this game Arthur Rowe, the Tottenham manager, spoke in my defence when a journalist asked him to comment on my style. Rowe said: 'Dooley used his weight pretty freely but I don't think there was anything vicious about his play. He is the sort of player who never gives up and his persistence is always likely to lead him into situations not encountered by a less tenacious player'. Obviously Mr Rowe didn't think I was 'yellow'!

There were others like Ditchburn who made it plain they did not appreciate my style, and it was amusing sometimes to recognise how two players in the same team had opposing views about me. When Portsmouth came to Sheffield and beat us 4–3 in one of the games when I earned two penalties, I was surprised that opposing centre-half Jack Froggatt refused to shake hands at the final whistle. However, his colleague Jimmy Scoular came up and put an arm round my shoulder. He grinned: 'You've upset Jack today, Derek, but don't worry about it, son. Keep playing just the way you do'. As Scoular was one of the hardest players in the game, I appreciated the compliment.

Frank Brennan, the man who had tied me in knots in the first game of the season, was similarly complimentary when I helped us to a 5–1 victory in the return fixture at Newcastle. At the final whistle he congratulated me and commented: 'I've had an awful afternoon thanks to you, but you keep playing like that, son. Don't let anybody change you'.

The record books show that my senior career with Wednesday spanned a mere sixty-three games and what might be called my golden phase was limited to barely fourteen months of League football before my playing days were suddenly ended three months after my twenty-third birthday. Perhaps because I packed so much into such a short spell, even nearly fifty years later I still remember almost every detail of the period between October 1952 and February 1953.

When I think of the 1952–53 campaign and the months immediately preceding the unfortunate event that occurred at Preston on Valentine's Day, it is more often with a smile than a frown. It was a happy phase from which I recall many moments tinged with humour and, while most were trivial incidents, for me they capture the essence of a time I shall always treasure because it was special.

Everybody who saw me play will claim I scored a few of my sixty-three senior goals with my shin, my knee and even my backside, but if anyone ever suggests the equaliser I hit at Bolton in November 1952 was a fluke, don't you believe them. I must admit I did intend to cross the ball as I moved in from the wing along the goal-line, but, when I saw goalkeeper Stan Hanson step forward in anticipation of a centre, I suddenly decided to shoot for the gap he left at the near post. The angle was difficult and, if I'm honest, I must say I was as surprised as anybody when I hit the target exactly where I had intended. It may not have been a typical Dooley goal and it probably left even my witty mate Dennis Woodhead lost for words, but it was no fluke—just pure genius!

A first-half header from Redfern Froggatt earned us victory against Chelsea in November 1952.

Challenging Robertson, the Chelsea goalkeeper, for a high ball from Alan Finney.

The Chelsea defence is again under pressure, but Ron Greenwood and John Harris watch as Robertson holds my shot. Harris, of course, was later manager of Sheffield United and had a spell with Wednesday.

*Rag Day in Sheffield in 1952 saw one university student create an effigy of me,
but, as I told him, I was never as big-headed at that!*

In terms of remarkable goals, a week after our trip to Bolton we drew 2–2 with Aston Villa. Stan Lynn, the Villa full-back, stunned us early in the game with an incredible strike from all of fifty yards. I think it was intended as a cross rather than a shot but it bamboozled Ron Capewell, our goalkeeper, and Lynn would certainly have been upset if anyone suggested it was a fluke.

The funniest thing about that Villa game was the way their centre-forward Derek 'Doc' Pace got away with consistently charging Capewell while I was penalised every time I touched the Villa goalkeeper Keith Jones. It was amusing see Pace, a stocky little man, keep barging into Capewell, a man-mountain at six-feet four-inches tall and all of fifteen stone. Unfortunately, we ended up with little to smile about because Pace's persistence paid off when he barged into Big Ron, who dropped the ball and could only watch as it rolled into the net for the goal which salvaged a 2–2 draw.

There were times when we tended to be over-generous to the opposition at Hillsborough, our Boxing Day game with West Brom was a classic example. Despite leading three times and being 4–2 up at one stage, we lost a thrilling duel 5–4 when Ronnie Allen snatched Albion's winner three minutes from the end. I know it was Christmas and an occasion when the festive spirit was at a peak, but we seemed to go over the top in terms of handing out gifts! Our defenders Norman Curtis and Eddie Gannon both scored own goals and, while it was never confirmed in the record books, I'm convinced one of Albion's other goals was turned in by Mick Kenny.

Opposing teams did not share our tendency for showing goodwill in the festive season, as I remember when we visited Middlesbrough on a wet and miserable New Year's Day when Albert Quixall took some terrible stick from Jimmy Gordon, the home left-half. Jimmy is probably best remembered now as a key member of the Derby and Nottingham Forest training staff in Brian Clough's golden years as a manager, but he first made his name as a tenacious and fearless player raised in a hard school on Tyneside and Teeside.

'Quix' complained to me at half-time: 'Derek, that bloke keeps kicking me'. I knew it was no use telling Albert to kick him back, so I told Gordon: 'I'll sort you out if you don't leave Albert alone'.

Gordon pointed to the main stand in the Ayresome Park ground and said: 'You see over there? That's where my directors sit, and they expect me to get stuck in'.

I replied: 'Well, my directors are sitting up there as well, and they don't just expect me to get stuck in. They also expect me to look after my mate Quixall and I'll sort you out if you keep having a go at him'.

Scoring against Aston Villa in November 1952.

Jack Sewell takes to the air during the Villa game in which I scored two first-half goals.

Action during our home game with Wolves as Pritchard clears while I look poised to pounce and poor old Dennis Woodhead (right) falls to the ground.

This picture was taken before our Christmas game at West Brom in 1952 when Slater and Storrar (between me and Cyril Turton on the front row) came into the side because Froggatt and Woodhead were injured.

Howells, the Cardiff goalkeeper, failed to hold this cross and I was able to pounce to score our first goal in a 2–0 win in January 1953.

On target for the second time in the match against Cardiff with a low shot past the goalkeeper.

Heading for goal watched by Stan Montgomery, the Cardiff defender.

In training before the FA Cup tie with Blackpool in January 1953. The line up is (left to right) Marriott, Dooley, Turton, Curtis, Witcomb, Sewell and Gannon.

I am looking on as Blackpool's Eddie Shimwell prepares to clear the ball.

This was a close call for Blackpool as we put them under pressure in our cup game, but George Farm, their goalkeeper, makes a spectacular save.

The last full ninety minutes I played for Wednesday in an away match came at Wolverhampton on the final day of January 1953 and I shall always remember it as a game which the referee abandoned but was then persuaded to complete. I think Wolves, who were leading and in sight of only their third win in eleven games, were keener to see the match finished than might otherwise have been the case.

The players were taken off in the second half because a blizzard made it impossible to continue. We were kicking into the snowstorm and couldn't see a thing. Most of our lads were stripped and poised to plunge into the bath, and I was actually already enjoying a soak when, to our astonishment, we were called back onto the field. Well, they do say it's a funny old game sometimes!

Here I am enjoying a tussle with Burnley's Tommy Cummings in what was to prove my last home game for Wednesday. Sadly, we lost 4–2 and I didn't manage to score.

Chapter Eighteen

Deepdale,
February 14th 1953

Those sudden and unexpected twists of fate over which we have no control but which shape our lives are a puzzle to most of us. I am sure the majority of people often look back on those crucial incidents and wonder whether things might have been different with just the slightest change in the pattern of events leading to what you might call our moments of destiny.

Over the years I have reflected many times on the circumstances in which my playing career was brought to a sudden end when the surgeons had to amputate my right leg to save my life. Of course, it was a shattering and traumatic experience but I have never felt sorry for myself and at no stage have I ever felt bitter. Once I came to terms with the situation I just got on with my life, I knew it was no good looking back and regretting something that had happened and couldn't be changed.

All the same I have often believed there is a sense in which I was simply a victim of the circumstances which existed in those days. In another time or place it might not, indeed would not, have happened. I was probably unlucky in that the match at Preston in which I broke my leg could easily have been postponed because of the conditions, yet, ironically, I was remarkably fortunate in the way the gas gangrene, caused by an infection in the leg, was accidentally discovered just hours before I was due to leave hospital and travel home.

Let me go back to the day before that fateful fixture at Deepdale on St Valentine's Day 1953. The weather across the whole of northern England was dreadful and there was so much snow on the Pennines that the exposed road routes from Sheffield into Lancashire were blocked. The Wednesday party had planned to travel by coach, but when Eric Taylor learned that Woodhead was closed, he hurriedly arranged for us to make the journey by train. We stayed overnight at Blackpool where, to our surprise, there was far less snow and ice than we had seen everywhere else.

However, as we made the short trip to Preston by bus on the Saturday morning the conditions seemed to worsen by the mile and I think most of the players half expected to learn the game had been postponed. I don't think I am mistaken when I say the prospects of the match being played remained doubtful right up to the kick-off.

I doubt whether anybody in the Wednesday camp would have complained if the game had been put off, for we were set to face one of the best teams in the First Division without Eddie Gannon, Redfern Froggatt and my pal Dennis Woodhead. Gannon's absence meant Tommy McAnearney, a promising young Scottish half-back, was making only his third senior appearance, while Woodhead's replacement was a young winger from Oswestry, called Bill Shadbolt, who was set for his Football League debut. It was some consolation that Albert Quixall, who was doing his National Service, had obtained leave from the army and had travelled from Catterick to join us.

Deepdale in those days had a reputation for being a heavy ground at the best of times and we arrived to find the groundstaff had been working on the pitch all morning. They had cleared away the ice and snow, but the pitch, softened by the salt peat intended to combat the frost, still didn't look too good. However, by the standards of the time, it was playable.

Had the year been 1993 instead of 1953 I have no doubt the game would not have been played. This is no reflection on Preston North End, referee Arthur Ellis or anybody else who was involved in the decision to go ahead, and it is no criticism of the very different attitudes in the modern game to the same situation. It is much easier to reschedule matches nowadays and at the start of the 21st century nobody would be expected to play in conditions considered quite acceptable forty or fifty years ago. There were no floodlights then and so clubs were keen to avoid a backlog of fixtures and a subsequently crowded end-of-season programme. As re-arranged midweek games were often played in the afternoon when people were working, clubs also faced the prospect of reduced gates and a loss of revenue. It all meant that conditions had to be exceptionally bad to prevent a game going ahead on its scheduled date.

I have to stress that the fact that I broke my leg in the game had nothing to do with the conditions. It was an accident which could have happened on a fine day on a perfect pitch.

Incidentally, in the light of the significance of this match for me, it was not without irony that it was one of the few away games in my Wednesday career when my father and my wife Sylvia were not present. They usually travelled to most matches, and Syliva had every intention of going to Deepdale on a Supporters' Club bus. Unfortunately, because of the conditions and the closure of the Woodhead route, the coaches were cancelled.

Sylvia has never forgotten that she decided to compensate by watching the reserves play at Hillsborough, and it was when she left the ground afterwards and was standing in Herries Road waiting to catch the homeward-bound Outer Circle bus that she overheard someone in the queue say it had been reported on the radio that I had been carried off at Preston with a suspected broken leg.

She rushed home to Addison Road to tell my parents, and Dad tried to calm her by saying it was only a rumour. I think a headline in the *Green 'Un* that evening confirmed what had happened, but the family did not accept is as fact until Sam Powell, the club's trainer, arrived at our house to say I would be spending the weekend in Preston Royal Infirmary.

The record books show that Preston North End were pipped to the Football League championship in 1953 on goal average. I mention this fact to emphasise what a strong team they were in those days. Tom Finney, the England star, was still their king-pin and they had strengthened their attack by signing Jimmy Baxter, a Scottish inside-forward, from Barnsley. It is also relevant to note a crucial factor in their progress was a sound defensive organisation featuring an astute use of the off-side game by full-backs Bill Cunningham and Bill Scott and Australian centre-half Joe Marston. This trio were ably supported by Scottish wing-halves Bill Forbes and Tommy Docherty.

However, good as they were, we didn't consider them unbeatable. Indeed, we felt we were getting on top in the latter stages of a first half during which I hit the home crossbar, while Jackie Sewell had the ball in the net only to be frustrated by an off-side decision.

During half-time Alan Brown, our coach, stressed that the way we could overcome Preston's off-side trap was by playing earlier through balls from midfield and ensuring I timed my runs to coincide with the moment the home defenders moved forward. If we got it right, I would burst clear with only the goalkeeper in front of me and be free to power in towards the ball and the target with the home backs left stranded.

About fourteen minutes into the second half we worked this move with a sweet and sudden simplicity, although, when Albert Quixall released his long pass and I dashed off from the half-way line in pursuit of the ball, I remember thinking the goalkeeper, George Thompson, looked sure to win the chase if he left his goalmouth quickly. George, however, hesitated just long enough to make me believe I could reach the ball first even though it was only just beyond the penalty area.

I was in full flight and George was now speeding in the opposite direction. Because George could not use his hands I knew he had no option but to go for the ball with his feet. I was close enough to stretch for it at just the same moment with my right leg. I managed to make the first connection with the ball before George but never knew if it was with my foot or some other part of my leg because in the same instant the two of us collided and my leg took the full impact.

I knew immediately the leg was broken, but, in those few seconds before the realisation dawned and I felt the sudden pain, my eyes followed the ball as it rolled across the goalmouth and just wide of a post. Before other emotions engulfed me I just had long enough to regret failing to score. I have to admit that, all these years later, I never re-live those moments without wishing I could say the last time I ever touched a ball as a player at least I had the consolation of putting it in the net. Moreover, had that one gone in we might not have lost the game to a late Tommy Finney goal!

Getting me off the pitch and into an ambulance seemed to take an age. I don't know how long there was between the collision and the start of the journey to Preston Royal Infirmary, but I don't think many people in the ground realised my leg was broken. Of course, the players knew and I have never forgotten that Albert Quixall was close to tears.

The break was a bad one, I suffered a double fracture, but, in normal circumstances, it was an injury from which I would expect to have recovered. It is history now that the broken leg turned out to be only the beginning of a story with far more serious implications but, whatever the unfortunate developments over the following days, I have to stress that the incident at Deepdale was simply an accident. When two well-built footballers, both totally committed and intent on getting to the ball first, collide there is always the threat of injury. The irony is that a similar situation might occur a hundred times without anyone being hurt.

Certainly I never blamed George Thompson and never for a moment throughout nearly fifty years since have I ever borne him any malice. I remember him only as a brave and courageous goalkeeper who loved football and tackled his job with the same passion and dedication as myself. Goalkeeping was in George's blood. He and his brother Des had followed their father into League football, and George, having served a long apprenticeship with Scunthorpe United, had only moved into the First Division with Preston the previous October.

Frankly, I always felt if one of us had to get hurt in that collision it was better for it to have been me. I had this public image as a rough and fearless player and, though it was totally unjust, there were those who regarded me as a dirty beggar. I would have hated to have had anyone pointing a finger at me, and, had it happened that way, I have often wondered what the effect on me would have been.

I went off to hospital, soon found myself in bed with a pot on my leg, and, as I prepared to settle down for a night's sleep later in the evening, I tried to view the situation philosophically. Okay, I thought, the season is over for me, but I shall have the summer in which to complete my recovery and ensure I am fit for the start of the 1953–54 campaign.

How could I know it was not the double fracture that was soon to threaten my career, and, indeed, my life, but a trivial cut on my calf which had become infected, probably due to some innocuous chemical used on the pitch? I could barely remember the circumstances in which I suffered the cut during the first half of the match and I did not learn until more than twenty-four hours later how lethal the rapidly spreading infection was. If I had any good fortune that weekend it was a nurse discovering the problem in the nick of time. Like the accident in the match, that, too, was pure chance.

Chapter Nineteen

'We've Got Some Bad News...'

The period between the late evening of Sunday the 15th of February and the morning of Tuesday the 17th marked a painful peak in the most traumatic and testing phase in my young life as the doctors at Preston Royal Infirmary discovered gas gangrene in my broken leg and knew they had no option but to amputate the limb.

The drama started in a light-hearted atmosphere of laughter and good humour at about ten o'clock on Sunday night. As I was scheduled to leave hospital and travel home on the following morning, the nurses took turns to say their farewells. An Irish nurse asked for my autograph, I invited her to return the favour by signing the pot on my leg and I remember thinking then that I must not forget to persuade Sister Winifred Hampson to sign too before I left. Miss Hampson had gone off duty but I especially wanted to remember her because we had got along famously and she had already proved to be quite a character during my short stay in the ward.

I looked up to see the Irish nurse frowning. 'Your toes are cold and look a bit blue' she said. 'Can you feel anything when I touch them?' I had to admit I couldn't. She suggested the pot was probably too tight, and subsequently, after she had been to find a doctor, there suddenly seemed to be a lot of movement and dashing about in the ward.

It soon transpired that an over-tight pot was not the cause of the problem and when they sped me into the operating theatre to open up the leg and investigate the problem, I didn't need telling that something had gone wrong. However, while it dawned on me that perhaps this was now about rather more than just a broken leg, I was unaware of the full implications and didn't feel any fear or alarm. I imagined it was just a minor medical hitch.

It was sheer chance that Sylvia, who had travelled over from Sheffield earlier in the day, witnessed this development. At this period in our lives she was working in a city centre wholesaler's office and it had been her intention to return home in the evening to be ready to go to her job the following morning. Unfortunately, the weather, which was already pretty bad, took another turn for the worse, a journey across the Pennines was deemed impossible and arrangements were made for Sylvia to stay overnight in the hospital. We didn't know it then but she was destined to remain in Preston for nine weeks—she never did go back to her position with Richardson's on Snig Hill.

With hindsight I can see there had been clues to the seriousness of my condition earlier on that Sunday. All through the morning and afternoon I didn't feel well, indeed I felt quite poorly, but I took the view that this was normal and remained convinced I would begin feeling better once I was back at Addison Road. My main fear was the bad weather might delay my departure. I was desperate to get home and anxious not to let anything happen to delay the journey, so when I suffered bouts of sickness I made discreet use of a handkerchief and asked Sylvia not to let the nurse see the evidence.

Many times since then Sylvia and I have both hardly dared contemplate what might have happened had I left the hospital before the infection was discovered. What a stroke of luck it was that I had asked the nurse to sign my pot and she had playfully tickled my toes! As I learned later the gas gangrene was racing up my leg so rapidly I might even have failed to survive the journey across the Pennines. If it was a shattering blow to learn exactly what I was fighting against, it was even more chilling to realise I could so easily have gone off home unaware of the lethal nature of my condition.

Long afterwards I was shown some X-rays taken at this time and it was strange to think that what looked like innocent whisps of smoke had threatened my life. I was told it was something which had affected thousands of soldiers who suffered shrapnel wounds on wartime battlefields. However, it was a million-to-one against it happening to someone injured on a football pitch.

On the day I had been expecting to go home my parents were instead travelling in the opposite direction. When I came round after the operation during which the gangrene had been found and saw them at my bedside I knew my condition must be causing grave concern. It was only later that I learned the surgeon, R.S. 'Bob' Garden, had asked for a second opinion, which explained why Sheffield Wednesday's orthopaedic specialist, F.W. Holdsworth, had dashed over to Preston. Arrangements were made, too, for some serum to be rushed from Manchester by police escort.

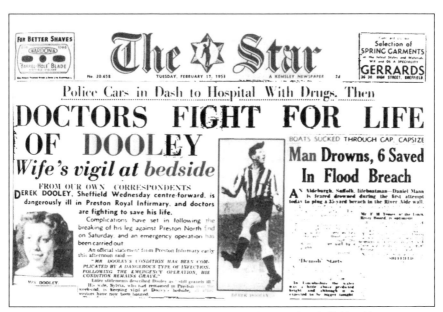

How the dramatic news from Preston was relayed to the Sheffield public.

On the day I broke my leg at Preston, William Fearnehough, the Wednesday chairman died. On the following Saturday the Wednesday players wore black armbands as a mark of respect, and, when the team lined up before the game with Stoke, acting chairman James Longden took time off to send a special message to me in hospital.

I have never forgotten overhearing the two surgeons as they discussed the situation in the hospital corridor just a few yards from my bed. They were speaking very quietly but I heard every word and remember thinking 'that's me they're talking about'. When Mr Garden walked in and said 'I'm afraid we have some bad news, we're going to have to amputate'. I told him 'Yes, I know'. The source of the gangrene was an infection in a scratch on my calf, apparently caused by something used in the treatment of the Deepdale pitch. It must have got into my system while I was waiting to be carried off.

In those moments immediately after I was told the bad news I felt very low both physically and mentally. Indeed I remained unwell in body and spirit for quite some time afterwards. However, while I was shaken by the turn of events and the implications of what was happening, I knew they were fighting to keep me alive and I was grateful for that. All I wanted was for them to get the emergency operation over and done with.

When I went into the theatre on that Tuesday morning I thought I was going to lose my foot. When I awoke following the operation the first thing I saw was a cage holding up the blankets over the bottom half of the bed. I have never forgotten the shock of feeling around with my hand and finding my entire leg had been removed. Mr Garden explained they had been forced to amputate the limb six inches from the top because the gangrene had already reached my knee joint and beyond.

Mr Garden told me later that I might not have survived the operation had I not been a professional footballer and a very fit and healthy young man with the physical and mental strength to battle through the trauma. Even so, the hospital staff endured a tense twenty-four hours after my return from the theatre and Sylvia kept her fingers crossed while everyone awaited confirmation that the gangrene had been caught before it had spread into my upper body.

I must admit that when the surgeon said he had no choice but to amputate my leg and the implications began to dawn on me, my first reaction was to feel they might just as well take me outside and shoot me. I lived for football and the prospect of never again chasing down the field in pursuit of the ball and scoring goals was overwhelmingly unbearable.

If I had ever felt depressed at any earlier stage in my life it was nothing compared with the sense of loss I felt now. I was just turned twenty-three years old and my playing days were finished. I doubt if I shall ever forget the sense of vulnerability and uselessness that suddenly hit me when I began to realise that not being able to play football again was only a part of the story. Sylvia and I had been married for only eight months and here I was with no money, no trade, no house and no means of supporting her.

On the day of our wedding in June our world could not have been happier and it had seemed that nothing less than a golden future beckoned. So soon afterwards I lay in my hospital bed and thought: 'I'm a right catch now! Poor Sylvia, she married a football hero and within a few months ends up with a cripple'.

The truth, of course, was Sylvia had immediately come to terms with the dramatic change in our circumstances and, though still six months short of her twenty-first birthday, the mature, totally selfless and positive way in which she adapted and coped during that time of personal crisis was a tremendous source of strength to me. For all my worries about the future, somehow I knew I could overcome any problem because I was lucky enough to have the best wife in the world at my side!

I drew strength from Sylvia's spirit and courage and, with my parents and other relatives rallying round and giving us every support, I knew we could get through the present and face whatever the future might throw at us.

As I have said, Sylvia remained in Preston throughout the nine weeks I spent in hospital. The dramatic change in our circumstances was as much an ordeal for her as for me and, frankly, I never recall that phase without marvelling at the way she took everything in her stride and maintained a cheerful and positive outlook which was a constant comfort to me. Of course, we had each other, but I cannot forget that this was a phase during which Sylvia had to endure spells alone and must often have felt a long, long way from home.

Apart from a couple of nights at the outset when she was accommodated in the hospital, Sylvia slept at a local pub called the Black Bull where, unfortunately, she did not feel comfortable or at ease. Wednesday were good enough to pay her bill but I must admit I was disappointed they did not arrange for her to stay in a small residential hotel.

Her room was along a dark corridor and to reach it she had to pass close to the pub bar. She has often told the story of how, when she returned there at about closing time on her first night, she discovered to her horror there was no lock on her door. I think my mother eased Sylvia's fears of being confronted by an unwelcome intruder by showing her how to position a chair to serve as a very adequate substitute lock!

I was also worried when I discovered the pub was a fair step from the hospital, about as far as from Middlewood to Hillsborough, and Sylvia was walking back there on her own on the dark evenings. Every night when she left the hospital I found myself whittling about her safety and I could seldom get to sleep until the middle of the night. I invariably ended up feeling extra tired the next morning, and, what with my lack

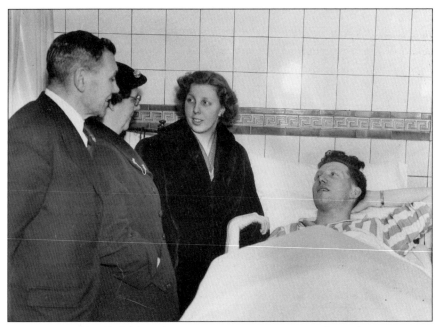

*My wife Sylvia and my parents were a constant source of strength
during my time in Preston infirmary.*

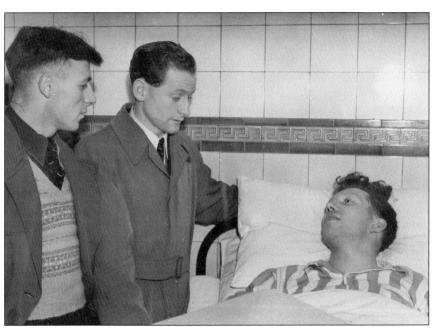

*It was always good to see football friends, and Preston players Tommy Docherty and
Tom Finney were regular visitors to the hospital.*

of sleep and the sense of relief at seeing her step into the ward, the irony was I often slept until lunchtime while my ever-patient wife sat silently at my bedside!

Of course, she could have travelled part of the way to and from the pub by bus, but what we forget now is how limited our funds were in those days. Syliva knew she had to count her pennies and accepted the situation without complaint. Like most women in similar circumstances, she preferred to save her coppers to ensure she stretched her money to buy little luxury items for her husband. Once, for instance, a doctor spotted me drinking some orange squash which Sylvia had bought at a local shop. He frowned and told her fresh oranges would do me a lot more good, and, somehow, she saw I got a regular supply even if it was more expensive.

As I have said, we had we never lacked the unstinting support of our parents. However, they too had to count their pennies but, as often happens in families, they were invariably generous beyond their means. Sylvia was moved to tears one day when her mother sent a card bearing the simple message 'Keep your chin up' and the envelope included a ten-shilling (50p) note we knew Mrs Barber could not afford. She was delighted to learn the money had helped maintain my supply of oranges.

Of course, I was not short of visitors. Two of the Preston players, Tom Finney and Tommy Docherty, dropped in to see me at least once a week. They usually called by after training on Friday and it was good to see them and catch up with some football talk. Sadly, they were unable to persuade George Thompson to join them on their visits even though I said I would be glad to see him and have the opportunity to tell him personally that he was not to blame for what had happened to me.

One day I was particularly lifted by the sight of four or five of the Wednesday lads walking into the room, it was a wonderful tonic to share in the laughter and banter which followed their arrival. I have never forgotten how empty the room seemed after they left and how depressed I felt when it suddenly struck me that I would never again play with those lads.

Of course, it was an emotional time but, frankly, as Sylvia and myself whiled away the long days in the Preston hospital, I think the over-riding emotion we shared was one of gratitude. I doubt if anything heartened me more than the reaction of the public at large. Goodwill messages arrived by the sack-load, not just from Sheffield but from all over the country and abroad. I knew I was popular with Wednesday fans and was aware of enjoying the high regard of many people in my home city, but I was staggered by the evidence of the affection and concern of football supporters and sports lovers from far and wide.

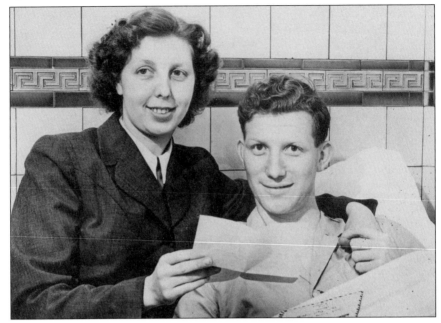

We received lots of mail from well-wishers and Sylvia made sure every letter was answered. People were very generous, and it was at this time that Jack Coulton, a man from Battersea who won £109,000 on the pools, sent us a cheque for £3,000.

Even fans who had booed me wrote to wish me well. Some of the notes I received, from small boys and pensioners, from old players and even people who had never seen a football match, were wonderful examples of human kindness and thoughtfulness.

Later, when we were back home in Sheffield, Sylvia happily undertook the marathon task of answering every letter personally. The postage came out of her modest housekeeping budget, but she didn't mind. We were grateful that the local *Telegraph & Star* were good enough to run off some small prints of an action picture of me so we could send signed copies to everyone.

I had plenty of time to think during those nine weeks in hospital and I wouldn't be honest if I didn't admit to spending many hours worrying about the future and, when I pondered on how I was going to make a living in the years ahead, I felt rather pessimistic about my prospects.

There were times when I could not imagine anything other than being destined to disappear into obscurity once the present attention and publicity died down. What kind of job was I equipped to do considering I had no

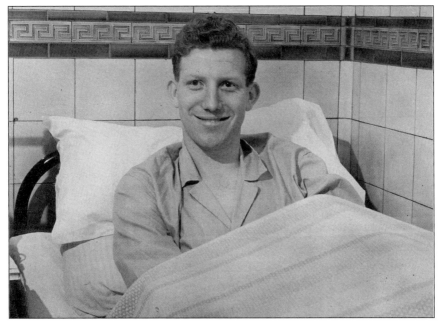

After the trauma of my first ten days in hospital, it was good to be sitting up and smiling again.

training or qualifications? I desperately hoped I might get the chance to stay in football because that was all I had ever wanted from the start of my career but, frankly, I questioned whether there could be any kind of place in the professional game for a man with one leg. I said they could stick me in the ground and use me as a corner flag so long as I could still be involved in something which meant so much to me—but I was not hopeful.

As things turned out, the fates chose to smile on me again and I can look back now and say I had the good fortune to remain a football man and have the opportunity to make a useful contribution. However, it took a while for a pattern of rehabilitation and adjustment to evolve and the first challenge was to come to terms with my situation and learn to take the positive view that only the right attitude could ensure I made the best of things.

At the age of twenty-three it could have been tempting to feel sorry for myself. During those long days in the hospital it was difficult, especially in the spells of solitude late in the evenings, not to dwell on the past and the career I had lost. In my heart and mind I was still chasing the ball down the middle.

I don't deny I shed a few tears, but by the time I was starting to get about on crutches I began to recognise it was no good looking back. I had to accept what had happened, take it on the chin and get on with life. There were many people far worse off than me and I had to start looking forward.

Over the years people have occasionally asked if I haven't sometimes felt bitter towards football because of the injury and its consequences, and I think some of those folk have been surprised when I have said the thought has never occurred to me. I have never stopped loving the game with the same passion I gave it as a raw teenager, and now, at seventy, I still cannot resist the lure of a football match whether it is a League fixture or a parks game involving schoolboys.

In any event, how could I not continue to love a game in which there were so many good people? I had so many friends, colleagues and well-wishers who shared my enthusiasm for football. I have mentioned the part my family and friends played in helping me to adjust, but I must stress, too, that the public, especially the people in and around Sheffield, gave me the kind of support which helped make readjustment easier. If others had faith in me I could not fail to have faith in myself.

Chapter Twenty

A New Beginning

The weekend when I returned to Sheffield after nine weeks in hospital was an emotional one. It felt so good to be back in familiar surroundings at last and at home again with Sylvia and my parents, also I was overwhelmed by the genuine warmth of the welcome from so many friends, neighbours and colleagues.

The following few months constituted a crucial phase in a period of adjustment in which I knew I had to make a new beginning, but, while I hadn't a clue what I was going to do with the rest of my life, what really mattered was knowing I couldn't fail because my family, so many friends and the great Sheffield public were all rooting for me.

Having lost a leg, it might sound like an attempt at misplaced humour to say I knew I had to learn to stand on my own feet, but this was exactly the case. When Eric Taylor told me to 'go out into the world and be independent', he wasn't being cruel. After a spell of convalescence, some people may have expected me to be given a job at Hillsborough, but, as Eric said, that would have looked like I was living on sympathy.

Over the following years I got to know Eric better than most people, and now, when I look back to the spring of 1953, I can well imagine that when he told me I had to make my own way, he was saying I had to show what I was made of. Nothing was said at the time but I suspect he had it in mind that, once I had proved I could adapt to my new situation, there might one day be a suitable role for me with Wednesday. Indeed, it was Eric who subsequently invited me to look after Wednesday's Juniors, which was an important psychological step for me. Eric was the key figure, too, when, in 1962, a situation arose which prompted my appointment as the club's first Development Fund organiser.

These things have a knack of dropping into place as part of a pattern which evolves over a longer period. When that happens it invariably seems just right, but, of course, in the meantime you have to take things as they come because you cannot know what is around the corner—anyway, if you did, you couldn't hurry it along!

In truth, when I look back on the phase between the spring of 1953 and the day in 1962 when I became a full-time Wednesday employee again, I remember it as an eventful, enjoyable and fulfilling period in my life. I made a fair job of picking up the pieces, and, frankly, there was a time when I began to believe, without any sense of disappointment, that I might spend the rest of my working days as a bakery executive with my football links limited to a part–time role.

All this, however, was a long way ahead of me on that Easter Sunday when Sylvia and I travelled home from Preston in an ambulance.

It just happened that Wednesday were playing Manchester City on the following day. Naturally, I was keen to be there and Eric Taylor didn't hesitate to arrange for a car to collect Sylvia and me from Addison Road

My Wednesday team-mates were delighted to see me on my first trip to Hillsborough after leaving hospital. Here I am talking to Jackie Marriott, Norman Curtis, Albert Quixall, Dave McIntosh, Jack Sewell and Cyril Turton before the game with Manchester City.

to take us to the ground. I could not have had a greater tonic. It was brilliant to be able to pop into the dressing room and see the lads, to watch the game from the director's box, and to savour the welcoming cheers of the supporters. A few of us, including some of my old team-mates, shed a few tears that afternoon and I have never forgotten how, with my crutches laid to one side, I sat and mentally kicked every ball as I saw the Owls share a 1–1 draw in which my old pal Dennis Woodhead scored the second-half equaliser.

Of course, while the occasion did me a power of good, I could not escape the reality of my situation. There was more to the challenge of adjusting to my new situation than learning not to forget that I only had one leg when I jumped out of bed in the morning! Sooner, rather than later, I would have to find some means of earning an income.

Wednesday paid me until my contract expired in June and, having subscribed one shilling (5p) a week as a member of the PFA, I received £200 from their provident fund. However, unlike in modern times, there was no other insurance or compensation to draw upon. Moreover, having ceased to be a player, I no longer qualified for a place on the club's housing list.

The Wednesday supporters gave me a tremendous welcome when I took my seat in the directors' box on my first visit to Hillsborough.

In the event, it was the generosity of the public, then and later, which ensured I did not lack some significant financial aid. The support of the people of Sheffield, and others well beyond the city, was a tremendous boon for which Sylvia and myself have been eternally grateful. Immediately after my accident the local *Telegraph & Star* launched a Shilling Fund which raised over £2,700 by October 1953 and enabled us to buy the house in which we still live. Then later, in March 1955, when a testimonial match was staged to coincide with the launch of the Hillsborough floodlights, a crowd of 55,000 rallied to my cause.

I shall never forget what so many ordinary people did for me at that time, and I hope I have given something back in different ways over the years.

I remember that while I was still in hospital, a man who won the football pools on the day of my accident made an anonymous donation through the *People* newspaper and Joe Hulme, the famous old Arsenal and Spurs player, travelled up to Preston to hand over the cheque to my wife Sylvia at a little ceremony in Tom Finney's house.

There were many other examples of people's kindness. I have not forgotten how people who had known us only briefly got in touch. For instance, dear old Mr and Mrs Evans, at whose boarding house we had spent our honeymoon, wrote to ask us to be their guests for a short holiday in the Isle of Man.

We were also staggered by the generosity of strangers. I recall dozing in my hospital bed one day when a man called Arthur Cronshaw came to see me. I had never met him before, but he was a keen football fan and simply wanted to offer his best wishes in person. Arthur was in insurance in Liverpool but it transpired he also had an hotel, the Portland, in Jersey. As he was leaving he said: 'When you get out of hospital, come and have a month with us'.

I had almost forgotten the invitation, but, not long after I returned to Addison Road, a letter arrived from Arthur repeating his offer. Within days of confirming that we would like to join him for two weeks and noting the most convenient dates, a couple of complimentary air tickets arrived from BOAC. Sylvia and I enjoyed a wonderful holiday. Arthur went to the trouble to ensure that when we arrived at St Helier we were accorded the red-carpet treatment, with a limousine waiting to take us to our hotel. The highlight of our stay was a banquet staged in our honour at which officials of the Jersey Football Association were present.

Sylvia and I had never been to Jersey before, and simply going there was a great adventure, but after that experience we were keen to go again and did so subsequently as paying guests. We enjoyed the friendship of Arthur and his family and were flattered that, when our second visit coincided with the birth of a daughter, the Cronshaws decided to call her Sylvia in honour of my wife. Unfortunately, it was some years before we had another holiday in Jersey and when I tried to trace Arthur on our next visit I found his family had moved back to Liverpool.

The generosity of the public certainly eased my rehabilitation and ensured we would have something to fall back on, but my top priority in the short term was to find some gainful employment, while my aim in the longer term was to find a new career. For a while I wondered if I might not have achieved both targets when I was given a 12-month contract by the *Daily Mirror* to work as a sports journalist.

In fact, one of the first job offers I had after arriving home from hospital came from William Stones' brewery, who offered me a public house. It promised a reasonable living and over the years the trade had attracted many ex-footballers, the majority of whom had gone on to enjoy successful careers as publicans. However, it didn't appeal to me. I didn't drink and felt that running a pub would not really suit me.

It was true that I had enjoyed occasional visits to Pitsmoor WMC with my father, but I had only become a member in order to participate in the fishing section. I had never been a social drinker. Sometimes I had joined my father at boxing matches staged at the club, but on those occasions, contrary to what some people may have thought, I never touched a drop of alcohol. There was one instance during my playing days when a so-called Wednesday fan had spotted me at a boxing event on the eve of a match and reported me to Eric Taylor, but the boss knew I was a non-drinker. Now, when I had the chance to take a pub, I think Eric shared my view that I wouldn't look quite right behind a bar.

The opportunity to try my hand at newspaper reporting came about quite casually and in the beginning it seemed likely to be just a matter of a couple of one-off commissions. I was asked to do a few articles for the *Daily Express*, then soon afterwards the *Daily Mirror* invited me to do something for them at the 1953 FA Cup final.

Curious as it might seem, I did not make my Wembley debut as a pundit with a seat in the Press box, but watched the match from the stand. The *Mirror* put Sylvia and myself up in a London hotel and we were chauffeured to the stadium in a car along with their top writer, Peter Wilson, but I actually bought our tickets from Sheffield Wednesday—the *Mirror* recompensed me later.

Wilson and Bob Ferrier did the formal coverage of the match and my role was limited to answering questions about the game which enabled them to produce an article under my name.

The twelve months I spent working for the *Mirror* in the 1953–54 season were certainly interesting, and I think the experience enabled me to have an appreciation of the Press which stood me in good stead in later years.

At the outset I was put in the care of an experienced reporter called Arnold Howe, who was based at the paper's Manchester office. He and I always met up at whichever ground we were working, we sat together in the Press box, and afterwards I would give him my views and impressions while he 'ghosted' my match report. Arnold was a friendly, helpful chap and a very good writer who was more than capable of doing an excellent report off his own bat and under his own by-line. He never once expressed regret that I was getting the credit while he did all the work.

Of course, at the grounds we attended I was viewed by the clubs as a privileged guest and Arnold reaped the benefits on a number of occasions when I helped him get a few scoops he might otherwise have missed. For instance, when I was invited into the boardroom after one match at Doncaster I took Arnold with me, and we met a couple of Irish selectors. The Northern Ireland team was being announced within a couple of days and Arnold couldn't believe his luck when our friends told us who was going to be picked. He was able to predict the line-up with an accuracy which must have surprised many of his rivals!

Unfortunately, after a couple of months of working with Arnold, one day I was told: 'Right, from next Saturday, you're on your own'. It was quite a change to have to write my own copy, but I had picked up the formula by watching Arnold operate and I don't think I made a bad job of it. The only thing that niggled me was I had to telephone my report on Sunday morning, which meant I wasn't able to go fishing.

My adventure into journalism was an eye-opener in several respects and it was intriguing to get an insight into the world of newspapers and see things from the viewpoint of the average football writer and their sports editors.

I recall being puzzled when I submitted my first month's expenses and received a call from the office in which I was told in no uncertain terms: 'Derek, you'll have to adjust these'. Although the sum I had claimed was modest, I feared I must have overcharged. But, no, they explained that if I didn't charge a good deal more I would be letting all the other lads down!

In those days I didn't drive because I had never learned and, anyway, I couldn't afford a motor car. If I had to get somewhere quickly when working for the *Mirror*, I was allowed to take a taxi but, for the most part, I used the train or the bus. If it cost 1s 9d (about 9p) to get to Doncaster,

I claimed that sum exactly. Now, however, I was told I must claim for a few extra taxi fares even though I hadn't spent them.

I soon learned, too, that covering a football match didn't necessarily mean I had to concentrate totally on the details of the game. As I discovered very soon after I began working alone, reporting a Saturday fixture for Monday morning consumption meant looking for a new line and finding a different angle. It was often a case of highlighting something which the average fan would consider incidental to the football. For instance, I watched an awful match between Doncaster and Oldham during which, apart from the goal that won the game for Rovers, the only interesting thing to say about the action was that the players kept complaining about the ball until the referee finally replaced it. In the final paragraph of my report I commented that the most exciting incident of the afternoon occurred after the final whistle when a home fan challenged George Hardwick, the Oldham player-manager, and pushed him before being removed by a policeman. I knew George, of course, and later he offered me a lift to Doncaster railway station on the team-bus. We discussed the spectator incident and George said he hadn't been hurt so didn't intend to take the matter further.

Of course, what I considered a footnote to the match the *Mirror* saw as the focus of the piece and I got an urgent call asking for more details. They were far more interested in the bother at the end than the game itself. It's called 'human interest'!

I must admit the episode raised my doubts about whether I was cut out to be a reporter and I did feel troubled on some occasions by the ethical aspect of my role. There was a conflict between Dooley the ex-footballer and Dooley the journalist.

I was still going down to Hillsborough and mixing with my old team-mates. Because the lads considered me one of them and talked openly to me as a pal I picked up a lot of knowledge which could have made a few good headlines. One day, for example, Jackie Sewell said he was unhappy and thinking of asking for a transfer, but he spoke to me in confidence and I could never have betrayed his trust for the benefit of my newspaper work.

I enjoyed a good relationship with the majority of my fellow reporters, but a few of the regulars in the Press boxes viewed me an ex-footballer taking a journalist's job. The late George Follows, who died in the Munich disaster in 1958, was among those who welcomed me to the fold with genuine enthusiasm and was all for supporting an application for me to join the National Union of Journalists. Alas, I never sought membership of the NUJ because I gradually reached the conclusion that journalism was not for me. I couldn't see myself reporting matches for the rest of my life.

It was when I was covering Wednesday's matches that I recognised that, as well as my other misgivings, I also lacked the essential neutrality of the best football writers. Once, when the Owls were playing Manchester City, I couldn't resist standing up and cheering when we scored. My action provoked a stern rebuke from Eric Todd of the *Manchester Evening News*. Eric was quite nice about it but made it plain that a good football reporter never reacted like a supporter while working in the Press box.

It is amusing now to recall how, in the last months of my contract, the *Mirror* sent me to a few cricket matches. I love cricket, but in terms of writing about it I hadn't a clue how to begin. Somehow I managed to produce something they were able to use, but it was further evidence of my limitations. The *Mirror* wanted me to do a second year for them on the football circuit but when they said it would be on a more casual basis and without a contract I felt it was the right moment to quit.

The year when I worked for the *Mirror* coincided with a time when I was travelling regularly to the Limb Centre at Chapel Allerton in Leeds, where eventually I was fitted with an artificial leg. It was also during this period that Sylvia and I moved into our new house at Norton.

The loss of a leg didn't prevent me from joining the lads in training, but if I had to settle for playing in goal I was never likely to challenge Ron Capewell or Dave MacIntosh for a first-team place!

After leaving hospital, I was on crutches for about three months, then I was fitted with what they call a 'pylon' but what is better known as a 'peg leg'. It was, quite literally, a giant step forward when the time arrived for me to have a leg which would enable me to walk again. I started to feel my new life was taking shape, and our readjustment felt complete when we found a home of our own.

There were no restrictions on how we used the money raised by the *Telegraph & Star*'s Shilling Fund but our priority was always a house. I wanted us to have a permanent roof over our heads along with the security and independence that goes with it. We knew we couldn't live with my parents for ever.

I received my testimonial fund cheque from the Lord Mayor of Sheffield, Councillor Oliver S. Holmes, on the Hillsborough pitch. Others in the picture are Colonel R.L. Craig, deputy chairman of Sheffield Wednesday, and Eddie Gooseman, editor of the Star.

A delivery of carpets at our new home in Norton.

Settling in at Norton...and learning to master the lawn mower!

We have lived in the same house at Norton since October 1953 and have never regretted our choice. However, I must admit that neither of us really wanted to leave the Firth Park area and when we first travelled out to look at the Norton property it seemed half a world away from our roots. I have never forgotten my mother's reaction when she came to take her first look at the place. She said: 'Well, it's very nice but I don't think we'll be coming up here very often—it's too far!'

We did look at a semi-detached house in Hereward Road, less than a mile from where my parents lived, and it was not only a comfortable, solid building but had one advantage which attracted me—it overlooked the football field where Firth Park Grammar and other schools staged matches. Indeed, I had played on it for Owler Lane and felt it would be fun to be able to watch games from the bedroom!

Having also looked at a house in Millhouses, we spotted an advertisement for an early post-war semi-detached property at Norton and embarked on what seemed a marathon journey to inspect it. We travelled on a tram into the city centre, then took another to Meadowhead, and by the time we reached our destination we felt exhausted. At that moment the omens did not seem very good. However, we had been in the house barely a couple of minutes when something about the place made us fall in love with it and long before we had inspected every room we had decided this was where we wanted to live. Amusingly, while the lady of the house was showing us around, her husband was entertaining another couple who were also prospective buyers. When we told the woman we wanted it, she promptly told her husband: 'Billy, the house is sold!' and the other couple left.

The house cost £2,100 and we paid a £100 deposit the following day. I would happily have paid it on our first visit but I only had £5 on me. Next morning I dashed to the bank very early to be sure of getting the deposit money to the woman before she changed her mind!

The move to Norton proved the right one on all counts, not least that it was very convenient for my next career move.

I found myself in demand as a cricket umpire in the summer of 1953, and here I am taking the field at Bramall Lane with George Pope, the first-class umpire and former Derbyshire and England all-rounder. The occasion was a benefit match for Cyril Turner, a famous old Yorkshire cricketer.

The arrival of our first child, Martyn, was a source of great joy to us—a joy which was later compounded with the birth of our daughter Suzanne.

Martyn and Sylvia see me off to work.

The day the Dooleys played host to the legendary 'Have a Go' couple, Wilfred and Mabel Pickles.

Martyn always shared my enthusiasm for football and loved nothing better than displaying his skills to his dad.

Chapter Twenty-one

The Gunstone Years

Eric Taylor once told me that immediately after he had seen me into the ambulance when I broke my leg at Preston in February 1953, he was called to the telephone in the Deepdale office and learned of the death of William Fearnehough, the Wednesday chairman. Mr Fearnehough, whose family links with the club dated back to the Olive Grove era, had been at a dinner with Eric only two days earlier and his sudden death in the Royal Hospital was a shock to everyone at Hillsborough.

I mention this now because Mr Fearnehough's place on Wednesday's board was subsequently filled by Dick Gunstone, and this proved a significant development for me in that Dick eventually came up with an offer of a job in Gunstone's bakery. It presented an opportunity to embark on a new career and marked the start of a phase in my working life that I remember with great affection.

Dick Gunstone was one of the most genuine and sincere people I ever met. I can only describe him as a real gentleman, always kind and ever considerate. He was one of the 'old school', a gentleman and a good friend. In becoming a Wednesday director he followed in the footsteps of his father, who had served on the club's board for twenty-five years. Dick never sought the limelight and was always a modest man who preferred to remain in the background, but he had a great passion for Wednesday. Like most of his colleagues he did a lot of good work for the club which went largely unnoticed except by those who mattered and were best fitted to appreciate his contribution.

It might not sound much when I say the position I accepted at Gunstone's was that of an £8 a week telephonist. However, it was a start, it gave me a base and an income, and I welcomed the offer. As I lacked the qualifications and training that might have enabled me to pick and choose when seeking a new career, it was essentially a case of being grateful for the chance to get into a business where I could begin to learn and, hopefully, eventually climb up the ladder into a more senior and fulfilling role.

I spent eight years with the firm and by the time I left I was assistant sales manager and earning £20 a week. Had I chosen to stay I would have become sales manager and, while it was not the career I had envisaged for myself when I was a player, I was content and had no complaints about the way things turned out. As I have said, there came a time when I felt I was destined to remain a Gunstone's man for the rest of my life and I would have been happy to do so if the opportunity to return to Hillsborough had not arisen.

As had happened in my days with Alfred Peters, I was comfortable and always felt at home and among friends in my years with Gunstone's. From the moment I started work on the switchboard at the Duke Street factory under the tuition of dear old Esme Loukes I never had a moment's regret about joining the firm and I soon found a niche that suited me after my move to the company's Dronfield premises.

Naturally, perhaps, after working as a telephonist-receptionist for about two years I began to feel I ought to be extending my range. I think Eric Gunstone, the brother of Dick and my boss at Dronfield, was already thinking of a new role for me, but, anyway, I precipitated a promotion by pressing my case. The upshot was a switch into a job working for Fred Smith, the sales manager.

Working in sales got me out and about and it was good to be involved and mixing with people again. I might not have liked it if I had been stuck in an office all the time and I was delighted to find a role in which I could excel and get satisfaction. I wasn't the world's top scholar but it is surprising what you can learn when you are genuinely interested in a job and keen to prove you can do it. My work taught me an appreciation and understanding of the overall function of the bakery. Even little things like dealing with the van men proved a useful grounding as I learned not only how many loaves there were on a bread tray but soon found I could rapidly calculate how many there were on six, seven or as many trays as you cared to mention!

Of course, it helped that football remained a part of my life, not only during this initial phase but later, and if my practical involvement in terms of running teams was a spare-time activity between the mid-1950s and 1971 it was nevertheless something which contributed significantly to my well-being and gave me a sense of purpose.

Eric Taylor's decision to ask me to share with my old colleague, Hugh Swift, the duties of looking after the newly-formed Wednesday juniors, for instance, did wonders for my morale and self-confidence. I also got a terrific kick from my association with a local club called Birley Amateurs for about eight years, while the creation of what became Dooley's All Stars was all the more satisfying in that it kept me in touch with other ex-professionals and had the added bonus of helping charitable causes.

Our role with the juniors at Hillsborough was ideal for Hugh Swift and myself. Like me, Hugh had suffered the blow of seeing his playing days end prematurely and as a couple of passionate Wednesday men we threw ourselves into the challenge with great enthusiasm,

I should mention that the people at Gunstone's, especially my immediate boss Fred Smith, were very sympathetic towards my involvement with the juniors. Travelling to away games often meant taking Saturday mornings off and Fred readily allowed me to make up the lost time by re-arranging my hours. It sometimes meant working at the firm until midnight on a Friday to justify my Saturday absence, but I was grateful for the facility. The biggest problem was at holiday times such as Christmas, when the factory was on double shifts but, somehow, we managed to

Hugh Swift...like me his playing days were cut short by injury, and we both enjoyed being involved in running Wednesday's junior team.

organise things so I could fit in my football without failing to fulfil my duties at Dronfield.

My connection with the juniors extended into the periods when Harry Catterick, Vic Buckingham and Alan Brown managed the club, and it was a rewarding and enjoyable spell during which we built a fair side, launched our Northern Intermediate League era, and tasted some success. I also had the pleasure of seeing lads like Peter Eustace, Vic Mobley, Wilf Smith, John Hickton and David Ford progress from the NIL side into the first-team. 'Swifty' and myself got great satisfaction from spotting the promise of these boys and encouraging their development.

We had a fair team but, in the early days, we were conscious that Sheffield United had an especially successful youth policy which was the envy of many other clubs. I recall one occasion when we faced United's juniors at Bramall Lane and, because they boasted such outstanding youngsters as Tony and Barry Wagstaff, Len Badger, Bernard Shaw and several other stars of the future, nobody gave us much of a chance of winning.

Before the game, just as I was chatting with the lads in the dressing room, we were taken by surprise when Harry Catterick walked in. The presence of the manager is always a boost for boys to whom 'the big boss' is someone normally quite remote and invariably regarded with awe, and Harry's impact that evening was remarkable.

You could hear a pin drop as Harry made a little speech in which he said:

> *Right, boys, tonight we're playing Sheffield United, and I want you to remember a few important things. First, there's a ball and there's two teams, which means you're entitled to fifty per cent of the ball to start with. Second, you're wearing a blue and white shirt, which gives you the right to another twenty-five per cent. Third, you're playing for me and for Derek Dooley, and that entitles you to claim the other twenty-five per cent. It means the other side isn't going to win any tackles at all, they're not going to see the ball, and if that doesn't happen, I'll be down here at half-time wanting to know why.*

We won the game 5–1!

Harry Catterick is remembered as the manager who led Wednesday to runners-up spot in the old First Division in 1961. It has often been said the points Wednesday gained that season would have won them the Championship in any other year but it was their bad luck that this just happened to be the campaign in which a magnificent Spurs side was at its peak and achieved a famous League and Cup double.

Harry was very much his own man. It is history now that he walked out and went to Everton at least partly because of a rift between him and Eric Taylor. I don't think I'm breaking any confidences when I say Harry and Eric simply did not hit it off, because at the time most people were aware of the situation.

There was one occasion when, during a discussion about the juniors, Harry turned to me and said: 'I want to know whether you are with me or Eric Taylor'. I replied: 'Look, Harry, all I do is my job. I work for you and I work for Eric Taylor and I'm not taking sides. I'm not sitting on the fence, but I'm not saying I'm with Eric or with you'. I think Harry was a bit peeved because I hadn't said I would side with him, but he just said: 'Okay, that's all right'. I like to think he respected me for refusing to be drawn into their feud and I must admit we always got along pretty well. Of course, our relationship was limited to a mutual interest in the juniors but, in that context, he never questioned my knowledge or judgement.

I recall a time when I told him about Peter Eustace and he accepted my suggestion that we should take Peter's case seriously and sign him as a professional. Peter had shown himself to be a youngster with great potential but the lad, who was then doing a five-and-a-half day week with Samuel Fox's at Stocksbridge, was having problems getting time off work to travel to many away games. Peter's employers were more or less saying he must make a choice between his job in the steel industry and football and it had reached a stage where I feared he was about to play his last match for us before reluctantly turning his back on the game.

I told Harry: 'I think he's a good player and he'd love nothing better than to play for us, but he can't get time off work and we might lose him. Can you have a look at him and consider offering him professional terms?'

Harry sometimes tended to think that if a lad was prevented by circumstances from turning out, it meant he didn't want to play for him, and he could be impatient of that kind of situation. However, I knew he had taken on board my pleas on Peter's behalf when he suddenly turned up at Owlerton Stadium in his car and sat in it watching the game. I doubt if he saw more than five minutes' action but it was obviously enough.

Still sitting in his car, he beckoned me over and said: 'I want to see Eustace in my office'. I said: 'His Dad's here'. He replied: 'Well, bring them both'. A hour or so later Peter Eustace had solved his personal dilemma by signing for Wednesday.

Vic Buckingham, who succeeded Catterick and spent three years at Hillsborough, was a very different type and had a style of management which contrasted sharply with both his predecessor and his successor, Alan Brown. Vic always gave the impression of being very laid back, but he

Vic Buckingham.

was very astute and nobody who worked with him was ever in any doubt that he knew exactly what he was doing. Vic had a rather theatrical touch about him and sometimes you felt he might be more at home among actors and show-business people, but he was still a great football man.

It was typical of Vic that he would say 'Come on, I'll take you to lunch' and then, when the time came to pay for the food, he remembered he had come out without any money. Once when he invited me to the Gate Inn on Penistone Road, we stood at the bar and he said: 'Have you got sixpence? Put it in the juke box and play Peggy Lee singing Mister Wonderful'. As the record began, I asked: 'Do you like this, Vic?' He said: 'Yes, that's me—Mister Wonderful!'

By coincidence, when Alan Brown returned to Wednesday as manager in 1964, in his first week he also invited me to have lunch with him at the Gate Inn. In this instance, there was never any doubt Alan would pay the bill and I don't recall him taking any special interest in the juke box. In fact, Alan simply wanted to talk about the players he had inherited and, as I found, he wasn't interested in my opinion of their abilities.

'Right' he said, 'we're in a war, I'm the captain and we're coming out of the trenches preparing to go over the top. Which of these lads will be right behind me and which of them won't? Tell me who are the brave ones.'

I was working in the club's pools office by the time Alan returned to Sheffield, and we got along very well because we went back a long way and understood each other. There was a great mutual respect between us and, unlike those who tended to view him as cold and intimidating, I could see his warmth and especially appreciated the dry sense of humour which showed he was far more human than some people thought.

Even so, Alan was not a man given to allowing you to influence his judgement on football matters. There were times when he might listen and take heed of your views, but that was usually when he was already of the same opinion. If he had made his mind up about something it was well-nigh impossible to alter his decision, and seeking to persuade Alan to think again was not a challenge to be relished.

When Wednesday reached the FA Cup final in 1966, for instance, I don't think Alan welcomed the debate about who should replace Vic Mobley when it became clear the big centre-half would not recover from the injury he suffered in the Villa Park semi-final.

Having watched the reserves on a regular basis in this period I had no doubt that John Hickton's displays at centre-half in the Central League made him an obvious candidate to fill the role in the first-team.

John was a product of Wednesday's juniors and I was familiar with his character, ability and versatility. He started out at full-back, but I had converted him into a centre-forward and he had made such a success of it that he had eventually enjoyed an excellent if short spell in the role in the first-team. Proof of Hickton's talent as a striker came in the following years when, after being sold for a giveaway £25,000 in the autumn of 1966, he emerged as a prolific marksman with nearly 200 goals for Middlesbrough.

Unfortunately, John was one of those players who never managed a long senior run at Hillsborough and it was always a mystery and a disappointment to me that things didn't work out for him as they should. He seems to have suffered because he was too versatile. In the spring of 1966 he was back in the reserves and, being a dependable and adaptable lad who accepted everything without complaint, he had not only agreed to being switched to centre-half but made a very good job of it. John, I knew, would never let anybody down, and I told Alan Brown so.

'Brownie' just looked at me and said: 'Go back to your pools office and look after that. I'll look after the team'. John Hickton did not play against Everton in that unforgettable FA Cup final and I had to be content that at least such other of my 'old' boys as David Ford, Peter Eustace and Wilf Smith did.

If my period in charge of Wednesday's juniors gave me tremendous satisfaction, I must admit the eight-year spell when I served as chairman of a local club called Birley Amateurs was just as rewarding, all the more so because it renewed my links with football at grass roots and gave me an opportunity to make a contribution alongside people who loved the game solely for its own sake.

I would have liked this phase to have lasted longer but, unfortunately, there came a time when my increasing duties at Hillsborough severely restricted my free hours. It was particularly sad that this coincided with a pattern of circumstances which eventually caused the club to fold. Our consolation was at least we all took away some very happy memories.

As my wife's sister lived at Birley, we often visited the district, and I was flattered when some members of the club called round and invited me to be their chairman. I was impressed with their enthusiasm and dedication and, in running teams in the Amateur, Sports & Athletic and Friendlies leagues, we enjoyed a good deal of progress and success over the next few years.

I have fond recollections of the lively meetings we used to hold at my Norton home. Sylvia would make several plates of sandwiches and cakes, then go off to spend an evening at the cinema, leaving us to discuss club matters. What I liked was that while lads like Frank Ackroyd, Geoff Burgess, Bob Towel and the others simply wanted to play for fun, they were serious about their football and their club. We were never short of fund-raising ideas at which everyone worked hard to ensure success, and we took as much pride in our activities as any professional club.

The lads played in blue and white striped shirts and, off the pitch, they sported blazers which bore a special badge comprising crossed corner-flags in blue and white plus a white Yorkshire rose. We had our share of frustrations, not least because it sometimes seemed that every time we

Talking football with the lads at Birley Amateurs was always a delight because they loved the game.

acquired a new pitch we soon lost it when the Council chose to claim the land for housing, but we survived the majority of what problems we faced. In the end it was the loss of a regular pitch that proved the final straw.

I have never forgotten the day a lad called Mike Bostock came to see me and, having explained that he had been born deaf and dumb, said he had learned to speak at the Maud Maxfield School for the Deaf where a special bonus was playing in the school team. Sadly, the team was being disbanded owing to costs and a shortage of players. Mike wondered whether the seven or eight lads affected by the development might be able to keep playing football by joining Birley Amateurs.

'Of course' I said. I knew my colleagues at Birley would welcome the boys with open arms. In fact, within a few weeks everyone was delighted with our new 'signings' because some of them were excellent players.

Cyril Davies, a slightly-built lad with red hair, was an especially notable 'find' for he had played for England Deaf against Italy. Incidentally, it is worthy of note that Cyril's talent was inherited by his son, Kevin, an outstanding young striker who has gone on to play for Chesterfield, Blackburn and Southampton.

It was really satisfying to be involved in both the professional and amateur sides of the game at the same time, and the Birley experience was particularly refreshing because it was so far removed from the Football League scene and you saw a very different world. I always found it such a tonic to be among people who reminded me of my sporting roots and it was wonderful to witness their passion for the game and their club.

It is appropriate to mention here that, some twenty years later, I had another enjoyable association with the amateur scene when I was roped in to manage the Rowlinson Youth Club's Sunday side. I had started watching them because my son Martyn was involved and, having become a regular on the touchline in the early 1980s when I was recovering from a broken hip, I unexpectedly found my services in demand.

The lad who was managing Rowlinson was planning to pack up and apparently someone said to our Martyn: 'Can't tha get thee Dad to manage us?' They kept pressing the case and I finally allowed myself to be talked into it. I filled the role for about eight years and only gave it up after my promotion to managing director at Sheffield United made it impossible to devote the necessary time to the youngsters.

For me the experience was another classic example of the terrific camaraderie you invariably find among a group of people involved in running and playing for an obscure little amateur club. When I packed it in, the lads went to the trouble of organising a surprise party for me at

Bramall Lane and, despite the passage of time since we went our separate ways, there are still occasions when we find an excuse for a reunion and I get as big a kick out of seeing those old Rowlinson friends again as I do from meeting up with old Wednesday colleagues.

It was, of course, some of my old Hillsborough team-mates who inspired the formation of what became Dooley's All Stars in the early 1960s, and we could not have imagined then that it was the start of something which is still a part of the local sporting scene nearly forty years later.

I was involved for about ten years until I became Wednesday's team-manager and handed over to Johnny Quinn. As everyone knows 'Quinny', who is the epitome of enthusiasm and the true spirit of football, has done a wonderful job and helped raise thousands of pounds for good causes over the past thirty years.

It all began because some of the lads wanted to keep playing after the end of their professional careers. They were always talking about forming a team to play matches for charity. Old players seldom want to hang up their boots and walk away from the unique dressing room atmosphere they have savoured for so long, and this seemed an ideal way of staying together.

Once we launched the operation it just snowballed. Initially it was mainly ex-Wednesday lads who were involved but soon we recruited old players from Sheffield United, Barnsley, Rotherham and Chesterfield. Indeed, it wasn't long before we reached a stage when I had so many players to choose from it was necessary to make a succession of substitutions during a game to ensure everyone got a piece of the action. The lads loved it and we shared some happy times together. I should mention, too, that we invariably had the free services of several top local referees who were as keen to be involved as the players.

We played the majority of our early games on Sundays and at that time, before football on the Sabbath became a normal part of the sporting scene, you were not allowed to take money at the gate. This meant the people who were organising the charity or cause for which we were playing had to print programmes and sell them in lieu of an admission charge.

One of my earliest memories of this phase is of a day when we travelled to Blunham in Bedfordshire to play a game which had been arranged by a pal of mine who lived at a place called Sandy. Our hosts, who wined and dined us in great style, also paid to hire a coach to take us down for a fixture being staged for a worthy cause.

I have not forgotten either that Eric Morecambe, the famous comedian, was not content simply to make a brief guest appearance at the event but insisted on staying to watch the entire game. Incidentally, in later years I was to meet up with Eric on several occasions in his capacity as a Luton Town director—he was not only one of the great comedy talents of his era but a wonderfully warm human being. You always felt uplifted after just a few minutes in his company.

Such was our enthusiasm for our new charity team, we never gave a thought to the fact that what we were doing was technically in conflict with the Football Association regulations. After we had played two or three games I received a telephone call from Ernest Kangley, the secretary of the Sheffield & Hallamshire CFA. He gently pointed out that we needed to be affiliated to operate. We soon put that right and for twenty-one shillings (£1.05) registered as Dooley's All Stars.

Our main problem in the early days was insuring the players against injury, and, in fact, this was something that was not formalised until Johnny Quinn took over. However, we never lacked a qualified first-aid man and Sheffield Wednesday were good enough to provide a first-aid box.

Frankly, the matches we played were essentially the sort of games in which we did not anticipate any serious injuries. We never expected the opposition to stop tackling or wanted them to lie down, but we did feel these were charity fixtures and should be played in an appropriate spirit. Not surprisingly perhaps, there were occasions when we might visit a village and find the local side wanted to play it tough because of the 'big' names in our side. I recall a few afternoons when I was concerned at the sight of someone wanting to cut up rough but, happily, we invariably found a quiet word from big Les Moore was enough to calm things down. Even the toughest amateur seldom fancied getting on the wrong side of Les, for he was a centre-half who had survived in the hardest of schools!

At the outset we played in kit borrowed from Wednesday and it was a nice gesture when they insisted on taking it back every week for washing in the club laundry. Later, of course, we invested in our own kit but stuck to the familiar blue-and-white stripes. Some of the lads who had passed their professional days with clubs other than the Owls thought we ought to wear different colours and, naturally, the ex-United men felt we should invest in some red and white shirts. I insisted there was only one strip synonymous with Derek Dooley—though had it all come about twenty years later, I might have taken a different view!

By late 1961 my playing days had been over for almost nine years and at nearly thirty-two years of age I had settled into a routine which was comfortable and fulfilling. I liked working at Gunstone's and enjoyed being involved in football every weekend and on at least a couple of evenings a week. Moreover, it was a nice bonus to still be remembered and regarded with affection by the people of Sheffield. I was conscious that what I had achieved during my brief Football League career and the circumstances in which it had all ended had given me a unique status in the hearts and minds of the local public, and I felt proud and grateful.

However, I did not think my fame extended much beyond my home region and never imagined myself as a potential subject for a national television programme such as This Is Your Life. When it happened, I was staggered. I thought I was far too young to qualify and, in any event, all I had done was play football and lose my leg. There didn't seem much of a story to tell!

It is amusing now to reflect on this episode and recall the curious little incidents that occurred during the build-up to my surprise appearance on millions of black-and-white television sets all over the country. People suggested afterwards that I must have known what was happening but, honestly, it was a complete surprise and only in hindsight did the advance clues click in my head.

By coincidence, the programme was one I seldom missed watching because it was invariably screened on a Monday evening when I was alone in the house as Sylvia went to a city-centre cinema with her sister. On the Monday prior to my appearance the subject who received the famous big red book from Eammon Andrews was a priest who had founded a boys' town in Rome. It was a particularly moving show and, having been impressed with the story of how this priest had worked with orphans and under-privileged lads, I couldn't wait to tell Syliva about it when she got home from the pictures.

Sylvia, of course, knew I was to be the next subject and, during our chat about the priest, she asked me how I would react if I ever found myself on This Is Your Life. I laughed and said: 'Well, that's unlikely because I've done nothing compared with the bloke who's been on tonight'.

Much later Sylvia admitted she had been scared stiff that she might give the game away and inadvertently reveal the secret plans that were afoot. On at least a couple of occasions I awoke in the night and found her staring out of the bedroom window. When I asked what was wrong, she said she couldn't get to sleep. Like most men I hadn't the nous to see something was troubling her.

In those days I was going down to the juniors' training sessions at Hillsborough on Tuesday and Thursday evenings, and one day when I rushed home from work, had tea and began to prepare for my trip to the ground, I spotted my son Martyn drawing a figure on a sheet of paper.

'Who's that supposed to be?' I asked. He said: 'Oh, it's the man who had a cup of tea here yesterday'. I cannot remember how Sylvia explained the mystery man who had made such an impression on my son. Only long afterwards did I discover it was a researcher from the BBC!

I have to smile now when I remember how annoyed I was by an incident which occurred at work, little realising it was all part of the plot to get me on the show.

On the Friday afternoon, I was called into Eric Gunstone's office and he said: 'Derek, I want you to go to London with Fred Smith on Monday. There's this bakery which has a new type of retail van and I would appreciate your opinion'.

I have to admit my initial reaction was: 'It's a bit late, isn't it, leaving it while Friday afternoon to tell me I've got to go to London on Monday morning?' Poor old Fred must have been lost for words when I returned to his office and said: 'Why didn't you tell me earlier about this trip? Were you afraid to mention it? Why didn't you give me more warning?'

It didn't help that we were scheduled to travel on the Master Cutler train, which meant I would have to be up at six o'clock. In the meantime, I faced a long trip with the Wednesday Juniors on Saturday and, with only Sunday in which to relax, I was disappointed at the prospect of such an early start on Monday.

When I told Sylvia about the visit to a London bakery she didn't seem as surprised as I had anticipated. I never for a moment suspected she had known about the plan before me, and it didn't occur to me there was anything even faintly odd about the way she insisted I should wear my best suit for the trip and take an overnight bag. I insisted: 'I'm not wearing my best suit to go round a bakery, and there's no need for an overnight bag because, whatever time we finish, I'm coming straight home'.

Arrangements had been made for Fred Smith to pick me up in his car on the Monday morning so we could travel down to the station together. I wasn't feeling best pleased really, and, when I was getting dressed, the small metal catch on my trousers broke. 'Well' said Sylvia, 'now you'll have to put your best suit on.' I said: 'Oh, no. Just put a safety pin in, it'll do'. How could I know I was going to meet Eammon Andrews wearing a working suit with trousers held up with a safety pin!

The journey passed without incident and, with hindsight, I can say the only thing which didn't go quite as had been planned was the position in which our carriage finished on the platform when the train reached St Pancras. For some reason the driver pulled up short of the buffers. Although I didn't know it, I was supposed to step out of the carriage and find myself facing Eammon Andrews and the TV cameras. In the event, we stepped

This Is Your Life, Derek Dooley…and Eric Taylor (seated) explains my Wednesday story to Eamonn Andrews (left) and a television audience of millions.

onto the platform twenty yards or so away from Eammon and his crew. Unaware of what was supposed to have happened, I stopped to light my pipe and, spotting the cameras, turned to Fred and said: 'It looks as if they're expecting the Queen or some big celebrity'. Imagine my astonishment when we started walking down the platform and Eammon suddenly stepped forward, smiled at my colleague and said: 'Hello, Fred!'

I remember thinking: 'They must be old pals. I wonder if Fred served with Eammon in the army or something like that?'

Even when Eammon turned and shouted me over, I didn't realise what was happening. I thought 'I must be going to appear on somebody's This Is Your Life as a guest'. I have never been more surprised in my life than when that familiar Irish voice said: 'Derek Dooley—This Is Your Life!'

The shots of me arriving in London were recorded as the introduction to the show, which went out live from the Television Centre at Shepherd's Bush the same evening. Once the drama of being dropped on at St Pancras was over, Fred disappeared and I found myself passing the day in the company of a BBC official. We had a coffee at the station buffet, later went

A full line up of all the guests who appeared with me on This Is Your Life.

for lunch at Simpson's on the Strand, then whiled away the afternoon at a cinema watching a film which I have long forgotten.

Appearing on the programme was an experience I have never forgotten but, like so many of the memorable moments in your life, this one flashed by in something of a whirl. Only when I returned to Sheffield and got back to normal was it possible to savour the privilege and pleasure of a very special occasion.

I can understand why so many of those who appear on this programme seem so overwhelmed with emotion, because it is a uniquely moving experience to meet up again with so many people from the past—and all the more so when they all walk back into your life at the same time!

Chapter Twenty-two

Back at Hillsborough

Not long after my appearance on This Is Your Life the opportunity arose to rejoin Sheffield Wednesday as a full-time employee and when Eric Taylor offered me the job of running the club's newly-created Development Fund in 1962, I knew there was only one answer I could give. It was like going home again at last and my return to Hillsborough was something which seemed as if it had always been destined to happen sooner or later.

At the time the Fund was launched I was working with the juniors on a part-time basis and, like everybody else connected with the club in some way, I was asked to take a few books of draw tickets to sell to family and friends. When I learned Eric Taylor was looking for someone to organise the overall operation, I joked 'I'm the man to run that' without really giving the matter much thought.

However, if my initial comment was little more than a flippant remark, Eric took it on board. Within two weeks he approached me after a juniors' training session and asked: 'Were you serious about running the Fund?' I admitted it was something I had said off the top of my head but added: 'If you're serious about wanting me to do it, I'm definitely interested'. He invited me to pop in for a chat the next time I visited the ground.

Of course, I told Sylvia what had happened, and when it came to discussing Eric's subsequent formal offer I think she knew I had already decided to accept it. Sylvia always understood me better than anybody, including myself, and she was aware that the chance to go back into football was an opportunity impossible for me to resist.

As I have said, I was happy at Gunstone's and they were happy with me. They were disappointed by my decision to leave and stressed I had a bright future with them, but they accepted my choice was as much about my heart as my head and we parted the best of friends. Ironically,

I went back to Wednesday for a wage of £20 a week which exactly matched what Gunstone's were paying me, and not even the promise of an immediate increase could persuade me to stay at Dronfield. This was not something I was doing for the money.

These days, the extensive commercial activities at football clubs are a normal part of the scene, so much so that many young people cannot believe there was a time when such things as sponsorship, replica kits and similar promotions were unknown. Football now is a multi-million pound business and everybody is familiar with the fact that no club in the modern era can survive on gate money alone and accepts that generating income from non-football sources is essential to financial stability and survival. It is a far cry from my playing days when the maximum wage meant clubs could budget for large playing staffs without breaking the bank. They knew exactly how much they were likely to spend on salaries and the annual figures seldom varied by more than a few pounds.

My return to Hillsborough in 1962 came at just around the time things were beginning to change. The removal of the maximum wage in the professional game a year earlier marked the starting point for all that has happened since. However, when we greeted the first £100 a-week footballer, Fulham's Johnny Haynes, I doubt if anyone could have imagined a time would come when some players would earn as much, and even more, in a week as most supporters manage in a year. Forty years ago a lot of people in football felt the players deserved a better deal but few can have anticipated it becoming normal for so many top footballers to be millionaires. We certainly didn't expect things to get as out of hand as has happened!

Anyhow, it was in the early 1960s that clubs started to adapt to the implications of the new wage structure and began to look for ways of boosting income from outside sources. The development fund at Hillsborough was one of the first in the Football League and the system we operated was based on one which had been pioneered and copyrighted by a man called Royle, who was chairman of Wigan Rugby League Club. We made such a success of the system that I was invited up to Celtic to help launch their fund and the Scottish club was so impressed they offered me a permanent job and a big pay rise. However, I insisted I would never dream of leaving Wednesday!

Setting up the kind of system we operated then was not simply a matter of doing something which you knew would bring in some cash, for there were all kinds of laws and regulations with which we had to comply. It is relevant to note that there were severe restrictions on how the money could be used and it had to be channelled into building and related developments. It couldn't be spent on players. Much has since changed to enable the concept of fund raising to be viewed in a very different climate and, of course, the range of commercial activities at football clubs has expanded beyond anything we could have envisaged nearly forty years ago.

Happily, we created one of the most successful development funds in the game. After reaching six-hundred books in the first fund, we obtained a licence to launch a second, spanning another six-hundred books, and over the following years the operation simply went from strength to strength. Our progress was seen in the fund's contribution to the building of the gymnasium, the new West Stand and other major developments in the 1960s.

My first office as development fund organiser was under some old terracing on the south side of the ground towards Leppings Lane. Here a turnstile was knocked out and a door fitted to create makeshift premises which opened for custom on Monday and Friday evenings. As the place had a concrete floor it could get very cold in winter, so we acquired some duckboards to ensure I didn't freeze to death! Later, of course, a specially-designed office was built just inside the Penistone Road gate and I felt very privileged to have not only ideal working facilities but a toilet and kitchen.

In all my years in the job I was the only full-time employee doing the work, although as the operation expanded I did enjoy the help of some part-time people on a couple of evenings a week and Saturday mornings. With my agents constantly calling in I was never lonely, indeed, one of the joys of the job was having regular contact with so many genuine Wednesday supporters. Numbered among them were some of the finest people I have ever known, even all these years later I can still remember not only their faces and names but how many books of tickets they each sold every week.

It was a big help in ensuring the success of the fund that I was Derek Dooley and synonymous with the Owls but, if I didn't have to 'sell' myself to the fans, the thing that made a significant difference was I had always had close links with the Supporters' Club.

We live in a very different world today and it is easy to forget the contribution the Supporters' Club made over many years. They organised coach travel to away games and a range of regular social functions to which all the players were invited. The people running the Supporters' Club were encouraged to feel an essential part of the scene and the good work they did, without any thought of payment or personal reward, is something that ought to be remembered.

Back at Hillsborough…All smiles outside the main entrance on the day I rejoined the club as development fund organiser.

Getting down to work in my new office.

In modern times many clubs boast their own travel clubs and have taken responsibility for organising transport to away matches for their fans. There has been a logical and practical reason for this development but it is sad to think that one effect of this and other related changes is supporters' clubs as we knew them now tend to be kept at a distance and, in many cases, they have no official encouragement to make a contribution.

In the old days, of course, there wasn't the gulf between the players and fans as sometimes seems to be the case nowadays when huge earnings have put footballers in a different financial bracket. In my day players and supporters were pretty much the same kind of people, and me and my team-mates had some happy times at Supporters' Club events.

I especially remember going on what was then a traditional five-day trip to the Isle of Man arranged by secretary Reg Crapper and his committee shortly after I finished playing. I still recall with affection some of the social functions staged by the branches at High Green, Deepcar, Swallownest and Hoyland. People like Bill Anderson at High Green, George Percival at Swallownest and Arthur Hawley at Deepcar, epitomised the true Wednesdayites of their era, and their enthusiasm for the club's cause was emphasised by the way they supported the fund.

It was a source of considerable pride to me when I was asked to become President of the Supporters' Club and my long spell in the role only ended in the mid-1970s when it seemed incongruous to continue—considering I had by then become an employee of Sheffield United!

The hard core of Wednesdayites were always keen to help the cause but, naturally, to make the fund work it was necessary to seek to extend it beyond the supporters who were, so to speak, immediately on hand and ready to serve as agents. I sought to recruit agents in local steel works and other major firms and was fortunate enough to find many personnel and sports officers at these companies especially helpful.

One of the difficulties in wanting to get out and about and spread the gospel of the club's fund was my inability to drive. Frankly, up to that period in my life I had never had the slightest inclination to get behind the wheel of a car, and owning a vehicle was not an ambition I had harboured. I suppose I was one of those people who had grown up always believing I could never aspire to buy a car.

Fortunately, Sylvia did learn to drive and she took on the task of driving me round on my tour of local firms, as always she simply wanted to help me make a success of my job. In this context, I should mention that she also often dropped into the office to assist me with my administration. She did all this without pay and never once asked for, or was offered, petrol money.

I've passed my driving test and have my own car for the first time.

Eventually, what with the fact that I was working until late on several evenings and I had to make regular trips to the bank to deposit our takings, I decided I had better take driving lessons. When I passed my test I invested in a blue Austin which did some sterling work on behalf of Sheffield Wednesday without ever being granted the status of being a club car.

Following my return to Hillsborough in 1962 I was destined to spend nearly twelve years connected with the administrative and management side of things at Sheffield Wednesday. It was a period in which I considerably extended my knowledge and experience while learning a great deal which stood me in good stead for the rest of my working life.

I have many happy memories of this phase. As well as doing my job as Development Fund organiser, I often helped out in the ticket office when Hillsborough was staging an FA Cup semi-final or being used as a neutral venue for some other big occasion. I have not forgotten what a hectic time we all had in 1966 when, all in the space of a few weeks, we had to deal with ticket arrangements for Wednesday's FA Cup final date at Wembley and then prepare for a series of World Cup games at our own ground.

The thing I remember is what a good atmosphere there was behind the scenes at the club, with those occasions when we had to pull out all

Eric Taylor.

the stops invariably bringing out the best in everybody. Naturally, our fans were more interested in activities on the pitch, but I can tell them there was plenty to admire about the teamwork in the offices. It was good to be a part of all that.

The key figures behind the scenes were Eric Taylor and his assistant Eric England. They were probably the finest administrative partnership in football in their era and I was lucky enough to enjoy their friendship and benefit from their example and influence. No man could have had better mentors and many times since I have profited from applying the methods and know-how they taught me.

Eric Taylor was the boss, the king-pin and the public figure, while Eric England was the loyal and ever-dependable lieutenant, invariably content to remain an unsung hero in the background. Taylor took the limelight but, for me, you could not separate the two Erics. They were the perfect combination and, as the senior Eric often said, he could not have achieved what he did without his partner.

When Eric Taylor told me Eric England had stopped him from committing suicide he was not overstating the younger Eric's influence. What he meant was he had frequently been grateful for his colleague's common sense on those occasions when he was tempted to act first and think later. Eric England was the restraining force, the man who tempered his partner's enthusiasm for a project by saying 'Let's sit down and talk it through'. Happily, the boss was not reluctant to admit at the end of a discussion: 'I think you might be right, Eric'.

Wednesday built a tremendous reputation for the quality of the club's administration and, especially, the superb organisation of big matches. Eric Taylor certainly knew how to stage-manage those major events and prided himself on seeing them through without a hitch, but much of the credit for the smooth operation belonged to Eric England.

The distribution of tickets for big matches invariably went like clockwork because the younger Eric was brilliant at overseeing the task. He never panicked, never lost control, and nobody was more thorough or meticulous.

Of course, I had known both Erics fairly well long before I rejoined the club, but working alongside them enabled me to understand and appreciate their qualities and get to know them not just as colleagues but

Eric England (right), who was Eric Taylor's right-hand man and a key figure behind the scenes at Hillsborough. Here he is seen with author Keith Farnsworth.

as people and friends. They worked together at Hillsborough for about forty years and what they did for Wednesday merits a lasting place on the club's roll of honour. Certainly those of us who had the privilege of being in the same team treasure the memory and know the true value of their contribution.

Eric Taylor was the finest administrator I ever met, a tremendous organiser and a man of foresight and vision. In many ways he was years ahead of his time. Many of the ideas he put forward, as long ago as the late 1950s and early 1960s, are now considered an essential part of the scene yet seemed so revolutionary when he raised them. He took a lot of stick because he wanted to turn Hillsborough into a top stadium, a venue fit for the best, but with hindsight everyone came to recognise how wise and astute he had been. I doubt if many people who know the full details will dispute that Wednesday benefited from what Eric had created long after he had passed from the scene.

When the Cantilever Stand replaced the old North Stand around 1962, many people regarded it as a white elephant and a waste of money. In fact, it set a lead which many other top clubs followed, and, as for the cost, the cash was raised by debentures. Later, when the West Stand went up and seats were placed on the South Stand terracing, the development coincided with plans for the 1966 World Cup, so Wednesday benefited from the special Government grants. Moreover, as I have mentioned, the proceeds of the Development Fund, which could only be used for building work, were invested with the long-term well-being of the club in mind.

Eric did not live to see some of his ideas come to fruition, but putting a roof on the Kop was one of his dreams made reality by his successors, while filling in the corners of the ground, expanding catering and restaurant facilities, and turning Hillsborough into much more than just a football stadium were just a few of the things he talked about. There was a time when he envisaged putting a dome above the playing area, he suggested a mono-rail transport system to carry supporters to and from the city centre, and he pondered on the possibilities of a huge rebuilding operation if only he could buy up all the houses in Vere Road.

Watching Eric in action on big occasions was to see a master at work. He was a showman who paid attention to the smallest detail. He loved to surprise visiting dignitaries with novel gifts at the lunches he staged with such style ahead of major fixtures. He revelled in showing guests from the Football Association how well Sheffield Wednesday could perform when hosting top events.

A trivial memory of my testimonial match in March 1955 serves to illustrate the typical Taylor touch. The game, in which a Sheffield XI played an International XI, coincided with the official opening of Wednesday's floodlights. The lights were novel then and when the 55,000 crowd started packing into the ground the fans thought they looked brilliant. What they didn't know until later was the lights were only at half-power. When the teams came out and lined up, I was announced, and as I walked out a switch was pulled to produce full power. The impact was tremendous and it lent a sense of wonder to a moment charged with emotion. I doubt if anyone present ever forgot the experience—and it was all down to Eric's planning. It served to emphasise the effect of the sudden difference in power that the Wednesday team wore some fluorescent blue shirts. Eric knew exactly how to put on a show.

Eric's flair, knowledge and talents made him one of the most respected figures in football. He was a great ambassador for his home city, for the club and for the game he loved. I sometimes thought there seemed to be no place in the world where Eric Taylor's name wasn't known and admired, and one of the secrets of his success was the people he knew in so many different fields of activity. They were invariably people who could always be depended upon to respond to his requests for help and support.

Those who knew Eric well will confirm he was a shrewd and wise man. He knew his football, understood people and, if he was a stickler for discipline, he was also a guy with a great sense of humour. He was an excellent companion, full of wit, someone who made you feel better for having spent time in his company.

I have mentioned how, when my playing days ended, Eric was sympathetic but realistic. Some people might have considered him cruel to tell me to go out and learn to stand on my own feet, but he was simply being honest. When the job with the *Daily Mirror* came up, it was Eric who urged me to take it. He said it would assure me of an income for twelve months and give me time to sort out what I really wanted to do. Whenever I had a problem Eric invariably offered advice which, while it might not be what I wanted to hear, was always sound and sensible.

OFFICIAL SOUVENIR, SIXPENCE

DEREK DOOLEY TRUST FUND

Floodlight Match

WEDNESDAY, 9th MARCH, 1955, Kick-off 7.30 p.m.

SHEFFIELD XI.

v.

INTERNATIONAL XI.

The Derek Dooley testimonial match programme cover.

When I became team manager at Hillsborough, some people seemed to think Eric told me how to do the job and interfered in team selection. I can only say they didn't know Eric. In general terms I knew he was always there with a helping hand if I needed it. Indeed, I made use of his huge knowledge and experience, but no way would he seek to influence me on playing matters. In any event, Eric knew I had a mind of my own and respected me for that.

There was one occasion during my time in the Development Office when Eric must have smiled at my tendency to speak my mind, and it summed up the way he was always one step ahead of his staff and more aware of what was going on than we sometimes imagined.

I have noted how we had to pull out all the stops in the spring of 1966 when not only did Wednesday reach the FA Cup final but Hillsborough was chosen to stage four World Cup matches. Over a fairly extensive period the staff ended up working some very long days and we seldom got home before midnight. I noticed no increase on my monthly pay slip and there was no mention of any bonus. Once when I asked Eric England if he thought we might be getting some extra payment, he could only say 'I should think so'. I told him: 'Well, nobody's said owt. Are you

Sheffield Wednesday's 1966 FA Cup final team. Back row: McCalliog, Eustace, R. Springett, Young, Ellis, Smith. Front row: Pugh, Fantham, Megson, Ford, Quinn.

going to see the boss and ask about it?' Eric said: 'No, but I expect he'll sort something out'.

Anyhow, I decided somebody needed to say something and, of course, I bounded in to Eric Taylor's office. I went on at length about all this extra work and nothing extra in my pay packet. Eric listened with great patience to my torrent of words, then quietly passed me a letter which had just been prepared ready for posting to me. It stated that Sylvia and I were going with Eric and the directors on an all expenses paid weekend trip to London linked to the World Cup final! That stopped me in my tracks, and when Eric also handed me a packet containing a £200 bonus I was frankly lost for words. I described it to Sylvia as a case of being shot down in flames and wishing I had kept my mouth shut!

Chapter Twenty-three

A 'Dream' Invitation

The fourth Friday in January 1971 started as just another working day in the Development Office. Then an early phone call from Eric Taylor suddenly changed all that and signalled a remarkable transformation in my status at the club. To say I was flabbergasted and amazed by the unexpected turn of events would be putting it mildly.

At this time I had a chap called Arthur Percival giving me a bit of a hand in the pools office. Arthur, a retired employee of Davy United, shared a handicap similar to mine in that he also had an artificial leg. I was glad of his help and he enjoyed making himself useful about the place. As usual, that morning I had picked him up from his Norfolk Park home and brought him with me to Hillsborough and once at the ground we soon settled down to our normal routine.

When Eric Taylor telephoned and asked me to pop along to the boardroom, I left Arthur 'minding the store' and made my way towards the main office. 'What's wrong now?' I wondered, thinking there was some problem connected with my department. Once in the boardroom I saw Eric had company in the form of club chairman, Dr Andrew Stephen. It was then that Eric uttered the words which left me speechless: 'What would you think if we offered you the job as the manager?'

It probably sounds like something out of a piece of schoolboy fiction when I say the prospect of managing the club I'd supported and played for was like a dream come true, but I cannot explain my feelings in any other way. It was as if some fantasy from my boyhood had suddenly become reality and it took me a while to absorb the significance of what was happening. I was tempted to respond with an instant 'yes' but instead said I'd like to talk about it and learn more of what they had in mind.

I especially wanted to know what was happening about Danny Williams, who was only in his second season as manager. Danny was a brilliant lad to get along with and he and I had become very friendly. He had often popped into my office to invite me to join him on a scouting trip to a match and I seldom said no. I welcomed the opportunity because Danny was not only always good company but had a sunny outlook on life. He had the knack of making people laugh and he was the sort of lad who didn't have an enemy in the world. The last thing I wanted was to be responsible for him losing his job.

However, 'Doc' Stephen said Danny would be leaving and stressed that whatever my answer to their invitation the decision about Danny's future had already been taken. I hadn't seen anything about it in the newspapers and I recall wondering whether he had yet been informed of his fate.

Nobody needed to tell me things were not going well for Wednesday on the pitch and I was well aware that some fans had been expressing their dismay and mounting frustration in no uncertain terms at recent games. Frankly, the club's fortunes had been slipping for two or three years and it summed up the situation that since Alan Brown's departure, in early 1968, the first team had played 125 League matches and won only twenty-nine. It all seemed a long way from the optimism inspired by Wednesday's FA Cup run in 1966 when so many people believed the club had a team with the potential to really start going places.

Danny had followed Jack Marshall into the job in 1969 and, considering what he had achieved at Swindon, many felt the Williams era would mark a dramatic upturn. Sadly, in Danny's first season in charge he had been unable to prevent Wednesday from dropping out of the old Division One for the first time in twelve years. Danny was an honest, down-to-earth guy who loved his football and had a great passion for his work, and I really felt for him when his efforts didn't succeed.

I had watched Wednesday, on that wet and miserable April evening in April 1970, when their relegation was sealed with a home defeat against Manchester City. Like many others, I shall always remember it as a game we ought never to have lost. Alas, it seemed as if the fates had delighted in conspiring to doom Danny's team just when an escape had looked within our grasp. I went back to the pools office at the end of the game with tears in my eyes. What with the disappointment I saw in the faces of so many passionate supporters who were my friends and my own sense of abject misery, I felt like throwing myself in the River Don alongside the ground.

Our first campaign in the Second Division since 1959 had not started well. We won only two of our first seven games, suffered a particularly painful 5–1 defeat at home to Luton in October and, when the match with Oxford a week before Christmas attracted the lowest League crowd at Hillsborough since before the war, it confirmed how glum the situation had become. At the time I was called in to see Eric Taylor and Doc Stephen, we had twenty-five points from twenty-six games.

Nothing was formalised at that Friday meeting. Eric and the chairman urged me to go home and talk things over with Sylvia. We arranged to resume our discussion at Doc Stephen's Wisewood House home on Sunday morning when Keith Gardiner, the vice-chairman, would also be present.

Once again it was a case of Sylvia knowing exactly what my reaction to the offer would be and she agreed it was a golden opportunity I could not dream of rejecting. There was a sense in which it would have been easy to remain in the obscurity and security of the pools office for the rest of my working life, and I knew some people might question the wisdom of accepting the pressures and the potential risk to my reputation of stepping into the hot seat. Of course, there was, too, the fact that eighteen years had passed since I had played. However, I never doubted I had the capacity to do a good job as manager. I was familiar with the club, I had watched Wednesday regularly, and I knew all the players fairly well.

There were some people, I know, who felt that Eric Taylor and the chairman were taking advantage of my status as a Wednesday hero and 'using' me to stem the growing tide of criticism of the board and themselves. I never felt this was so and I was sure I could make a success of the task. Certainly I knew I would regret it for the rest of my life if I didn't accept the challenge, and I was delighted to get the opportunity.

When I went to see the chairman and vice-chairman on the following Sunday, I anticipated it being essentially a formality, just a matter of confirming my acceptance, discussing aspects of the job and listening to their views on what they hoped for and expected from me. In the event, I faced such a grilling for two hours that I began to feel I was on trial and they were viewing me as an applicant for the job when, in fact, it was they who had invited me to take it. The questions got so pertinent I ended up saying: 'Hang on a minute, you've already asked me to be the manager. I haven't applied, and if you don't think I'm the man...'

The chairman said: 'Oh, no, Derek, you've answered all the questions we wanted to ask. The job's yours, and we'll announce it at a Press conference tomorrow'.

Doc Stephen and Keith Gardiner were two of the most decent people I ever knew and I shall always remember them with admiration and affection. Even in those days it was fair to describe them as being of the 'old school' but if their manner and style inspired respect they did not lack a sense of humour or humility. The more you got to know them the more you appreciated how human and genuine they were, and I can only call them gentlemen, educated people who stood for honest virtues and high principles. They had a touch of class.

They were men of character and trust, invariably absolutely straight and sincere at all times, and it was my good fortune to be able to look upon them as friends. There was always a mutual goodwill between us and, while this did not guarantee me an easy ride, I soon learned that their tendency to question some of my decisions was intended more as a help than a criticism.

Dennis Woodhead and I were great pals and I was delighted when he stepped in to run the development fund after my appointment as team-manager.

The Wednesday board shortly before I became team-manager. Back row: Eric Taylor (general manager), Stan Ashton, Arthur Broomhead, Danny Williams (manager). Front row: Cecil Turner, 'Dick' Gunstone, Dr (later Sir) Andrew Stephen, Keith Gardiner and R.E. Peasegood.

By the time I became manager, Doc Stephen had, in addition to his duties at Wednesday, been chairman of the Football Association for four years. Indeed, it was during my spell as team boss that he was knighted for his services to football. He was widely regarded as a great ambassador for the English game, a man of dignity and quiet wisdom who not only had a great passion for football but, by virtue of his medical background and experience, boasted a deep understanding of people.

His links with Wednesday dated back to some years before the war, for, soon after moving to Sheffield from Scotland at the start of his medical career, he succeeded his partner, Dr Rhind, as the club's doctor. He was invited onto the board in the mid-1950s and, as a consequence of an unexpected pattern of circumstances, suddenly found himself elected chairman within a very short time. His elevation coincided with a difficult spell for the club, but he proved himself the ideal choice as leader. I think one of his strengths was he was a genuine football man who knew the game and left nobody in doubt about his devotion to the Wednesday cause.

Wednesday always had a reputation for doing everything strictly by the book, and Doc Stephen was the epitome of a philosophy of fair and honest dealing which went back to the era of the legendary Sir Charles Clegg. As I discovered to my eternal embarrassment on one occasion, he was appalled by even the slightest suggestion of bending the rules.

We were one of a number of clubs chasing a very promising youngster, and at a board meeting I reported there was talk of perks and 'extra' payments being made available to the lad and his family by some of our rivals for his signature. During our discussion, the chairman asked what did I suggest, and I made the error of saying something on the lines of well, if you can't beat them, perhaps you should join them. Dear me! I thought I had lined myself up for instant sacking!

I had spoken without really thinking and I wasn't suggesting the club should do something illegal. What I was trying to say was Wednesday had no chance of getting the player because he would join a club prepared to offer him incentives which meant bending the rules. Doc Stephen's dismay at my comment troubled him long after the meeting and he told me later: 'Derek, I'm amazed at you. I hope I never hear you talk like that again'.

Doc Stephen was never a man who wanted to make people conscious of his eminent status in the game. Indeed, he was a modest and reserved sort of person and, unlike some other prominent football figures, he refrained from courting personal publicity. Frankly, I always felt he abhorred the posturing of those of his Football Association colleagues who constantly bent over backwards to get their names in the newspapers.

He was, however, a stickler for ensuring the way his staff acted in public reflected the standards expected of anyone from a club whose chairman was also top man at the FA. Once, for instance, he spotted me angrily rebuking a referee and both linesmen as we went up the tunnel after a 3–3 draw at Brighton in October 1972. While he didn't say anything at the time, later he said he was surprised and saddened by what I had done. I knew I had let him down. It was no excuse that the reason I had got upset with referee Oliver was because he had allowed Brighton's Ken Beamish to grab an 88th-minute equaliser when the lad was at least five yards off-side. I envied the ability of the Doc to stay calm when he had seen us score three goals away from home and then be denied victory by a late and unjust strike!

Keith Gardiner's role as vice-chairman did not bring him into the spotlight in quite the same way as Doc Stephen. As a consequence I don't think the majority of supporters knew much about his distinguished background or were aware of his considerable knowledge of football. Keith, of course, was very well known in the business community because for many years he was a top man in the Neepsend Group owned by Sir

Stuart Goodwin. He was also known as a former editor of the old *Sheffield Telegraph* and, indeed, he had devoted all his career to journalism before turning to industry.

There cannot have been many football club directors who could claim to have reported on the game from the Press box. Keith did so for some years before coming to Sheffield in 1929. In truth, he didn't talk about these things very often, but just occasionally he might be persuaded to reminisce about the FA Cup finals he covered in his time on the *Sheffield & Rotherham Independent* before the war.

He always said Wednesday's Ernest Blenkinsop was the finest full-back he ever saw and insisted that Sheffield United's Jimmy Hagan was the best footballer he ever watched on the local scene. I don't think he ever claimed that his knowledge of the game matched that of the professionals but, like Doc Stephen, he was much more knowledgeable and perceptive about football than the average director. He knew enough to be well aware when anyone was trying to confound him with claptrap and he was never slow to speak his mind on those occasions! He did, however, belong to that breed of men who respected that opinions expressed in the boardroom should not be repeated elsewhere.

To be honest, before I became Wednesday's manager, I had little to do with Keith Gardiner and I tended to view him not without a certain fear and trepidation. He was a huge chap physically and, from a distance, he gave you the impression of being a man who might not be easy to deal with. In fact, he had a great warmth and once you got to know him you discovered a thoughtful and kind person whose keynotes were loyalty and trust.

At board meetings he was given to asking questions that were invariably pertinent and straight to the point and he made it clear he expected honest answers. A grilling from FKG seemed to be an essential item on the agenda of every meeting I attended and he would never rest until I had given him satisfactory replies to his questions. Keith was not an easy man to please and he was never slow to tell me when he thought I was wrong about something. However, if he felt I was justified and believed there was merit in what I said or did he always backed me to the hilt.

What mattered to me was I always knew exactly where I stood with both Doc Stephen and Keith Gardiner and, while I was well aware that in the final analysis I would be judged by what I achieved, I was also never in any doubt about the strength of their support.

With Eric Taylor on the day of my appointment as team-manager.

Chapter Twenty-four

In at the Deep End

The distance between the Development Fund building and the office I now occupied as Wednesday's manager was probably little more than a couple of hundred yards, but moving from one to the other was like stepping into another world in terms of responsibility and the expectations of my employers and the club's supporters.

However, I think I took the transformation in my stride. I knew the task was far from easy but never for one moment did I believe it was beyond me to do a good job. I had faith in my ability to adapt to the challenge because I knew myself and felt I had the qualities required to succeed in the role.

I may have spent eighteen years away from direct involvement in League football but I had remained a close observer of the game at that level and understood it because I had continued to watch with the eyes of a professional. Over the years, too, I had enjoyed the advantage of viewing things as an insider at the club and thus picked up much that might have escaped others. People may have said my only experience of management was running the juniors but, in terms of rules and tactics, football is the same at any level. I knew how I wanted my teams to play and at the end of the day every manager stands or falls by how well he transfers that personal concept into reality.

However, I think the crucial key is gaining the respect of the people with whom you have to deal, and on that count I had no qualms. Looking back now, I believe I had the knack of getting the best out of my players and they respected me as a person and as a football man. Of course, respect is something which has to be earned. No doubt when I first took over there were some players who questioned my credentials and wondered how a man who had just moved from the pools office could become the manager. I think I won over the majority of those who had started out asking 'What does he know about football?'

Experience had taught me how to handle people. Frankly, until I got the manager's job I don't think I was conscious of any particular ability in this direction but I found myself reacting instinctively and spontaneously to situations. I got it right more often than I got it wrong and, reflecting on that phase, I feel I owed much to the lessons I had absorbed from the people I had worked under over the years. At the age of forty-one I had lived through circumstances which had developed a maturity and an appreciation of other people as individuals.

Confident and relaxed on my first day in the Hillsborough 'hot seat'.

Moreover, in football and life at large, I had benefited from the example of some very capable man-managers. I especially felt the influence of Eric Taylor had rubbed off on me. Indeed, then, and later, much of what I picked up from watching Eric at work stood me in good stead and helped me assume the responsibility of management with common sense and confidence.

I have always believed that you win the respect of people if you are honest and fair. I don't think I ever ducked a fight to get a player or an employee a deal I felt they deserved. However, while I didn't always succeed, I never promised anyone anything I knew I couldn't deliver. I have gone through life telling the truth and if the truth sometimes hurts, and there have been occasions when people haven't liked it, I have always felt it far preferable to any alternative.

One of the things I was particularly conscious of when I became Wednesday's manager was not so much that I had an artificial leg but the fact that it prevented me from participating in training sessions. In truth, this was not really a handicap because I could witness all I wanted to see from the pitchside. Some journalists seemed to think it undermined my ability to manage because I lacked the mobility to demonstrate things, but I made the point that there were many older managers in the game who had long passed the stage where they got involved in training.

Indeed, most of the old-timers who insisted on taking part in five-a-sides and suchlike were simply seeking to re-live their youth—and risking a heart attack in the process! In my case, I didn't have to pretend.

Even so, there were a few instances when I threw caution to the wind, probably prompted by the frustration of seeing the lads struggling to master a move we were practising, and the sight of Derek Dooley limping onto the pitch no doubt astonished some of the players but I think it proved that where there's a will there's a way!

I particularly recall one day at the Middlewood Road ground when we were working on defending corner kicks and making a right pig's ear of it. When I took the field in my suit, the lads probably imagined I was simply going to talk to them. However, once in the goalmouth I shouted to John Sissons or whoever was taking the flag kicks: 'Right, cross the ball'.

In fact, though the cross was only fractionally too high, I didn't have the mobility to jump and head the ball. In my prime I would have reached it and got a header on target because I was left totally unchallenged, and that was the point I was trying to emphasise. 'Look' I said, 'I've only got one leg and yet I caused you problems, so goodness knows what would have happened if you'd been facing someone with two good legs.' John

Watching Ron Staniforth during a training session. Ron is talking to Tommy Craig, John Sissons and Dave Clements.

Holsgrove's excuse was: 'I didn't want to make a challenge and knock you down, boss, you might have got your suit ruined in the mud!'

When you become a manager and have to deal with players every day you soon see the differences in character and get a much more rounded view than the one drawn from watching from the director's box on matchdays. Being able to see the whole picture and getting to know players almost as well as members of your own family is an illuminating experience. We are all learning about and from each other all the time and nothing hastens the process of mutual understanding better than working together in various circumstances.

One way or another I think the players recognised my commitment and their response was exactly what I hoped for. In my time a positive atmosphere prevailed, the dressing room combined harmony and discipline, and I can always say the lads never gave less than their best for me.

As I have noted, I tend to respond spontaneously to many situations because it is my habit to trust my natural instincts in certain circumstances. For instance, the day my appointment was announced coincided with a major Supporters' Club function at which all the Wednesday players, management and directors were present. It was my first public engagement as manager and, not unexpectedly, I was called upon to make a brief speech. For some reason I cannot explain, because it was not anything I had planned, my first words were to ask the players to stand up and toast the supporters. It was a small thing which may seem rather trivial but that gesture had a remarkably stimulating effect on proceedings.

In my first week as manager there was another minor incident which I recall with amusement because my reaction surprised some of the players. During a practice match a couple of the lads suddenly started scrapping. They ended up rolling about on the pitch, but when some of the others prepared to pull the pair apart I shouted: 'Leave them!' Within seconds the duo suddenly stopped fighting, stood up and shook hands.

Ron Staniforth, my senior coach, explained the pair invariably had a ding-dong during practice matches and somebody always had to pull them apart. I doubt if they expected me to let them fight on but, once they saw I was prepared to see the scrap continue until someone won and someone lost, they seemed to think it wiser to stop without delay and call it a draw!

When I took charge, we had sixteen games left and our situation in the table was far from healthy. Turning things round was not going to be easy. The priority was to ensure we didn't end up embroiled in a relegation battle and, with little in the way of money to spend, it was essentially a case of soldiering on to the end of the season with the players I had inherited.

It didn't help that our neighbours at Sheffield United were clearly heading for promotion back to the top grade, but the way I saw it was if we could keep out of trouble at least we would have the summer break in which to get things sorted out ready for an attempt at a long-term improvement in the following season.

The eleven points we collected from our remaining fixtures hardly constituted a major revival, but there was a distinct upturn in spirit and discipline and, in finishing fifteenth, we comfortably achieved our safety target.

My first match in charge was a home fixture with Swindon Town. We came from behind twice to draw 2–2 and I believe John Sissons notched our second equaliser twelve minutes from the end. However, when I look back, the players I most readily associate with this game are Graham Pugh and Peter Rodrigues.

Pugh was a tenacious midfielder who is best remembered as the teenager who suddenly burst into prominence late in the 1966 FA Cup run. Later he was often dogged with injuries which prevented him from fully exploiting his exciting early promise and by the winter of 1971 he was in and out of the team. He was a player I had always rated since the days when he was one of my juniors, and I didn't hesitate to call him back into the side to face Swindon, simply because I felt we might benefit from the sort of spirit he epitomised.

Soon after the team-sheet had been pinned up in the dressing room, he knocked on my door and said: 'You know I'm not fit, don't you, boss?' I replied: 'Even at less than 100 per cent, Graham, I know you'll give me everything, and that's all I ask'. He celebrated by scoring our first equaliser, his first senior goal for fifteen months.

Rodrigues was an experienced Welsh international full-back who had been signed by Danny Williams three months or so before I took over. Apart from Tommy Craig, I don't think anybody played in more matches for me than Peter, but, on that first occasion, I wondered if he wasn't trying to put my authority to an early test.

Before the game I happened to mention something he was well aware of, that Swindon's outside-left, Don Rogers, was probably their most

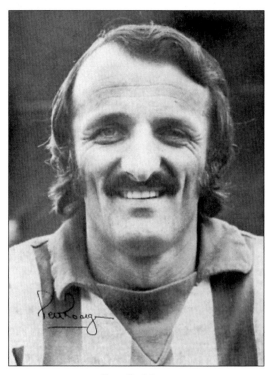

Peter Rodrigues.

dangerous player. 'You'll have to mark him very tight, Peter' I said. He suggested he might need some help or back-up, but I declined to discuss ways in which that might be provided. 'With the speed and experience you've got you're perfectly capable of looking after him on your own' I told him. His reaction clearly suggested he was not happy. However, he went out and did a good job and afterwards he even thanked me for my pre-match comment. Perhaps he hadn't been testing me after all and was grateful someone had helped him regain some self-belief by telling him how good he was!

If Rodrigues was invariably a regular in my time in charge at Hillsborough, one of the first names I put on the team sheet was always that of Tommy Craig. Ironically, although Tommy figured in all but fourteen of my League matches as Wednesday's manager, when I took over he was on the transfer list and insisted he wouldn't withdraw his request for a move.

Tommy Craig.

I made a point of arranging one-to-one interviews with all the players within days of taking over and I have not forgotten that Tommy's first words to me when he walked into my office were: 'I'm not coming off the list, boss'. I think it surprised him when I said I wasn't going to ask him to do anything he didn't want.

Tommy had arrived from Aberdeen shortly before the appointment of Danny Williams. At the age of eighteen he had been saddled with the burden of being the costliest teenager in British football. Moreover, because Wednesday had paid a record £100,000 for him, many people had assumed the club had bought the finished article instead of a talented lad who had great potential but was still developing. Tommy always knew he had a lot to learn and he was unlucky in that his early months at Hillsborough coincided with a time when the team was struggling. It was hardly an ideal scenario and Tommy felt circumstances were preventing him from playing to his strengths.

When I asked him what his problem was, he said he was being denied the freedom to go forward, which was his natural game. I said: 'If you feel like a run up the Kop and that is in the interests of Sheffield Wednesday, do it, Tommy. What I mean is, I'll give you the freedom of the park and guarantee you'll play in the next four games. So now it's up to you to prove I've made the right decision'.

It wasn't long before Tommy was knocking on my door and asking to come off the transfer list because, he said, he was enjoying his football again.

Tommy Craig was a player I always knew I could rely on to give his best whether it was on the training pitch or in a match. He was an honest, genuine lad, and while he has said since that his greatest regret is not having touched a peak in his Hillsborough days, I'm sure many supporters share my view that his qualities were greatly appreciated. Nobody had a sweeter left foot and some of the goals he scored with volleys and free-kicks were stunning and superb. He was, too, my penalty man and whenever we were awarded a spot-kick I could guarantee the ball would finish in the net. The record books show he converted fifteen penalties in my time and I still find it hard to believe he also missed three.

We didn't set the world on fire in my first full season as manager. On paper, finishing fourteenth in the table in that 1971–72 campaign was probably considered modest, but when I viewed the situation in the context of the circumstances I didn't feel we had done too badly. I reached the end of the season convinced we had made more progress than the statistics suggested and was confident that all we needed was a bit of fine tuning. We had created a basis from which to take things forward and, while I know every manager invariably says he is just short of a couple of players, I felt two more signings would be enough to make a considerable difference.

Our problem was that while we recovered from a poor start and enjoyed a fifteen-match run in which we lost only once between late September and late December, we were plagued by inconsistency in the second half of 1971–72 and were left frustrated by a spell when we managed just two wins in fifteen games. It summed up my sense of frustration that at one stage late in the season we lost the services of both our senior goalkeepers, Peter Springett and Peter Grummitt, through injuries. This happened just after the March transfer deadline and the Football League refused us permission to sign an experienced goalkeeper on loan. For four games we ended up using a local amateur, called Trevor Pearson, who had played in our reserves.

I think we lost about a dozen games by a single goal and drew too many matches we might easily have won. Like all managers, I didn't think we got the rub of the green on many occasions when we deserved it, and, if I savoured the pleasures of victory, I did rather tend to take our setbacks much more to heart, especially when they left me with a sense of injustice.

It is fair to say one of my hardest lessons after I became a manager was learning not to over-react to unfair refereeing decisions or, at least, to control my emotions when expressing my views to the Press!

I remember a game at Norwich when we lost to a Duncan Forbes goal in the last eight minutes on a day when young Allan Thompson was sent off. Frankly, I didn't have any sympathy for Thompson because he didn't need to get himself in trouble but, all the same, he was the victim of two trivial bookings by referee Oliver and I didn't hesitate to describe the official's decision as 'diabolical'!

We managed only one win in our first nine games, and the last match in this sequence, at Millwall in late September, was typical of our lack of luck. The record books show Millwall, adopting a Route One policy, began the campaign with an unbeaten twelve-match run. However, we were well on top that day and a superb free-kick from Tommy Craig should have been enough to give us the points. Alas, early in the second half when a linesman flagged for off-side against Millwall, Peter Rodrigues was penalised for picking up the ball before the referee had blown his whistle, and the resulting free-kick led to Barry Bridges scrambling an equaliser.

There was one famous occasion, at Burnley in February, when John Sissons notched a hat-trick but we ended up losing 5–3 and I felt we owed our defeat to the referee's harsh decision to send off Tommy Craig. Burnley had a winger called Leighton James who tended to dive about, and I felt the official, John Yates of Redditch, had been taken in by the winger's theatricals. I knew Tommy was the victim of a raw deal and, wanting to tell Mr Yates so, I ended up on the pitch. However, I had only got halfway to the referee when I was collared and escorted back to the dug-out by a policeman. Had I had two good legs, I might have got to Mr Yates to tell him what I thought before the long arm of the law could reach me!

That was a day when, but for Tony Pritchett from the local paper, I might well have said a few things to the Press which would have landed me in hot water. Fortunately, Tony persuaded me to temper my public criticism and, of course, with hindsight, I appreciated the wisdom of keeping my real feelings private.

Incidentally, one of the games we lost by a single goal was at Preston in November 1971. It was my first visit to Deepdale since my accident in 1953 and I took the opportunity of inviting Bob Garden, the surgeon who had amputated my leg, to the game. I was surprised to learn that Bob had never watched a football match since the day I broke my leg. In fact, he took some persuading to accept my invitation. I was delighted to meet him again and have a chat before the kick-off, but I seem to remember that he did not stay to watch the action.

A Wednesday squad early in my time as manager.

As I have said, I managed with the players I inherited until the end of the 1970–71 campaign but, in the summer, I made my first excursion into the transfer market. The funds available for new players were limited, but the club's directors were well aware that I needed to strengthen the team in a number of positions.

I was particularly keen to sign a centre-half and a centre-forward before the new season began but, in the event, I had to settle for signing only one newcomer, big John Holsgrove. John, who cost £50,000 from Wolves, had the experience of around 200 League games with Crystal Palace and Wolves and, as well as strengthening my defence, I saw him as the kind of leader I needed to take on the captaincy.

Had everything gone according to plan we would also have kicked off the 1971-72 campaign with a new striker but, unfortunately, my efforts to sign Welsh international, Wyn Davies, from Newcastle ended in failure.

I knew Wyn's days on Tyneside were numbered because Harry Haslam, the manager at Luton, had tipped me off that Newcastle were poised to take Malcolm Macdonald from Kenilworth Road for £180,000. When we managed to agree a fee with Newcastle for Davies, I was optimistic about getting my man and the situation looked promising when I met the player for talks in, of all places, the car park at Carmarthen Castle.

Unfortunately, Manchester City subsequently joined the chase for his signature and I knew the prospect of First Division football at Maine Road and the opportunity to play alongside the likes of Colin Bell, Francis Lee and Mike Summerbee would prove far more tempting to Davies than a switch to Sheffield.

Within a few weeks of the start of the 1971–72 season I did manage to compensate for missing out on Davies when I signed Brian Joicey from Coventry, and now, when I look back, I feel I actually ended up getting a much better deal. Joicey may not have been the 'big name' that Davies was but I always rated him one of my most successful buys. He scored forty-eight goals in his first 120 games for Wednesday, starting with sixteen in thirty-nine outings in his initial season with us. In my book that adds up to good value.

The irony of the Joicey deal was that I went to a match at Coventry simply because I was hoping to set up the signing of his colleague, Dave Clements. I knew I needed a centre-forward but my priority was Clements, an Irish international midfielder who could also play in defence. As things worked out, Clements didn't play that night, Joicey did, and I ended up buying two players instead of one.

As I mentioned earlier, Wednesday had not started the season very well, I think we had lost our first three games. The need to bring in some new

When comedian Eric Morecome arrived, with Luton Town, there was always time for a laugh and here he shares a joke with me and John Holsgrove.

On promotional duty with players Peter Rodrigues, Tommy Craig and John Holsgrove.

blood was getting urgent when Freddie Scott, our chief scout, alerted me to the availability of Clements. He was clearly a man who could strengthen our resources and give us extra options, and the £60,000 Coventry wanted was exactly the amount of money I had at my disposal to spend. Although Clements had begun the campaign in the reserves, when I was told he might play in the First Division fixture with Derby I decided to have one last look at him before attempting to finalise a deal.

If, when I arrived at Highfield Road, I was disappointed to discover Clements wasn't playing, by the end of the game I had been amply compensated by having seen the kind of persistent and positive centre-forward display I appreciated more than most. Joicey, who a couple of years earlier had been playing amateur football with North Shields, gave Roy McFarland, the Derby and England centre-half, a torrid ninety minutes. The lad played with the sort of spirit that warmed my heart!

When I met Noel Cantwell, the Coventry manager, after the game I told him I wanted to buy Joicey as well as Clements. As I recall, Noel didn't really want to part with Joicey and offered me another striker, John O'Rourke, instead. He only agreed to sell me the man I wanted when I said it was Joicey or nothing. At the time, Coventry were very anxious to generate the funds to invest £90,000 on Chris Chilton, a striker from

Brian Joicey.

Hull City, and it suited them to agree a £100,000 double deal to sell us both Clements and Joicey.

Cantwell and I shook hands on the deal and, as I drove home from the Midlands, my enthusiasm was tempered by the knowledge that the Wednesday board had given me only £60,000 to spend. I pulled up at the first telephone box I saw and called Eric Taylor to explain I had committed the club to an extra £40,000. Eric, thank goodness, promised to speak to a couple of directors ahead of the next day's board meeting and the upshot was I got the clearance to formalise the deal.

Even so, this was one of those transfers which still required a lot of work before it was completed. Brian Joicey was then a single man and he jumped at the chance to join us. However, while we had no problem settling personal terms with Brian, it took hours of negotiations to persuade Dave Clements to sign. I have to admit there were moments when I feared the deal would collapse.

Dave and his wife had just had their dream house built in the Midlands, and it wasn't enough that we had brought him into Sheffield via the scenic route to show there were some equally idyllic spots in this part of the world. He needed rather more than the prospect of a pleasant area in which to live.

Tension in the dug-out at Hillsborough. Physio Geoff Eggington and coach Ron Staniforth are also in the picture.

It was a welcome bonus that Dave and Brian were good pals and I think their arrival was a boost for us off as well as on the field because they were a positive influence in the dressing room. Although we managed only one point in the newcomers' first three outings in the team, when we beat Sunderland 3–0 at Hillsborough in mid-September I felt it marked a turning point. Over the following three months we lost only twice and, while the second half of the campaign saw our tendency towards inconsistency exposed, I did feel we had good cause to look forward with confidence and optimism.

Incidentally, one of the highlights of the 1971–72 season and an occasion which offered a break from the bread-and-butter business of Second Division football, was the visit of the famous Brazilian side, Santos, to Hillsborough in February, 1972. I think it is fair to say that, in terms of entertainment, the game never quite matched the unforgettable heights of the previous visit of the legendary Pele and his pals in October 1962, but it was nevertheless a fairly memorable and illuminating event.

When the Brazilians were negotiating their European tour, Eric Taylor didn't hesitate to invite them to Sheffield. His plan was to stage another floodlit epic similar to that which had thrilled a 49,000 crowd ten years earlier. Unfortunately, by the time the Santos party arrived in England, the country was in the grip of a power crisis and Wednesday had little choice but to play the game in the early afternoon.

Santos had been guaranteed £50,000, which was a lot of money then and, with many of our supporters expected to be working and unable to get to the game, Eric Taylor feared the effect on the attendance would be such that the receipts would not cover the sum demanded by the Brazilians.

The upshot was that, on the morning of the game, when the Brazilians arrived in Sheffield, Eric attempted to re-negotiate the financial deal. The Brazilians were asked to accept half the gate receipts and full payment of their hotel expenses. They did so, but only with great reluctance after Eric had overcome the problem of communicating with a Brazilian club president whose command of the English language suddenly deteriorated in mid-sentence when he started discussing money!

Then, at about one o'clock, Eric popped into the dressing room and invited me to go outside and see how rapidly the stadium was filling up. 'If this trend continues up to kick-off time' said Eric, 'the Brazilians' share of the receipts will be more than the original £50,000.'

He made straight for the Santos president and said: 'Further to our earlier discussion, I have spoken to my chairman and we think you are

The day Pele returned to Hillsborough. The great man signs autographs for Tony Pritchett, Jimmy Mullen, Allan Thompson, Tommy Craig and Eric Taylor.

right, we should stick to the original arrangement'. His offer was greeted with enthusiasm. Eric then telephoned the Grosvenor House Hotel, where the visitors were staying, and told the manager: 'Make sure the Brazilians pay their hotel bill before they leave tomorrow'.

The game was watched by a crowd of 36,996, which meant we made a fair profit. Eric hoped the Brazilians did not see the details in the newspapers and calculate the receipts before they left Sheffield!

The game itself, which Santos won 2–0, was a bit of a disappointment. Frankly I have forgotten most of the details, the only thing I remember vividly about what happened on the pitch is how Tommy Craig followed Pele all over the field to ensure he was able to claim the great man's shirt at the final whistle!

Chapter Twenty-five

Stars and Stripes

The 1972–73 season was one in which our fortunes and prospects took a significant upward turn and I felt we were definitely moving in the right direction. True enough, we rather let things slip in the closing weeks of the campaign and it was frustrating to finish in tenth place when three more points would have put us in the Second Division's top four, However, there were far more positives than negatives in the season as a whole and the atmosphere was one of genuine optimism.

This was the year when I persuaded the club to bring back the traditional blue and white striped shirts after a lapse of about eight years. It will also always be remembered as the season in which Peter Swan and David Layne returned to football after a long spell of enforced exile, and nobody will ever forget that the campaign marked the arrival at Hillsborough of the remarkable Willie Henderson, who made such a hit with our fans.

I should mention, too, that I brought Peter Eustace home again and, during the season, I recruited Jim Craig, a defender who had been a European champion with Celtic, and Roy Coyle, a promising midfielder from Glentoran. All three justified my faith and it was particularly satisfying to see Coyle gain his first Irish cap after only a handful of Football League outings. Incidentally, two of the youngsters I promoted, striker Rodger Wylde and goalkeeper Peter Fox, showed the kind of promise which made it plain they were destined for long and successful careers in the game.

Bringing Swan and Layne back to Hillsborough, once the Football Association lifted the life bans on the players, was not a step which met with universal approval and I must admit that the chairman, 'Doc' Stephen, and several directors were far from keen when I put the suggestion to them. There were many people who found it difficult to forget the events of 1964 when Swan, Layne and Tony Kay had been named as participants in a betting coup masterminded by Jimmy Gauld and involving at least a dozen players around the country.

I knew there were some people who remembered the shame the episode had inflicted on Sheffield Wednesday and still found it hard to forgive. At the time the story broke in the newspaper one Sunday in April, 1964, I had viewed it all with as much disbelief and dismay as everybody else. Wednesday had always been a club which did everything strictly by the book and were the innocent victims of a cruel blow to their reputation. However, by 1972, I was also aware that Swan and Layne had lost eight years of their careers. They had served their time and in my opinion had been punished enough. They didn't need telling that what they had done was wrong and knew it was something they would always have to live with. As they said themselves, they had paid a heavy price for what had been a foolish act of bravado which they didn't appreciate as having criminal implications.

Swan had played in some 270 games for Wednesday at centre-half and gained nineteen England caps before the ban halted his Hillsborough career. Layne boasted fifty-one goals in only eighty-one games and had

Welcoming Peter Swan and David Layne back to Hillsborough.

been rated one of the best centre-forwards in the country. He was a Sheffield lad but Wednesday signed him from Swindon for a fairly modest fee, and, by coincidence, when the club had first started looking at him I went to a match at Halifax to watch him at the request of Vic Buckingham. I now felt that if either player was half as good as he had been before, he would do a good job for Wednesday.

To the credit of the Wednesday directors, whatever their personal feelings, they supported my plan to give the pair a chance and the exercise was one we had no cause to regret. Unfortunately, Layne, who failed to make it back into the first-team, never enjoyed the same success as Swan on their return. In truth, the ages of the players meant neither could be considered a long-term investment. Indeed, Swan's senior outings were limited to fewer than twenty games. However, even that was enough and I always felt that doing what we did was the human and proper thing.

Layne was in reasonable shape after his long spell out of the game and he certainly worked hard to make a success of his comeback. His misfortune was that the intervening years had left him vulnerable to the sort of niggling injuries which had never troubled him when he was at his peak. Swan, on the other hand, had maintained a high standard of fitness over the years and at thirty-four he was still superbly fit. Moreover, he had not lost the enthusiasm and spirit that had once made him one of England's leading defenders. The moment he got the go-ahead to return to Hillsborough he volunteered to do some training with the apprentices and promptly showed he could match the best for fitness.

As the start of the season approached, I never had any doubts that there would be a place for Swan in the team for the opening match against Fulham. On the previous Tuesday at the training ground I told him he would play on Saturday. He was a bit overwhelmed with emotion and he thanked me profusely but, as I said at the time, my decision was not influenced by sentiment or because I wanted to do him a favour. Peter had proved himself on the pre-season trip to Scotland and he was in the team on merit. I would not have picked him if I did not think he could do a job for us.

We beat Fulham 3–0 and it was a lovely sunny afternoon which I am sure Peter will never forget. The reception the crowd gave him was marvellous and it summed up a day when everything went just as he wanted when, in the opening fifteen minutes, he had a hand in our first goal. As I recall, Brian Joicey knocked on Peter's upfield ball and Mick Prendergast stuck it in the net. The joy on Peter's face had to be seen to be believed.

Swan moved on to Bury in 1973 and helped them win promotion from Division Four. I would have been happy to have given him a contract for a second term at Hillsborough and let him play in the reserves, however, having waited so long to figure in the Football League again he wanted to prolong the experience. That he made a success of his comeback said a lot about Peter's depth of character.

Swan had first joined Wednesday as a youngster and I don't think he ever lost that special feeling for the club. The same could be said of Peter Eustace, who gladly took a big drop in his pay to rejoin the Owls after three unhappy years in London.

When Eustace went to West Ham for £90,000 in 1969, everybody thought his style would assure him of instant success with the Hammers. It looked to be the ideal move, but things didn't work out as expected and his heart remained at Hillsborough. He played in fewer than fifty games for Ron Greenwood's side and we were lucky to be able to bring him 'home' for a modest £15,000 fee. In fact, Greenwood asked us to keep the bargain price a secret and the media assumed we had paid three times as much for Eustace as was the case.

Of course, the biggest bargain of them all was signing Willie Henderson, the little Scottish international winger, who became such a tremendous favourite in his two years with Wednesday.

Willie was like a breath of fresh air, a wonderful tonic on and off the field. The fans loved him and he was brilliant for me. He was a positive influence in the dressing room because he was a bubbly character who had the respect and admiration of his colleagues. He had a terrific rapport with his team-mates and several of the lads hero-worshipped Willie as much as any of our supporters.

Willie gained every Scottish domestic honour and twenty-nine international caps in his career with Glasgow Rangers and Scotland but, by the time he came to Sheffield, he was at the veteran stage and had had a spell in South Africa. When Freddie Scott, our chief scout, said the player was available, I made haste to fix up a meeting and booked Willie into the Grosvenor House Hotel. I knew several other clubs were chasing him and this was one race I desperately wanted to win.

When the news broke that I was trying to sign Willie there were many people who asked me if I knew what I was doing. Willie had a reputation as a rebel and there were those who believed I was asking for trouble, As I recall, there had been a bit of a fall-out with Rangers when he felt he got a raw deal over some money he had been promised around the time

The day Willie Henderson joined Wednesday.

Willie Henderson.. he was like a breath of fresh air.

he left Ibrox. The upshot was a lot of publicity which didn't paint Willie in a very good light.

The man I knew and came to respect and admire was very different from the image that had been suggested. One of the first things he said to me was: 'Don't believe all you have heard about me'. I replied: 'Willie, I don't care what you've done in the past, but, if you once put your name to a Wednesday contract, I do care. If you step out of line, I'll fine you'. He gave me one of those famous Henderson grins and said: 'That's okay by me, boss'.

I have to admit Willie was no angel in his time at Hillsborough but I never had a problem with him. Indeed, I can safely say that all the headlines he made in Sheffield concerned the positive things he achieved on the pitch. I warmed to the man from the minute I met him and the way we instantly generated an atmosphere of mutual trust and respect left me with a gut feeling that this was one deal I would never have cause to regret.

After a long initial chat I told Willie the terms I could offer him, he nodded agreement and we shook hands on the deal. We arranged to meet again at the ground early on the following morning to complete the formalities. Alas, when he arrived I had been unable to put the details to the board for clearance and, as Willie was wanting to dash off to catch a train to Glasgow, I had no choice but to ask him to sign a blank contract.

To his credit Willie didn't hesitate. 'You're the first bloke I've ever signed a blank contract for in my entire career' he told me later. He had asked what would happen if the directors rejected what we had agreed. I said if they turned it down I would rip up the contract and nobody would know he had signed it.

I shall always remember Willie Henderson with great affection because he not only did the business for me but he was someone whom it was impossible not to like. He was the type of bloke who put a smile on your face. He even made inflicting a fine on him a pleasure!

As he didn't drive and depended on taxis to get to training, he would sometimes arrive five minutes or so late. He would burst through the dressing room door and, before I had time to look at the clock, say: 'How much, boss?' To the amusement of the other lads, he would pull out a five-pound note and hand it over, always paying his fine with a cheeky grin.

Some twenty-five years later I never think of Willie without evoking so many happy memories. On the field he was such a wonderful entertainer and for me certain games will forever be synonymous with the unique magic of the little Scot.

I think he first really stamped his personality on the Hillsborough scene in a League Cup tie with Bolton one evening in September. We won the game 2–0. Joicey and Eustace were the scorers but, while Willie was not directly involved in the goals, everybody present had no doubt this was 'Henderson's match'. The way he gave left-back Don McAllister the run-around in the early stages had our supporters drooling with delight.

Willie was always full of surprises and never without an answer when his tendency towards the unexpected sometimes left his team–mates and manager puzzled. In this particular game, having caused havoc on the right flank he suddenly drifted over to the left wing. When I asked him why he had made the switch, he said: 'Well, I was beating the first defender, then the second, but I was having problems with the third defender. So I thought I'd walk over to the other wing'. Only when I insisted that John Sissons was designated to operate on the left did he promise to stick to the right flank!

If there is one match from the 1972–73 campaign which will always be associated with Willie Henderson it is the February fixture with Sunderland. This was the season when the Wearsiders went on to a famous FA Cup final triumph over Leeds, and they arrived at Hillsborough boasting a nine-game unbeaten run in the Second Division. Bob Stokoe had recently taken charge and, as often happens when a new manager arrives on the scene, their fortunes had suddenly improved.

The game was still goalless at half-time and Willie had barely performed in the first forty-five minutes. In the dressing room I asked him: 'What's happened to you?' He said he hadn't had enough of the ball. I promptly ordered the other lads to ensure Willie had no complaints on that count in the second half. A minute past the hour mark Peter Springett made a save at the Leppings Lane end and, spotting Willie unmarked, he kicked the ball towards the little Scot. What happened next was pure magic. Willie set off dribbling down the right wing and left a string of bemused defenders in his wake before cutting in and finding the net with his shot. My abiding memory of this moment is the image of Willie on his knees with his arms raised in triumph towards the fans on the Kop, and Brian Joicey bending over him to offer his congratulations.

Bob Stokoe was not best pleased by Sunderland's defeat. When I walked up the tunnel at the end of the game he shouted 'Dooley!' and when I turned to face him he added: 'You're a set of **** animals!' I said 'Thanks for the compliment' and was ready to leave it at that, but Bob insisted on a right old verbal ding-dong. In the end I told him: 'The best thing you can do, Bob, is get in that dressing room and give your players a rollicking instead of me'.

Of course, my players had seen what had happened, and when I walked into our dressing room I found them all lined up awaiting my arrival.

They applauded and shouted 'Well done, boss!' Standing right at the end of the line was Willie, who thrust out his hand and said: 'I told you I'd win the match, boss, and I knew you'd want to congratulate me!'

It is well known that Willie's eyesight was not very good and some people said the reason he liked to hug the touchline on his runs was because it guided him in the direction of the corner-flag. This may have been an exaggeration, but the sight of him peering across the dressing room with that familiar grin was invariably amusing, especially when he had to ask an apprentice to help him locate his boots!

Willie's poor sight was particularly noticeable in floodlit matches. Once when I was shouting instructions to him he wandered to the touchline alongside the dug-out and squinted as he asked 'Is that you, boss?'

Henderson in his heyday must have been a marvellous sight and the Willie we saw in the twilight of his career left our supporters with some magical moments they will never forget.

In that 1972–73 season we won five of our first seven games, had a brief spell on top of the table and remained in the top two places until mid-October. After that we slipped a bit and the tail-end of the campaign was disappointing. The frustrating tendency to lose games by the odd goal and draw matches after being in front continued. We did well at home with fourteen wins and only three defeats, but we again struggled on our travels. The irony was that there was a stage when I really thought everything was coming together.

We looked good going forward because we had some good attacking players, and I felt one of the reasons for our loss of impetus was an injury to striker Mick Prendergast. 'Prendo' was one of the bravest of lads and he endured more than his fair share of setbacks in his career. In this instance he was sidelined by cartilage trouble and internal bleeding in his knee which required surgery. It meant he figured in only sixteen games and I'm afraid the club never addressed the implications of his absence.

This was the year when Queen's Park Rangers gained promotion and they and Burnley ran away with the Second Division. Early in the season QPR compensated for the loss of winger Martyn Busby through injury by paying £165,000 for Dave Thomas, and I felt that, if we wanted to stay in the promotion race, we needed to respond in a similar way to the loss of Prendergast. Unfortunately, when I told the board I really needed to buy another centre-forward they said there was no money available.

Rodger Wylde was a young striker who was given his first taste of senior football because of Prendergast's absence, and I never had any doubts that this tall local lad was destined to make the grade. However, while he had a good touch and could use his head, at that stage he was really one for the future. I always remember he scored the first League goal of his career on the December day when we drew 2–2 with Millwall at Hillsborough after leading 2–0. I was sure the lad would always have the goal-knack, the problem was that he needed to be given time to develop and, meanwhile, we lacked an experienced deputy for Prendo.

Wylde, of course, was keen to learn and his natural skill was matched by enthusiasm. There was a stage in his development when I felt he didn't get into a game as much as he might. Once, at half-time during a Central League match, I had a bit of a go at him. Unfortunately, he took me so literally that he was throwing his boots and head at everything. As I recall, he ended up getting kicked on the head. 'Rodger', I told him afterwards, 'I want you to get involved, but I didn't mean I wanted you to risk getting killed!'

We finished tenth in the table because we ended the season with only two wins in the last eight games. I shall always remember that one of those victories came against Orient at the end of March on the day when Peter Fox was given an unexpected League debut.

Fox was then four months short of his sixteenth birthday and his appearance ensured him a place in the club's record books as the youngest player in Wednesday's Football League history. With both senior goalkeepers, Springett and Grummitt, injured I had no choice but to promote the lad and the maturity and courage he showed that day confirmed my belief that he was another youngster destined for a long career in the game.

If I was impressed at the way he took the news of his selection in his stride, the manner in which he conducted himself on the pitch in what proved especially testing circumstances left me full of admiration. The lad played for all but three minutes of the second half with a dislocated toe! He won a race with Barrie Fairbrother as the Orient striker bore down on him at speed but was injured in clearing the ball just as the pair collided. At the time, of course, we were unaware of the dislocation and all I remember is Peter playing on in great pain like a real trooper.

Fox had to wait about another eighteen months for his next senior chance, by which time, of course, I had left the club, and it is history now that the lad was limited to barely fifty senior outings for Wednesday. He was unlucky in that the circumstances which developed didn't help his cause at Hillsborough but, happily, he went on to enjoy a fine career in which he played in some 600 games, including nearly 500 for Stoke. Those of us who knew him when he was starting out were delighted to see him eventually progress into management at Exeter City.

We took pride in the fact that Peter was one of a number of successful products of the youth team which was in the care of George McCabe. George is best remembered now as a former Football League and FIFA referee but in his younger days he had been a pretty good goalkeeper. This helped him spot the potential of Fox when he saw the lad playing schoolboy football in Scunthorpe.

A number of clubs were monitoring Fox's progress and when we signed him after he left school we were accused by Don Revie of stealing a player who had been promised to Leeds United. The truth was that Fox's parents much preferred to see their boy start his career at Hillsborough, and they always said their choice was entirely because they liked and trusted George McCabe.

I don't suppose reaching the fifth round of the FA Cup suggests a great run along the Wembley trail but I always felt that the circumstances in which we made it to the last sixteen of the competition, in 1972–73, served to show we had the potential to make an impact in the promotion race. We didn't lack the ability or the spirit and the Cup games confirmed we were not far short of a team equipped to end our exile from the top-grade.

As the loss of Prendergast had clearly highlighted, our undoing was being short on strength in depth. One of the ironies of our FA Cup campaign was that it generated a financial bonus which, had we been assured of it earlier in the season, might have enabled us to make a badly-needed signing.

The feature of our Cup run was a fourth-round three-match marathon with Crystal Palace who, at the time, were in the First Division. In fact, they were relegated at the end of that season but they had spent a lot of money and boasted some excellent players. We certainly viewed them as a major test and it was a challenge we met with a lot of character.

The first game, at Hillsborough in early February, came during a spell when I risked bringing back Mick Prendergast and, sadly, this proved one match too many for him. He lasted only eighteen minutes and didn't play again that season. However, before Prendo limped off, we had taken the lead with a Tommy Craig penalty after Willie Henderson was up-ended in the box. Unfortunately, Palace squared the scoreline with a second-half equaliser.

There wasn't a goal in the replay at Selhurst Park until seven minutes from the end of normal time, and, to my dismay, it was Palace who scored through Iain Phillips. I was standing by the dug-out when the ball went into the net and, having just lit my pipe, I threw my lighter to the ground in disgust. Peter Eustace, who was on the bench, went to pick up the lighter. As he handed it to me he said: 'Don't worry, boss, we'll get one back'. Happily, he was right, and in the very last minute young David Sunley celebrated his twenty-first birthday with a goal.

The second replay, at Villa Park, proved to be one of the most memorable occasions in my managerial career. We achieved a famous victory after twice being behind and the emotion and atmosphere of that night is something I shall never forget.

David Payne put Palace in front on twenty minutes but Brian Joicey equalised just after half-time. Then Don Rogers restored Palace's lead with a deflected effort and Joicey again levelled the score within six minutes when he headed in from a Henderson corner.

When the game went into extra-time I wanted to substitute Henderson because I thought he might have had enough. It was typical of Willie that he said: 'No, boss, I'll just stay on long enough to make the winner for you, then you can bring me off'.

In fact, it was John Sissons who provided the through ball from which Joicey hit our third and completed his hat-trick in the nineteenth minute of extra-time. However, needless to say Willie had a hand in the build up. The grin on his face when he walked off the pitch spoke volumes!

I replaced Willie with little Eric Potts, instructing him to try to keep possession and eat up a few precious minutes. Eric was known to all the lads as 'Billy Whizz' because he fizzed about a lot and his team mates did not always know what he was going to do when he got the ball. To be honest, on this occasion, worrying whether Eric would do exactly what I wanted got me more agitated than counting the minutes and shouting to referee Gordon Hill: 'Come on, ref, blow your whistle!'

That unforgettable victory on a night when at least ten thousand Wednesdayites travelled to the game was followed within a few days by a fifth-round clash with Chelsea at Hillsborough. A crowd of 47,000 packed into the ground and the tie was a tremendous climax to a great week. It made me feel that the good days were on the way back for the Owls, even though we lost the match as Chelsea came from behind to pip us to a place in the quarter-finals.

In modern times, of course, the kind of marathon we shared with Crystal Palace cannot happen. The trend towards ensuring matches in cup competitions are finished at the first attempt or don't go beyond one replay, with the deadlock ended by penalty shoot-outs, is something which saddens me. Marathon ties were a feature of the FA Cup and what amounts to outlawing them is tantamount to removing some of the magic and romance from the competition.

The FA Cup is all about the opportunity for the game's minnows to confront the giants, and if the little club could take a big club to two or three replays it was a situation which not only captured public imagination and created excitement but generated much-needed extra income for smaller clubs.

I can understand the reasoning which has prompted the changes and a number of circumstances have contributed to the development. One initial problem came when the police authorities in many areas argued the need for ten days' notice before a replay. That meant a threat to the completion of subsequent rounds on schedule, and then, of course, the overall increase in the volume of football at top level meant it suited the big clubs if replays were limited to one.

The tendency to pander to the wishes of the big boys is unfortunate and unfair on smaller clubs. My view is that if the clubs are playing more games now than was the case a few years ago, it is doubtful whether individual players are playing more football.

If you start totting up how many games some individuals play in a season it is surprising how often the figure barely tops thirty. Maybe I'm old fashioned but I must admit I have to smile when I read of players complaining of too much football and saying they are tired because they have figured in two matches in the same week. I belong to a generation of footballers who would gladly have played every day without complaint. I'm sure there are some lads in the game today who feel the same way but, unfortunately, they seem to be in a minority.

A 1973 dressing room shot of me with Willie Henderson, Peter Rodrigues, Colin Prophett, Tommy Craig, Peter Grummitt, John Sissons and Roy Coyle.

Chapter Twenty-six

Victims of a Mystery Virus

Ahead of the 1973–74 campaign the atmosphere at Hillsborough was positive and the mood of optimism was such that it was impossible to anticipate the drama and dismay that suddenly developed to haunt us in the following months.

I was confident I had something to work on and genuinely felt that, given the breaks, we could make a push for promotion. Certainly I would never have believed the fates could conspire to create the pattern of circumstances which occurred and I doubt if anyone could have predicted that events at the club would turn out as traumatic as they did.

We did not start the season as well as we might have wished and four wins in our first nine games left room for improvement. Our third and fourth victories came in successive matches at the end of this sequence and, at the time, those results seemed to suggest we were finally starting to click.

Unfortunately, in early October, we suddenly found ourselves in the grip of a mystery virus which swept through the club. Over the next two months sixteen or seventeen senior professionals and several other members of the playing staff were affected. At one stage I had thirteen players available for selection, including two goalkeepers, and I couldn't honestly say that all those capable of standing were really fit. The consequence was that between October 6th and December 22nd we played sixteen League and Cup matches and won only two, with just one victory in twelve Second Division fixtures.

When I look back on that painful phase I cannot help but feel I made the wrong decision in choosing to play down the depth of the crisis we faced. I have often wished I had made more of the seriousness of the situation because, remarkable as it might seem, few people really appreciated just how bad that mystery virus was. Frankly, even some of the directors, while they knew what was happening, seemed unable to comprehend the extent of the problem and the difficulties it was causing.

I must admit I was reluctant to make as much of the virus as I might for two reasons. First and foremost I felt that if I spelt it all out in detail and kept stressing the point I would be giving our opponents a psychological boost. I thought I was being a master psychologist and adopting wise tactics by consciously understating the situation.

Alas, once we were on the field the effects of the virus were evident in the way we played. Some of the lads were taking the field when they ought to have been taking to their beds and the cruellest irony of all was that most of those watching the games were unaware of the illness.

The second reason for my caution in revealing the full facts was I didn't think people wanted to hear excuses. In the context of Wednesday's history over the previous five or six years, I knew many of our fans had grown tired of excuses and it was particularly unfortunate that, in this instance, the reality constituted genuinely unfortunate circumstances which would normally have been received with widespread sympathy and understanding.

I should mention, too, that a curious aspect of the virus was that we never did find out exactly what it was and nobody ever discovered the

The Owls' squad in 1973–74.

source of the infection. We always felt it must have come from abroad, and some of us were inclined to wonder whether it was brought home from a foreign holiday by a relative of a member of the staff.

It would be unfair to name anyone now after all these years, but a few weeks before the virus struck one player returned from a trip to Mauritius and reported his wife had been rushed to hospital suffering from the effects of a mysterious infection.

The illness could not have come at a worse time and its effects in terms of our results simply compounded the frustration of our supporters. Events suggested their hopes of seeing the club pushing for promotion were being dashed yet again and they were not pleased at the prospect of another failure.

Their impatience was not entirely surprising and their pessimism was reflected in the dramatic drop in attendances at home games in November and December. By then the criticism being voiced at matches was loud and long. To be fair to the fans, I was never on the receiving end of any serious stick myself, the main target was the board. The fans were angry that the directors didn't seem to be doing anything to remedy a situation in which we were deprived of so many key players. Some investment at that point might well have changed the course of subsequent events.

Even without the mystery virus I knew we still needed to buy to strengthen the squad, but a lack of funds continued to be the stumbling block. I remember that around the time the virus was starting to pass its peak I reviewed the situation and came up with a plan. I decided that once everything was back to normal, I would look at the possibility of selling someone to raise a substantial amount of cash. Tommy Craig was the last player I wanted to sell but I knew Aston Villa were keen on buying him, and, all things considered, I was prepared to sacrifice Craig if it meant we could use the money to improve the team.

Incidentally, around this time, Liverpool were very keen on young David Sunley and there was a stage when a swap deal involving Tommy Smith and a cash adjustment in our favour was mooted. It was a phase when Smith, the original 'Anfield Iron', was supposed to have reached the end of his Liverpool days. In the event the deal broke down, with one of key reasons being Smith's high wages but, anyway, I doubt if he ever really wanted to leave Merseyside and the irony was that, almost immediately, his Anfield career revived and he went on to figure prominently in a famous European Cup triumph.

Now, when I reflect on the autumn of 1973, I can see that whatever my personal view of the pattern of events and whatever I did or sought to do about the situation, my destiny and that of the club was influenced by other people and circumstances over which I had no control. The climate of growing unrest on the terraces eventually induced unexpected developments in the Hillsborough boardroom with changes which, though I didn't know it then, were to have significant consequences for me.

To put everything in a proper context, perhaps I should go back to the summer of 1973 when, as I have said, I was in an optimistic mood and our immediate prospects certainly looked healthy.

I had strengthened the squad by recruiting Bernard Shaw from Wolves and Ken Knighton from Hull City, and, as they were both experienced players boasting nearly 600 League games between them, the total outlay of less than £100,000 looked a good investment. Shaw, of course, was well known to our fans for he had started his career at Sheffield United, while Knighton, a South Yorkshire lad who had served five clubs, was widely recognised as a tenacious, competitive performer.

In fact, I had been chasing Knighton for some time because he boasted exactly the kind of resilience I felt we needed. However, I learned that Luton Town were also in the race to sign him and it was looking as if we were getting involved in a Dutch auction. Fortunately, Harry Haslam, the Luton manager, was a pal of mine and I was able to phone him and tell him we both had to stop taking turns to up our offers. He appreciated that we were both losing out by creating a situation in which one of us would end up paying over the odds. Once we had agreed we would both offer the same fee, I knew I was the favourite to get Knighton because he was keen to return closer to his Barnsley roots and, anyway, he had been a Wednesdayite as a lad.

If there was one cloud on the horizon it was that Dave Clements, who had missed only four games in two seasons, was determined to leave— his departure had been on the cards for some months before it happened. It is history now that Dave's only appearance for us in 1973–74 was in the first match of the season and in September he moved to Everton, where his former Northern Ireland team-boss Billy Bingham had recently been appointed manager.

Dave had become a bit disenchanted because I wanted to use him at left-back but he preferred to play in midfield. He may have feared that if he didn't figure in the same position as the one in which he played for Ireland, it might affect his international career. Frankly I don't think there was any danger of this happening because everyone in the Irish camp valued his talents.

Long before the new campaign, Dave and I were lining up a new contract and I often wonder whether the pattern of subsequent events might have been different had he not gone off to play for Ireland before the deal was settled. When we talked he had said of the terms I had put to him: 'That's all right, boss. When I get back we'll sit down and have another chat, but we're near enough to agreement'.

Unfortunately, he returned to Sheffield a different person. He immediately made it plain he wanted to leave and I couldn't help but feel that somewhere along the line something had happened or been said during his absence on international duty which had suddenly and unexpectedly altered his attitude.

Because of the troubles in Ireland the national team was then playing some home games at Goodison Park and, just when I was puzzling over what had made Dave change his mind, I received a phone call from Billy Bingham at Everton which seemed to me much more than just a coincidence. I don't think I was putting two and two together and making five! Bingham made what I considered a ridiculous offer for Clements, barely half of the value I put on the player, and that call marked the start of a saga which dragged on over the following weeks.

Clements kept popping in to my office to ask if I had heard any more about his transfer. One day his regular enquiry just happened to follow a call I had taken from Sunderland manager Bob Stokoe and I think he was surprised when I said: 'Yes, you'll have to go up to Roker Park next week. Sunderland have come in with an offer which is far better than Everton's'. Stokoe's bid was £70,000.

Perhaps it was just a coincidence but, within three or four hours of talking to Clements, I received another call from Everton in which I was asked to state what I wanted for the player.

To cut a long story short, I finished up getting £88,880 for Clements. It meant that, after the levies which then prevailed had been deducted, Wednesday collected £80,000. Frankly, I would much rather have had the player than the money because I rated Dave very highly. He had always done well for me and I never held it against him that he should choose to leave. Indeed, I felt I couldn't blame the lad for doing what he considered best for his career. However, I must admit I was disappointed by the way it happened.

Of course, it didn't help that we managed only two wins in our first seven games. We then sealed two home victories in the space of five days but, just when we thought the tide was turning, we saw the first signs of the wretched virus which knocked us completely off our stride.

Nobody was more seriously affected by the mystery bug than skipper John Holsgrove, who collapsed in the shower after the second of our three League Cup games with Bournemouth in mid-October. He spent the following week in hospital under observation and it is a measure of just how debilitating the virus was that he did not play again until the following March.

Other key players were also sidelined for long spells. John Sissons, for instance, figured in only four of our first twenty-four games, while Willie Henderson missed fourteen matches. Jim Craig managed to start only three games and a particularly cruel consequence of his illness was that it shattered his hopes of making his mark at Hillsborough after such a promising start.

Some lads bounced back more quickly than others, including Tommy Craig and Brian Joicey, but the truth was that the majority returned far too soon. They didn't lack anything in terms of spirit and willpower but you cannot climb from your sick bed and walk straight onto a football pitch—well, you can, but you cannot expect to perform with any energy for long.

John Holsgrove.

The situation had a knock-on effect in several significant ways, not least in terms of restricting our training routines. We were limited to light training for several weeks because we knew we had to ensure the recovering players conserved their energies. As for practice matches, there was a spell when we didn't have enough men to make up two teams, and I was scared that someone might go and get injured just to compound our problems!

So many senior players went down with the virus that I could barely field a senior team, but few people outside the club were aware of how serious the situation was. The crisis was such that the players' area of the ground was closed down for a week with the dressing rooms and adjoining sections sealed off and fumigated. Meanwhile the players were told to stay away from the ground.

It was at this time, in late October, that we tried to get our home match with Notts County postponed. However, the Football League rejected our appeal and secretary Alan Hardaker insisted we fulfilled the fixture. We were bitterly disappointed by the League's lack of sympathy, and I must admit we felt the decision was influenced by that fact that Hardaker and Eric Taylor were hardly the best of friends.

Over the years Eric had tended to criticise many of Hardaker's pronouncements, especially when he believed they unjustly favoured some clubs at the expense of others. I think Eric resented Hardaker's autocratic style and it was widely known within the game that each had a knack of provoking the other, so whenever they met the atmosphere was decidedly lacking in mutual goodwill.

I had no option then but to use such untried youngsters as Danny Cameron and Eddie Prudham in place of Rodrigues and Prendergast, and while the likes of Jimmy Mullen, Eric Potts and Allan Thompson had a bit more experience to their credit than Danny and Eddie, throwing all those kids in at the same time was far from ideal. Of course, they didn't let me down and I was rather proud of the way everybody rose to the challenge and ensured we emerged from the Notts County game with a 0–0 draw. All the same, I believed we deserved more sympathy from the Football League.

We followed the Notts County match by finally disposing of Bournemouth in the League Cup with a 2–1 home win at the end of October. Alas, November proved a traumatic month in which we suffered five straight defeats, and while we were beaten by only a single goal in four of those fixtures, at the start of the month we had to endure the indignity of being thrashed 8–2 in a League Cup match at Queen's Park Rangers.

Because we had struggled to put a team together at QPR and several of those involved were not really fit, I knew we faced a mighty battle against strong and experienced opponents. Things didn't look good when we found ourselves two goals down after only fourteen minutes but we managed to hit back and level the score.

In the end it was one of those nights when we felt the whole world was against us. At a crucial stage we were denied a blatant penalty and I was especially dismayed by the circumstances in which QPR were allowed to go through and score while Danny Cameron was stretched full length on the pitch and clearly injured.

The irony was that, a few minutes earlier, when a home man, Terry Venables, had gone down injured, the referee had stopped the game instantly to allow him prompt attention. You can be sure that I told referee Tom Spencer there seemed to be one law for a star like Venables and another for a kid like Cameron!

The bottom dropped out of the game for us when QPR scored three times in six minutes just past the hour mark and we endured a very rough ride in the final third of the game. It summed up our nightmare that both Cameron and Mullen contributed own-goals to the home team's tally of eight.

You can only respond to circumstances as they exist at a particular moment, and, in the context of the situation we were then in, I don't think the way we played in the next three or four games reflected badly on anybody at the club. A heavy defeat like the one at QPR can shatter team spirit but the lads reacted with considerable character. We all knew things were not as we wanted them to be, but I still believed that once everyone was fit and available the outlook would begin to improve.

By early December there were signs that the crisis caused by the virus was starting to ease. Yet if the worst was now behind us, I knew we still faced an uphill battle and any improvement in our overall record would be gradual rather than sudden. I felt sure another couple of weeks would see us turning the corner and all we needed in the meantime was just a little bit more patience and understanding.

I soon learned that circumstances had already begun to create a climate in which patience and understanding were suddenly in short supply, and not just on the terraces but in some corners of the boardroom.

Chapter Twenty-seven

Sacked
at Christmas

Before the team had kicked a ball in December 1973 there was a dramatic development behind the scenes at Hillsborough which, although I didn't know it at that moment, marked the beginning of the end for me.

When Sir Andrew Stephen and Keith Gardiner resigned at a board meeting on the first Thursday in the month I knew my position as manager might be under imminent threat if there wasn't a rapid revival in our playing fortunes. However, even if I had taken the most pessimistic view possible of the situation, I could not have expected to be removed from my job within less than three weeks. Certainly I did not expect to be sacked on Christmas Eve.

I had never concerned myself with boardroom politics, but I was aware that some friction had surfaced among the directors and knew one or two people were flexing their muscles. I was only called into board meetings to deliver a brief manager's report and answer questions but I saw enough to sense that all was not well. The atmosphere was not as harmonious as it had once been.

Of course, I was not privy to the details of that fateful meeting on the 6th of December but, knowing 'Doc' Stephen and Keith Gardiner as I did, I could not imagine them choosing to quit without considerable provocation. They were the epitome of tolerance and understanding and I always believed their strength was a capacity to keep their heads when others were losing theirs. I knew it must have taken a lot to make them walk away. Neither man ever discussed the episode with me, but the following comment from Keith Gardiner which appeared in a newspaper offers an intriguing insight.

> *To say I retired or resigned is a euphemism. The truth is that a certain majority of the board decided heads must fall. I walked out with my head*

on my shoulders at least. I anticipated the inevitable. I don't like being pushed around so I departed. Things turned sour in relation to certain things. There was a long catalogue of trials and tribulations. The majority of the board felt they must put their heads on a pike. There was the usual talk of finding millionaires and so forth. I took exception to the methods they were adopting. That is why I said I would call it a day and walked out.

When I learned of the departure of the chairman and vice-chairman I was saddened because I knew Sheffield Wednesday had lost two good men, people of stature who had given their hearts and souls to the club's cause. Moreover, on a personal level I had lost two friends who, while they had never given me an easy ride, were allies and people I could trust.

Matt Sheppard, an accountant with a range of business interests, took over as chairman. His links with Wednesday went back a considerable time by virtue of his long service as the club's auditor for some years before he became a director. However, in the context of what had happened and what subsequently developed, the irony was that Eric Taylor had been responsible for persuading Doc Stephen to invite Matt to join the board two years earlier. Now even Eric's position was under threat.

Within a few days of becoming chairman, Matt Sheppard organised a buffet party at his home for the directors. Eric Taylor and myself, along with our wives, were invited. As Eric was rather more astute than me and sensed this was not really a social gathering, he chose to leave Emmie at home, but I took Syliva along. Eric's hunch that this was not an ordinary get-together proved right, for we found a couple of unexpected guests present. Moreover, Matt announced Bert McGee and Roy Whitehead as the successors to Doc Stephen and Keith Gardiner on the board.

Of course, as Eric noted, the pair's co-option had to be confirmed at a board meeting, but this was a formality and soon afterwards the public learned of their appointment. McGee, the boss of a tool firm then

Matt Sheppard.

called Easterbrook Allcard, was prominent in local industrial and business circles. Whitehead, who ran a small engineering firm, if less well known, was familiar to Wednesday supporters as a once-prominent member of a rebel shareholders' group. In fact, Whitehead was not unknown to me as I had played football with him when we were youngsters.

The new-look board met for the first time exactly a week after the departure of Stephen and Gardiner, the meeting coinciding with my forty-fourth birthday. I was not asked to make an appearance and, all these years later, it still seems strange that in my remaining time as manager I was never called into a board meeting to formally meet the newcomers. In fact, neither man ever spoke to me as an individual during this spell. They didn't know whether I was a good manager or a bad one and knew nothing of the true extent of the circumstances which had prevailed over the previous three months. Yet, remarkably, within ten days of arriving on the scene, without having asked a single question of anyone who had been in the front line, they were voting to sack me!

There were, of course, enough other people on the board who knew me well. Indeed, they had known me a long time and, what is more relevant, they were, or should have been, fully aware of the effects of the virus and the conditions against which we had battled for months,

I could appreciate that the newcomers wanted to be seen to be taking action and pursuing bold steps. Obviously they were keen to make an instant impression and create a new regime, but it was bitterly disappointing that the 'old school' of Arthur Broomhead, Cecil Turner and Stan Ashton did not rally to my defence. At least my one remaining loyal supporter, 'Dick' Gunstone, being aware of what was going to happen and knowing he would be hopelessly outnumbered, chose to miss the meeting at which he was required to vote for my dismissal.

The proposal to dispense with my services was apparently met with a unanimous vote, which meant the old and the new directors all put their hands up in agreement. Perhaps the trio of older directors believed they were doing the right thing, and if that is what they genuinely felt I cannot argue. They were, after all, honourable men.

However, it was not the decision to sack me that caused me the most lasting pain. What hurt me most deeply was that they allowed it to happen when it did. I shall always feel they might at least have tried to ensure the newcomers had the decency to defer the formal sacking until after Christmas.

I know it is easy for me to say I was sacked just when I really believed we had finally started to turn the corner, but on that last Saturday before Christmas I travelled home from Crystal Palace feeling far more optimistic than I had been for months. A goalless draw which earned us only our second point in seven games might not seem to suggest a major step forward but, with lads like Sissons, Eustace and Coyle back in the team at last, we displayed some of the qualities which had been missing.

I could see a big difference and was positive we would soon be climbing the table. The fact that three of our next four games, including an FA Cup tie, were at home seemed to offer an ideal platform for long-awaited evidence of progress in the form of vital points.

I should, perhaps, mention that it was around this period that Ron Staniforth and Gerry Young switched coaching roles, with Young promoted from the reserves to take on first-team duties. It was a step I considered for some time before putting it into effect and, in the context of our situation, it was the right decision.

The fact that we had struggled for so long was almost entirely down to the effects of the wretched virus but, when things do not go well over a long period, you tend to review and analyse every aspect of the situation time and time again. You find yourself looking beyond the basic cause of a problem and pondering all manner of ways to improve things. Sometimes the most trivial alteration in routine or the composition of your staff can have unexpectedly beneficial effects.

Circumstances meant I was limited in the permutations I could attempt with the players I had available. However, while the return of a number of key men was crucial to any sustained upturn, it did seem possible that a subtle adjustment on the coaching front might give us a psychological boost.

When I thought of asking Ron Staniforth and Gerry Young to switch jobs, it was no reflection on Ron. As older Wednesdayites will know, Ron had been one of the most respected full-backs of his generation, a player with a touch of class. Moreover, as a coach he knew his stuff and the lads not only recognised his knowledge but enjoyed working with him. He had a quiet and dignified way of doing things and was one of the nicest people you could meet.

If Ron had a fault it was he was too nice. His manner was more in the Tommy Walker mould than that of Johnny Logan. Laying down the law with an iron hand and a sharp tongue was not his style and there came a time when I began to think we might benefit from a bit more of the sort of toughness and straight talking that was in Gerry's make-up.

Gerry was also one of the most genuine and likeable guys in the business. However, as well as the advantage of having only recently reached the end of his days as a senior player, which meant he could talk the same language as everyone in the dressing room when it was required, Gerry could be as blunt and forceful as the best.

The irony was that, just when I was planning to try the Young approach and anticipating making the change, I attended a board meeting at which one of the long-time directors suddenly asked: 'Have you ever thought of promoting Gerry Young?' I said I had indeed been giving that very idea serious thought. However, as I didn't want the director to imagine I had been influenced by his suggestion I delayed the switch for a couple of weeks. It was important not to let him think he was managing the team!

Gerry's influence no doubt contributed to the added resolve with which the lads played at Crystal Palace, and the atmosphere on the homeward journey certainly indicated I wasn't alone in thinking better days were on the way. There were more smiles than frowns!

I remember Matt Sheppard asking me during the journey what my plans were for Christmas and I told him that, as we had a home match with Hull City on Boxing Day, I was having the players in for training on Christmas Eve and Christmas Day morning. In the course of our conversation we also touched on other matters and I took the opportunity to stress that I would like to make a couple of early signings. I said I would be happy to sell someone later to repair the outlay.

Gerry Young...after great service as a player he joined the training staff.

Christmas Eve was two days later and, on that Monday morning, I was in the dressing room when Freddie Scott, our chief scout, came in and said the chairman wanted to see me. I can put my hand on my heart and say I didn't for one minute think I was being summoned to be given the sack. I turned to Gerry Young and said 'Get the lads up to Middlewood Road and I'll join you when I've finished with the chairman'. Then I walked along the corridor feeling quite cheerful. I had been dwelling on the part of my Saturday conversation with Matt Sheppard in which we had discussed getting some new players in and, knowing the board had met on Sunday morning, I said to myself: 'Good, Matt's worked fast and he's going to tell me he's got some money for me'.

I do not remember exactly what Sheppard said to me when I walked into the room but I have never forgotten that he delivered his bombshell before I even had time to sit down. There were no frills, he got straight to the point and, if I cannot recall his precise words, they hit me like bullets bearing one blunt phrase: 'You're sacked'!

Moments earlier some of the lads had been talking in the dressing room about their plans for Christmas, but suddenly the season of goodwill seemed a million years away. I cannot explain the sense of shock and disbelief I felt in those seconds when the significance of Sheppard's words burned into my brain. I don't think I knew what to say and I was so nonplussed that, rather foolishly, I reached into my pocket and offered the chairman the keys of my club car. At least he had the decency to decline them after asking how I was going to get home without the car.

I recall asking for permission to remove my personal belongings from my office and to speak to the players, but what happened during the next few minutes is a blank in my memory. However, I have not forgotten that, after calling the lads together, I planned to say all sorts of things but instead failed to get beyond the first sentence before breaking down. When I had pulled myself together, I went to my car and drove home to Norton oblivious of the evidence in the streets that Christmas was just a few hours away.

The sight of my car pulling up in the drive so early in the day was a surprise to Sylvia and, not unexpectedly, her first words when I walked into the house were: 'What are you doing here?' If I broke down again and my emotions got the better of me as I tried to explain what had happened, I was soon sufficiently in control of my feelings to be more concerned about the effects of the news on my family than myself.

Our first thought was of our son, Martyn. He was a mad Wednesdayite and, as he was an apprentice at Barlow's the shopfitters, I feared he might hear the news of my sacking at work. We knew that, because it was

Christmas Eve, he was knocking off at lunchtime and had planned to have a few festive drinks with his workmates before coming home. I had this nightmare picture in my head of some fool walking up to him in a public house and saying: 'Do you know your Dad's been sacked?'

A couple of hours or so later Martyn walked into the house and I was grateful to note he was obviously unaware of my sacking. As he came in through the door I heard him ask Sylvia: 'What's Dad's car doing in the drive at this time of day?' When she told him he suddenly exploded. It is no exaggeration to say he went berserk. Sylvia and I had never seen him so angry and for the first time in our lives we heard our son swear. He ran upstairs and tore down his treasured Wednesday pictures from his bedroom walls. It was quite a challenge persuading him to sit down and regain his composure.

Martyn had arranged to go to a Christmas dance with his girlfriend in the evening and, although he was much calmer by the time we sat down to tea, I was worried that someone might deliberately provoke him when he was out at a crowded social event. As it happened, he had no trouble, but I felt it would help if I ran him to the dance and picked him up afterwards.

It was, of course, difficult to believe this was Christmas Eve. Somehow the seasonal decorations and the lights on the Christmas tree seemed out of place. The telephone was busy as friends and colleagues in the football world rang to offer their condolences but, as there were no newspapers being published the following day, I was spared the task of speaking to the Press.

However, one journalist, Keith Farnsworth, sports editor of the *Sheffield Morning Telegraph*, did take the trouble to visit me. Obviously, he wanted to talk about what had happened but he came as a friend as well as a trusted local scribe. During much of my time as Wednesday's team-boss Keith had written my programme notes. Indeed, some years earlier he and I had collaborated on a book about my playing days but been unable to find a publisher for the manuscript.

I have to say that if the bottom had dropped out of my world there were still moments during that day when I could smile. In both the professional and private senses, I felt shattered by the suddenness and the timing of my dismissal and my emotions were a mixture of disbelief, anger and the bitter hurt of betrayal. I could not escape the conclusion that what had happened was the work of people without feelings and blind to the date on the calendar. Yet a few words from my daughter Suzanne raised my spirits and made me recognise that life goes on and there is nothing more precious than one's family.

At the age of nine Suzanne was too young to understand the implications of what had happened. Indeed, she was quite pleased I had lost my job. 'Daddy, does that mean you'll be able to play with me on Christmas Day and not have to go to the football?' she asked.

Of course, when Boxing Day dawned and the media was back in full swing, my telephone never stopped ringing and suddenly everybody wanted to talk to me. I have always accepted that dealing with the Press, the radio and television is a part of my role in life, and normally I would have faced up to the challenge. However, I was still in a state of emotional turmoil and I was concerned that I might say something I would later regret. In any event I didn't want to expose myself to the possibility of breaking down in front of a television camera or when speaking into a radio microphone.

One of the calls I received on Christmas Eve was from my pal Harry Short at Sandy in Bedfordshire. He had asked me if, in the light of what had happened, we wanted to go down to his home for a few days to get away from it all. I was grateful for his kind gesture but, initially, I said we preferred to stay in Sheffield. Indeed, Sylvia and I did manage a quiet Christmas Day at home with Martyn and Suzanne. However, on Boxing Day, when it suddenly started to seem as if all hell had broken loose with constant calls from the media, I telephoned Harry and asked if his invitation was still on offer. It was, so we seized the opportunity to travel south in search of some peace.

Our daughter Suzanne was too young to understand what had happened to me on that Christmas Eve of 1973 when my Wednesday days ended, but she hoped it meant I could stay at home and play with her on Christmas morning instead of going to work. Her innocent pleasure in that fact made me appreciate that life goes on and there is nothing more precious than one's family.

Chapter Twenty-eight

Picking up the Pieces

Today, nearly thirty years after the event, my sacking at Christmas still hurts. The bitterness has diminished with the passage of time but the memory has never stopped hurting. Of course, I don't dwell on the episode very often these days but when someone mentions the subject I can still get upset.

I would not be speaking honestly if I didn't admit that at the time of my sacking the circumstances left me deeply bitter for the first time in my life. I felt more bitter about it than was ever the case when I lost my leg. My injury was an accident but my sacking was an act which could have been handled with compassion. For a long time afterwards I kept asking myself 'How could they do that?'

When I accepted the manager's job I knew I would stand or fall by the results I achieved and I never kidded myself that I merited any extra protection simply because I was Derek Dooley and was viewed as a local folk hero. I was no different from any other manager and accepted that if I failed I would get the sack.

However, I did not feel I had failed. I knew that in normal circumstances our record at the halfway stage of the 1973–74 campaign might have put my job under threat, but everybody knew the circumstances had been far from normal and nobody was more aware of that than the directors. That they had chosen to act as they did in the light of the true facts of the situation was difficult enough to accept, but what was much more hurtful was the timing. Even if I had deserved the sack I would never have expected the blow to be delivered on Christmas Eve.

The irony is that, whether I was unlucky or not to lose my job, it would have long been forgotten by the majority of people if the board had chosen a different moment to sack me. As it is, for many Wednesdayites and in the club's history, Christmas Eve will forever be synonymous with my sacking and every year the anniversary is remembered by many more people than just the Dooley family.

I was told that when Matt Sheppard read a short statement to the Press on Boxing Day he seemed genuinely surprised that some reporters questioned the timing of my dismissal. It seems the board took the decision on the Sunday and the chairman carried it out on the following day and the fact that it was Christmas Eve was viewed as just an unfortunate coincidence.

I don't know what their thinking was. As I said earlier, the sudden changes in the boardroom had created a mood in which the new regime no doubt felt they had to be seen to be doing something. They believed they had to act decisively and quickly.

Some people have suggested the timing was intended to exploit the fact that there were no newspapers on Christmas Day. I don't know about that because the story was still sure to make the headlines on Boxing Day. I have always felt that once they had made the decision they wanted to push it through promptly.

Of course I was dismayed that those directors who knew me well did not try to have the decision deferred for a few days. I don't mean to suggest they should have pleaded for me to keep my job, but I do feel they could have argued that it made sense to wait until after Christmas. Most people would have seen it was the human thing to do no matter who was being sacked. Surely they could see that choosing that moment to sack someone who had been connected with the club since 1947 and who had lost a leg playing in the famous blue and white stripes would be viewed as an insensitive action.

I don't want to do them an injustice but I could not help but feel they feared they might have to put the decision on hold for longer than a few days if the team went into the New Year on the back of two or three wins over the holiday period.

Whatever my feelings and however deep the bitterness I felt, I resisted the temptation to speak out in the weeks after my sacking. One newspaper invited me to write a series of three articles and, inevitably perhaps, they wanted me to stir things up. They were offering a large fee and I could have done with the money, but I could not bring myself to do it.

I didn't want to start slamming a club which meant so much to me and I'm glad I turned down the opportunity then and in later years. Even today, and in this book, I have no intention of slamming Sheffield Wednesday, or any individuals, and I hope my recollections of this episode will not be interpreted as an attempt to do so.

Of course, it is probably impossible to tell the truth and recall memories of any particular episode in one's life with honesty without sometimes appearing to criticise someone. Some things cannot be properly explained unless the decisions of others and the essential background are noted. However, I have tried to be fair and I think the benefit of being able to write at length in this book is that any details and comments have been placed in the fullest context with no intent other than to recall what happened and how I felt about it.

It was essentially a case of coming to terms with what had happened and starting to pick up the pieces. Once again it was a matter of accepting I had no option but to make a fresh start, only this time I was forty-four years old instead of twenty-three. My consolation was I had learned a great deal over the intervening twenty-one years and felt confident the knowledge and experience would stand me in good stead.

I always believed I would recover from the blow of losing my job at Hillsborough and I had good reason to hope I might find my way back into football eventually. In fact, at the outset, there was some talk suggesting there might still be a role for me at Sheffield Wednesday, although the climate was such that I always saw this as speculation unlikely to become reality.

Before the break with Wednesday was final, there were a few things to be sorted out, and in this context I should mention that when I went down to Sandy in late December, 1973, my pal, Harry Short, invited his solicitor to have a chat with me about negotiating some compensation from the club. I told Harry I didn't want to see a solicitor because I was well able to sort things out with Wednesday myself.

Harry's solicitor wanted me to take my case to court and promised to get me a good QC. When I asked what a QC would cost, I was told it would be about £3,000. I said that even if Wednesday paid me every penny that was left on my contract it would come to less than £3,000, so going to court didn't make sense. In any event, I stressed I had no intention of taking legal action against the club.

Incidentally, among the many letters of sympathy I received after my sacking was one from Lord Netherthorpe, the Wednesday president, who was very upset about what had happened. When I showed the letter to Harry's solicitor he said 'That's worth a few bob to you in court' but I knew I could never use Lord Netherthorpe's gesture of goodwill in an attempt to punish Wednesday.

I kept reading in the papers that Matt Sheppard was going to sit down with me and talk about finding me another job at the club. Unfortunately, the weeks rolled by without even a whisper of any meeting despite my attempts to arrange one. Frankly, I could not imagine there was a job available that I would find suitable or able to accept. The manner and timing of my removal as team-manager did not inspire me to believe I could take an optimistic view of any proposals which might be put to me.

After nearly three years as team-manager there was no way I wanted to go back to the Pools Office because I felt the eight years I had spent there had been enough. In any event, I never gave that possibility a moment's serious thought because the job was now being done with considerable success by Dennis Woodhead, and he was one of my best mates.

My mind went back to the time of my appointment as team-manager and I remembered how Eric Taylor had said that if things didn't work out there would always be a job for me at Hillsborough. Eric intimated that his plan was to take me in with him and give me a year or so as his understudy so I could take over as general manager when he retired. Had 'Doc' Stephen and Keith Gardiner not resigned from the board this might well have happened at some stage.

Of course, I knew Matt Sheppard did not have me in mind as Eric's successor. I felt that if the possibility had ever occurred to him, and if he had thought it a good idea, he would have seen the switch as the ideal way to replace me as team-boss with a touch of dignity. The notion probably never crossed his mind but, anyway, I doubt if there was any way the new regime would have considered me for the role. There was a sense in which it seemed they wanted to wipe the slate clean.

Had Eric Taylor been invited to discuss the subject he might well have mentioned to Matt Sheppard what he had once said to me. Unfortunately, Eric's position and influence had been weakened by the change in the climate in the boardroom. If Eric did raise the matter he probably did so knowing it would be in vain.

It was not long after my sacking that Eric announced plans to retire within a few months. I think he made the decision rather sooner than he might have done in other circumstances and, in truth, it didn't help that he was already in failing health. I doubt if many people outside the club were aware of how bravely he had fought to recover from the effects of extensive injuries suffered in a car crash seven years earlier. Now, in the late winter and early spring of 1974 he fell seriously ill and he died in September at the age of sixty-two without ever having the chance to enjoy his retirement.

True to character, Eric put up a brave fight and remained as witty and positive as ever right up to the end of his life. However, those of us who knew him well and respected what he had done for Sheffield Wednesday were saddened by the way his forty-five year career at the club ended. He deserved better and his misfortune was compounded by the tragedy of such an early death.

Over the years it was often said that the man they called 'Mister Sheffield Wednesday' had too much power, but even his critics admitted he was never guilty of abusing his authority and nobody could ever say he ever failed to give his heart and soul to the club's cause. Eric didn't do what he did for personal gain, he did it for Wednesday. You had only to walk down the players' tunnel and look at the stadium to appreciate Eric's achievement and any perceptive observer was well aware that the remarkable redevelopment of Hillsborough was only a part of his contribution. Sadly, there were people who found it too easy to forget.

Following the board changes of early December 1973, Eric soon got the message that the new regime no longer wanted him to be what he had been for so long. He saw the writing on the wall but, if he was saddened by the turn of events, he took the disappointment in his stride. On the surface he retained his sense of humour, but I must admit I was upset and close to tears one day when he joked 'I never thought I'd go from office boy to office boy in forty-five years'.

As things turned out, Eric's illness and early death meant he could not have continued to contribute for much longer anyway but, of course, at the time he announced his retirement nobody was aware that he didn't have long to live. For all anybody knew then he might have had many more good years ahead of him, and what was particularly sad about the decision to push him into retirement and away from the scene was that Wednesday deprived themselves of a vast fund of knowledge and experience.

At least on the administrative front they still had the wisdom of Eric England to call upon and I think they had cause to be grateful for this in the following years.

It is not intended as a criticism of Wednesday when I say that in my long career in the professional game I have found a consistent and debilitating tendency in football clubs to get shut of people with experience, simply because it is felt circumstances demand it when a new regime arrives on the scene. I am not against change and have long accepted that things cannot always stay the same, but sometimes change is too rapid. The fabric and the essential framework of a club suffers. Change for its own sake is unnecessarily damaging if it deprives any organisation of stability and the qualities which have long proved essential to its well-being.

When new directors arrive at a club without any knowledge or background in the professional game it is understandable if they are unfamiliar with many aspects of the business. Yet, instead of seeking to benefit from the experience and wisdom of the people best equipped to help, they so often choose to dispense with their services. Invariably the newcomers end up learning the hard way by making mistakes they could so easily have been spared.

I don't think I ever seriously thought that Matt Sheppard would offer me a job at Hillsborough which I could accept, and I could not imagine them creating a position likely to make the best use of my knowledge, experience and abilities.

When I finally met the chairman to discuss the matter I wasn't surprised it proved a let-down because it turned out much as I had expected. Matt must have known my answer would be a firm 'no' when he invited me to work in the club's ticket office. He suggested I had the advantage of knowing the supporters, but I'm sure he never believed there was any danger of me saying 'I'll take the job'.

As I drove out of the ground that afternoon I knew I was saying a last goodbye to a place which had meant more to me than anyone could ever be expected to understand.

After walking out of Hillsborough on that day in early 1974 when I went to see Matt Sheppard, I did not go back to watch a Wednesday match for nineteen years, and, if I am honest, I must admit that even when I finally agreed to visit the old ground again it was with great reluctance.

I vowed I would never return and I might have maintained that stance for the rest of my life but for the encouragement of friends who felt it would help heal a few wounds. Now I can go back and it doesn't worry me, but it wasn't always so, and I can appreciate why my wife Sylvia still cannot bring herself to visit Hillsborough again.

Between December 1973 and early March 1992 I saw only one game at Hillsborough. This was when I went to the 1976 FA Cup semi-final between Manchester United and Derby County, and the moment I passed through the turnstiles I knew it was a mistake to go.

I had not intended going to the game but it was one of those trivial episodes in which circumstances conspired to make it happen and I allowed myself to be pushed into something I would normally have resisted.

When the draw was made and Hillsborough was chosen as the venue, my pal from Sandy, Harry Short, said he would like to see the game and bring some friends. As I was a debenture holder and could claim five tickets, I bought my full allocation. When Harry came to Sheffield on the day of the match, I handed him the tickets and he surprised me by giving me one back.

'That's for you' he said. I insisted that I didn't want to go, but Harry would not take no for an answer and after a bit of persuasion I reluctantly agreed to join the party. Well, I thought, at least it's not a Wednesday match and, as I would not be sitting in the main stand and the teams involved were Derby and Manchester United, I convinced myself I was unlikely to see anyone connected with the Owls.

How wrong can you be! The turnstile operator was a man I knew and once inside I had barely walked a few yards before I was being greeted by people I had known for many years. Our seats were in the North Stand and I had completely forgotten that this was the area of the ground traditionally used by Wednesdayites and fellow debenture holders at FA Cup semi-finals and similar fixtures.

Being surrounded by what seemed a sea of familiar faces and suddenly finding myself in close proximity to places around the ground which had once been such a big part of my life stirred countless memories. Walking behind the stand I saw the gymnasium, then, taking my seat, I could hardly avoid looking straight across the pitch and seeing the South Stand and the players' tunnel. How can I describe my emotions when words cannot express the way I felt? It was like a bad dream. I could not settle to enjoy the match and I wished I hadn't gone.

Certainly I never wanted to repeat the experience. Time, it is said, is a great healer and the bitterness induced by the circumstances of my departure from Sheffield Wednesday eventually started to diminish, but for a long time I still could not bring myself to go to Hillsborough again. There was no way anyone could tempt me.

At last, late in that 1991–92 season when the Sheffield clubs were together again in the First Division after a lapse of more than twenty years and staging their first top-grade derby at Hillsborough since 1970, I was persuaded to go. Of course, by this time I had worked for Sheffield United for eighteen years, and it was largely due to the prompting of colleagues at Bramall Lane that I found myself sitting in the directors' box at the Wednesday ground.

I travelled to Hillsborough that evening in United secretary Dave Capper's car and we made a point of arriving early. We had barely parked up before I began to wonder if I had made another mistake but, in the end, I was glad I had gone for more reasons than the fact that United won the match in style with a 3–1 margin.

When I climbed out of Dave's car I was immediately greeted by a fan who wanted to welcome me. Within moments one of the turnstile operators left his post to rush across and say 'It's lovely to see you back, Derek. Tha should never have left'. Then another man walked towards me with his children in tow and told them 'This is Derek Dooley, the finest centre-forward I ever saw'.

People who know me will tell you I can be as hard as nails when the situation demands it, but at that moment I was close to tears. I appreciated the warmth of the comments of those fans but there was a lump in my throat as large as a football and I told myself 'I can do without this'. I feared the emotion of the occasion was going to prove too much, and when Winton Cooper from Radio Sheffield suddenly appeared and thrust a microphone towards me I wondered if I wasn't going to regret having come.

I thought I might have made the biggest mistake of all when I allowed Dave Richards, the Wednesday chairman, to persuade me to walk onto the pitch with him ahead of the kick-off. There were over 40,000 fans in the ground and I could not anticipate how I might feel if their reaction to my appearance was not positive. Happily, from every corner of the stadium the Unitedites and Wednesdayites roared their approval and a moment I had faced with trepidation and reluctance proved to be one I knew I would always remember with pleasure.

It has been a great source of pride and pleasure to me over the past twenty-five years or more that I am regarded with equal affection by supporters of both United and Wednesday. It is an honour bestowed on few people because the nature of football fans seldom permits the acceptance of someone associated with their greatest local rivals.

One of the ironies of my career is that there are many fans who insist I am still a Wednesdayite. Forgetting the fact that I have worked for Sheffield United since 1974, and despite what happened to me at the end of my time at Hillsborough, some people tend to believe that deep down I remain an Owl. Indeed, I have heard it said that if you opened up my heart you would find the word 'Wednesday' etched across it in large letters.

I don't think so. There was a time when this might have been true and I shall never forget those days when my passion for all things blue and white knew no bounds. As a boy I loved Wednesday more than anything in the world and to play for them as I did in later years was one of the most satisfying things in my life. However, make no mistake, I am a Unitedite now.

I never thought I could ever have an affection for another club to match the feeling I had for Wednesday in the old days yet that is exactly what has happened. I have now been connected with United as long as I was with Wednesday and, in terms of the management and administration, I have been more deeply involved with the Blades for much longer.

I will admit I still have some feelings for Wednesday, but they are largely linked to my memories of a distant and happy past. You cannot have a twenty-six year association with a club and remove all trace of the feelings you once had from your heart.

Since I went back to Hillsborough in 1992 to watch a match, I have returned on many occasions, and, so long as they have not been playing United, I have always wanted them to win. The acid test is watching a derby match between United and Wednesday. The way my heart has leapt when United have scored in these fixtures serves to show I am definitely a true Blade now.

Whatever happened at Christmas 1973 is in the past and, while I cannot deny that I felt bitter for a long time, I don't think I ever bore a grudge. I can honestly say that when Wednesday fell into the Third Division and endured a long period of decline I took no pleasure in witnessing their troubles. I must confess there was a time when I didn't care one way or the other. Indeed, when they lost it didn't hurt me the way it might once have done. Yet I cannot say I ever jumped for joy. In fact, when Wednesday's fortunes were at their lowest in the mid-1970s I did feel some regret, although my sympathies were essentially with the supporters. The Wednesday fans had been brilliant to me throughout my long years at Hillsborough and I had always enjoyed a great rapport with them. They were friends and I wanted them to have the pleasure of a successful team.

Our son Martyn has always been a Wednesdayite. I brought him up to be an Owls fan and I'm delighted he has remained a 'true blue'. He was bitterly upset when I was sacked by the club but I told him he should not let what happened to me affect his allegiance.

Martyn's son, Del, is also a staunch Wednesdayite. I have tried to convert him to the United faith but I have no chance of succeeding. Even when I took him to Bramall Lane as a small boy to attend my testimonial match, my grandson insisted on wearing his Wednesday kit, and, like his dad, whenever the opportunity arises he has a tendency to rib me about my support for the Blades.

Our daughter Suzanne was a Wednesdayite until I got the sack and, being nine years old at the time, she promptly declared herself a Unitedite. She has remained one ever since but, happily, it didn't prevent her from marrying a Wednesday fan.

My grandson Del is already very enthusiastic about his football and nothing gives me more pleasure than to watch him play. Whether he will grow up to be a footballer I don't know but, if he does, I have no doubt he might aspire to become the second Derek Dooley to play for Wednesday.

Martyn was always a keen player as a youngster but I don't think he ever dreamed of following in my footsteps. I think there was a sense in which he thought he might be letting me down by aspiring to make a mark in the game, and I remember that when I was managing the Rowlinson team in which he played he was anxious not to push himself.

He would always volunteer to be a substitute rather than suggest that being the manager's son should assure him of a starting place. In the final analysis perhaps he lacked the desire and dedication to become a professional but as an amateur he could have reached a decent standard. I'm sure that from time to time in his early years Martyn found it a problem being Derek Dooley's son, but he coped very well and I don't think he was unduly troubled when the inevitable 'thar't not as good as thi dad' and such remarks were aimed at him.

By the same token I think he came to terms with my departure from Hillsborough when it was not easy for a teenager to understand why it had happened to his dad in the way it did. I'm delighted he remains one of Wednesday's keenest supporters and I think he is glad I was able to rebuild my career—even though I had to join Sheffield United to do it.

A happy line-up of three generations of our family. Back row: Andrew and Suzanne Tabor, and Martyn Dooley. Front row: Georgie Dooley, Derek Dooley, Ben Tabor, Sylvia Dooley (holding baby Max Tabor), and Derek Dooley Jnr (who prefers to be known as Del).

Chapter Twenty-nine

Becoming
a Blade

I think it surprised more than a few people when I was installed as Sheffield United's commercial manager in November 1974. Frankly, joining the Blades was a step which I would once have considered highly improbable, perhaps impossible, and when it happened nobody was more astonished by the turn of events than Derek Dooley. However, when the opportunity came along I knew it was too good to miss, and I have to say I never had cause to regret deciding to take it.

It is fair to suggest that the sequence of events which prompted my switch to Bramall Lane started with an invitation to appear on a Yorkshire Television programme called 'Yorksport' a few months after I had left Sheffield Wednesday. In truth, initially I wasn't too keen on the idea of facing the cameras but I ended up pleased I had made the trip to the studio in Leeds because it led to an unexpected and welcome bonus.

When Keith Macklin, the presenter, asked me to be a guest, my first reaction was to wonder whether he expected me to criticise the Hillsborough board. I said if that was his plan, he could forget it. However, he assured me the idea was simply to discuss what a football manager did when he was out of work. As I explained to Keith when we finally went on air, most of my time was being spent looking for a job.

Later, while we were in the studio bar, a telephone rang and Keith answered it. 'It's someone asking for you' he said, and I found myself talking to Paul Ziff, the chairman of Stylo Matchmakers, a Leeds-based company which made ladies and gents shoes as well as some sports footwear that included a renowned range of golf shoes. Paul said he might be able to find me a job.

On the following Monday Sylvia drove me to Leeds for an interview with Paul, then later in the week he and I had a second meeting at which his managing director joined in the discussions. The upshot was the offer of a position as a sales representative at £5,000 a year.

I still smile now when I recall how apologetic Paul was when he said he couldn't afford to pay football wages. I had to explain that I had never reached the Don Revie salary rating as a manager and, in fact, his offer was only £500 less than Wednesday had been paying me when I finished at Hillsborough. Moreover, as I would have a company car plus travelling and telephone expenses, I considered the terms very acceptable.

My job was to sell Stylo boots to football clubs all over the country and, with the advantage of knowing most of the managers and many of the chairmen with whom I had to deal, it did not prove difficult. I was always assured of a warm welcome when I dropped in on clubs like Wolves, Fulham, Leyton Orient and others where I was known and among friends, and, apart from savouring my success as a salesman, I got a kick out of meeting up with so many football people.

My enthusiasm for the job is reflected in the fact that I clocked up over 13,000 miles in what proved to be a much shorter stay with Stylo Matchmakers than I had planned. I probably drove further and for longer than was necessary on some occasions because I always preferred to travel home rather than stay overnight in an hotel. I didn't really enjoy having to do so much driving, especially at the end of a busy day, but I could never resist the lure of my own bed at Norton!

John Hassall, the man who invited me to join Sheffield United.

It is curious to think that one of the shortest trips I made in my time with Stylo turned out to be the most significant. One day after I had left some samples at Sheffield United I received a call from John Hassall, the chairman, asking me to pop down to the ground to see him. I thought 'I've cracked it, they're interested in doing some business with me'.

I didn't consider it unusual when I went in to meet John Hassall and found he was joined in the room by vice-chairman Bert Jackson. However, I was intrigued when John looked at the bag of samples I was holding and said: 'You'll not need that, put it under the table and sit down'.

I was so taken aback by what he said next that I could only mutter 'Pardon?' which prompted him to say for the second time: 'We'd like to offer you a job'. He then explained he wanted me to become the club's commercial manager. To suggest I was lost for words would be an understatement. I had to admit I didn't know what to say and I think I ended up promising to think about their offer and talk to the people at Stylo.

Paul Ziff and everybody at Stylo had been brilliant to me and I was happy in the job. After joining them I had every intention of staying for a long time, but I had not anticipated that a job in football would come up so soon. If I am honest, at the outset I was a bit sceptical about going to Sheffield United but, as had happened before in my life, I knew this was an opportunity I would find difficult to resist.

When I saw Paul Ziff and told him the news, he offered to match United's offer of £6,000 a year, and I remember saying: 'Don't confuse the situation, the money doesn't come into it'.

It so happened that Sylvia and I were scheduled to take a holiday in Bournemouth, so I told John Hassall and Paul Ziff I would make a final decision on my return. As always, Sylvia knew what the outcome was long before I confirmed my choice. As we talked in our Bournemouth hotel she said: 'I know what you're going to do, you're going to go back into football. It's your decision, Derek, but just remember what happened at Sheffield Wednesday'.

We had not been back in our home at Norton for more than ten minutes when the telephone rang. It was John Hassall calling. 'Have you made your mind up then, Derek?' he asked. I replied: 'Yes, I'm coming'. He said: 'Right, start on Monday'. This, I explained, was impossible because that was when I was travelling to Leeds to give Stylo my decision.

Of course, Paul Ziff was not surprised. He admitted he was disappointed but he accepted my choice with tremendous grace, so much so that I felt a bit guilty about leaving. He knew this was not something I had planned. He said: 'You've done a wonderful job, Derek, and if things don't turn out as you want at Sheffield United I will gladly find you a place with us again'.

Happily I never had any need to ask Paul to keep his promise and everything worked out well for me at Bramall Lane. I couldn't imagine then that I would still be connected with United more than twenty-five years later, having in the meantime served as a director, managing director and chairman. In 1974 nobody could have predicted my passion for the Blades would soon match the feelings I had once had for the Owls.

The first anniversary of my Christmas sacking came up very soon after my switch across the city and it was, of course, a milestone tinged with sadness. Inevitably, the date on the calendar provoked some painful memories and I was grateful I was not needed at Bramall Lane and was free to spend the day quietly at home.

There was, however, a humorous footnote to my absence from the club. When I saw John Hassall shortly before United's holiday game with Arsenal, he handed me a present for Syliva and myself and said 'I came down to give it you on Christmas Eve, but you weren't there, Derek'.

I smiled and said: 'No, I've decided that is the one day of the year when I shall not be available to meet a football club chairman!'

I felt rather strange and more than a little apprehensive when I started working at Bramall Lane, and it took a bit of time to get used to being an employee of Sheffield United after a lifetime's devotion to Wednesday. However, my new colleagues made me welcome, so I soon settled in and felt at home.

Of course, I knew my duties would bring me face to face with the most fervent of United's fans and I wondered how they might react to dealing with someone who had been synonymous with the Owls for so long. In the event I had nothing to worry about. The majority of Blades supporters were brilliant and even those who enjoyed ribbing me about my Wednesday background welcomed me into the fold.

It's a lovely feeling to know you are accepted and respected as 'one of us' by people who might once have viewed you as a foe, but I have always found my fellow Sheffielders, be they red-and-whites or blue-and-whites, essentially fair-minded and friendly.

It was a period when significant changes were occurring at Sheffield United and my arrival coincided with the beginning of a new era for the club. Nothing served to emphasise this more than the fact that, a year or so earlier, Bramall Lane's association with Yorkshire cricket had ended after nearly 120 years, and now a new south stand was rising in front of the famous old pavilion to create a four-sided football-only ground for the first time in United's history.

Of course, the investment put enormous financial pressure on the club and because there had never been a time when a successful commercial operation was more crucial, I knew my task was to start laying the foundations and achieving results sooner rather than later. It helped that I had done a similar job at Hillsborough, and right from day one I knew what I wanted to do at Bramall Lane and how to set about it.

As I told John Hassall and Bert Jackson at the outset, I had not joined United simply to run the pools office, because doing so would be merely stepping back into a role I had filled for eight years with Wednesday. I wanted a much more demanding and satisfying challenge and expected my responsibilities to extend far beyond anything I had done in my time at Hillsborough.

All the same, getting to grips with the development fund was the priority because the existing system had been allowed to run down and was in urgent need of a complete overhaul. Having studied the books I had discovered that while the income looked reasonable on paper, the club was struggling to make it profitable once the running costs were deducted. Indeed, they were barely breaking even, and that situation didn't make sense.

My switch to Bramall Lane meant I was able to meet up again with dear old Harry Latham, the man who gave me such a hard time in the Sheffield derby match of 1952.

There are two reasons why I have not forgotten the day I faced the United board for the first time to report on my plans as the new commercial manager. For a start, until that moment I had not realised the Blades boasted so many directors, and then there is the memory of how they all looked aghast when I announced my intention to close down the club's lottery.

In my time as Wednesday's manager there were usually about five directors plus general manager Eric Taylor present at meetings. Now I found nine directors sitting round the boardroom table. As I recall, they were John Hassall, Bert Jackson, 'Dick' Wragg, Frank Melling, Ken Lee, Frank Price, Maurice Board, Jim Sterland and Professor Frank O'Gorman. Secretary Keith Walker, manager Ken Furphy, and John Harris were also present, and while everyone seemed pleased to see me I must confess I found a dozen faces rather daunting.

To be fair, they accepted my plan to ditch the existing lottery when I explained it was losing money and said I was putting another one into operation which I promised would be profitable.

By the same token, I think the supporters and agents saw the sense of the new lottery once we got it up and running early in 1975. At first, naturally perhaps, there were a few agents who accused me of bringing in my Wednesday ideas, but they were won over once they recognised signs of success.

I was lucky enough to inherit a good staff. Kath Mowat, for example, was a tower of strength because she was not only enthusiastic and supportive but knew all the agents and was familiar with the background and details of what had been done in the past. With Kath, her sister Brenda Wilshaw, and Yvonne Crawshaw to help me, I knew we would make things work smoothly.

The first pools office was in some old premises at the corner of John Street and Shoreham Street which we smartened up a bit with some essential alterations. Later, when Arnold Laver & Co. switched their operation to Queen's Road, we moved into a part of the Cherry Street property they vacated and converted it into offices which offered us a bit more breathing space.

When we were setting up the new lottery I arranged a series of meetings in the old Tudor Room with our agents to explain everything. Frankly, two meetings would have been enough to accommodate all the agents but I chose to have four separate sessions because I felt it might be easier to handle smaller groups. I also had a hunch that it might be wise to spread the risk of problems from critics over four meetings. Thinking ahead paid off because I ended up with three meetings which went without a hitch while the other get-together proved to be the one at which all the awkward customers, those who weren't too keen on the changes, turned up!

We launched a recruiting drive for new agents and doing the rounds on a succession of local housing estates enabled us to more than double our numbers fairly quickly.

This was a phase when I first appreciated just how enthusiastic John Hassall was about what we were doing. John took a very keen interest in everything connected with the development fund and I don't think he ever missed one of our commercial meetings in all his time as chairman. Moreover, he insisted on joining me and my team of workers when we went on our agent recruiting drives.

There was one occasion when he wanted to take on the task of knocking on doors himself but I told him I had plenty of 'troops' who were experienced in doing that. I explained I wasn't knocking on any doors myself but always ensured I was on hand to oversee the operation. I knew the chairman's presence was enough to encourage those who were, so to speak, in the 'front line'.

John Hassall, who was at the helm from 1974 to 1981, was not luckiest of United chairmen and he was desperately unfortunate that things turned out as they did in terms of the team's fortunes.

People forget that he was thrown in at the deep end when Dick Wragg gave up the chairmanship to concentrate on his Football Association duties. John had taken over shortly before my arrival on the scene, and his elevation coincided with a particularly difficult and testing time in the light of the club's decision to end the cricket era and build a costly new south stand which made consistent financial success imperative.

I doubt if any chairman ever put more effort into his job or gave more time to the club than John. He deserved a far greater reward and much more appreciation than he ended up getting. The fact that his seven years at the helm coincided with a decline in the team's playing fortunes did not really present a true reflection of his contribution.

John was well aware that while I revelled in organising the new pools and lottery systems, once everything was in place and running smoothly I needed to turn my attention to other things. Happily, circumstances enabled me to have a lot more scope than might have been the case a few years earlier. It was my good fortune that this was a time when the introduction of things like advertising boards, match and shirt sponsorship, and corporate hospitality were changing the concept of commercial activity in football.

It was at the start of the 1975–76 season that I handled my first sponsored match, and I have not forgotten how it turned out to be a rather more enlightening experience than I anticipated. When Alan Laver's firm undertook to sponsor the opening day fixture against Derby County, I probably thought I was going to kick off our new venture with an easy sponsorship mission because of the long Laver link with United.

In fact, Alan drove a particularly hard bargain and I knew it was especially important to ensure everything went smoothly on the big day, which, incidentally, coincided with the formal opening of the new south stand.

Part of the Laver package included a pre-match parade of trucks around the perimeter of the pitch. The trucks carried Laver products such as sheds and greenhouses. Everything went well until the leading truck got stuck when it was being driven behind the Bramall Lane goal. It may have inspired some unscheduled entertainment for the crowd, but I was getting a bit hot under the collar at the prospect of an embarrassing hold-up delaying the start of the match. Fortunately the line of trucks had just managed to disappear from sight as the teams lined up for the kick-off!

I found the work I was doing all the more satisfying because while on the one hand I was playing to my strengths and using my knowledge and experience, I was also getting the opportunity to stretch myself. In everything I did I knew it was an advantage to be known to so many people in Sheffield and to have lots of contacts, but there was still the challenge of undertaking tasks which were new to me.

For instance, about a fortnight before the opening game of the season we ran into a bit of a crisis with the match-day programme. When we held our usual meeting to discuss the progress of various plans, John Hassall was horrified to discover we had only one page of advertisements booked for the programme. He was so dismayed by the agency's lack of success that he promptly dispensed with their services. Then he decided I should take on the job.

Selling advertising space was not exactly a role for which I felt equipped, but while I was unfamiliar with the technicalities I knew which areas of the programme needed to be filled and I knew how much we were charging. Within two days I had sold every available space. I ended up dealing with the production of the match-day programme for some months and it gave me quite a kick to think I was making it pay so quickly without having had any previous experience of the job.

The success of our commercial ventures was a source of considerable pride to me. Indeed, we did so well that I began to wish I had negotiated a contract which gave me a commission on the income I was generating. Of course, when I accepted my appointment I had plumped for the security of a guaranteed salary and it was not without irony that I found I would have been better off taking a smaller basic wage and gambling on getting profitable results. However, what really mattered was I was happy in my work.

It was reward in itself to be back in professional football. Of course, I wasn't involved in the playing side of things but that didn't worry me. In truth, I made a point of keeping well away from football matters.

The last thing I wanted at that time was to concern myself with the playing side. It was not my business and I had no wish to change that situation. Naturally I watched the matches and, like any other spectator or supporter, I had my opinions on what I saw. However, if I expressed any views I did so privately and did not expect them to be made public.

Unfortunately, within barely a couple of weeks or so of starting work at Bramall Lane, something I had said found its way into a national newspaper, and it upset manager Ken Furphy.

In those days some of the Press lads used to gather in the John Street reception room after matches and one of the reporters must have overheard me make some comment to a friend following our 1–0 home defeat against Tottenham. I think I said we had been unlucky to lose and added some innocuous remark on another aspect of the match. I didn't know I was going to be quoted in the *Daily Express* on the following Monday. In fact, I was unaware that anything had appeared in print until I received a telephone call from John Hassall.

John said I had upset Ken and the manager was demanding an apology, but I told him I didn't feel I needed to apologise when I had not spoken to a journalist.

I thought Ken would get the message and forget the matter. However, our next home match was against Coventry and, after we had achieved a 1–0 victory thanks to a Billy Dearden goal, I was talking to some friends in the reception room when Ken walked past. 'Are you giving your report to the papers, then?' he asked.

'Hang on a minute, Ken' I said. 'I ain't going to apologise for what happened the other week because I wasn't guilty of speaking to the Press. Let me make it plain that I have a big enough job on looking after the pools office without getting involved in the football. I haven't come to Sheffield United to comment on team matters and don't intend doing so.'

Once Ken saw there had been a misunderstanding I think we got along quite well. Indeed, nobody was more delighted than me when he led the team into sixth place in the old First Division in my first season at Bramall

Lane. My only regret was the success did not prove quite enough to get the Blades into Europe, though it had seemed possible at one stage.

However, I refrained from saying anything in the papers. It might have been pleasing to say something in praise of the club, but I knew it was not my place to pass any comment, and in my nine years as commercial manager I made a point of never discussing any football matters in public.

Of course, I had my opinions and I was as saddened as anyone by the dramatic dip in the team's fortunes after the successful run of 1974–75 had seemed to suggest we were on the brink of better things. Who could have believed we would lose our First Division status within twelve months or have imagined that we were destined to fall into the Fourth Division inside six years? It proved a painful phase during which Furphy left early in the 1975–76 season to be replaced by Jimmy Sirrel, then in January 1978 Harry Haslam arrived and had a three-year spell in charge.

I felt Jimmy Sirrel never got the return he deserved, because he certainly worked very hard. It is one of the peculiarities of football that some managers seem to be ideally suited to one club but not another. Jimmy had done a marvellous job at Notts County before he came to Bramall Lane and, of course, when he returned to Meadow Lane he again showed what an astute manager he was. Alas, for some reason he couldn't do the same with United.

Harry Haslam, too, had achieved a lot with a little at Luton and he came to Sheffield with excellent credentials. Harry was someone I had known well as a fellow manager during my time with Wednesday, so I was able to tell John Hassall about his background when the chairman was considering candidates.

I knew Harry had been at Luton for ten years and was aware that after six as manager he was ready for a move. He brought Danny Bergara with him from Kenilworth Road and was planning to bring David Pleat as well. It is history now that Pleat decided to stay with Luton after he was offered the manager's job, and now, when I look back, I often wonder whether that was the development Harry had the most cause to regret. It is difficult to believe United would not have profited from Pleat's presence and have enjoyed a more successful time in the Haslam years than proved to be the case.

Harry Haslam will be remembered as the man who did more than anyone to inspire the start of the sudden influx of foreign players into English football following his appointment of Antonio Rattin as his scout in Argentina. Harry brought Alex Sabella to Bramall Lane and was responsible for recommending Ossie Ardiles and Ricky Villa to Keith Burkinshaw at Tottenham.

I always remember Harry coming home from a trip to South America and enthusing about a seventeen year-old player he had seen. 'Derek' he said, 'nobody over here has heard of this lad yet, but he is going to be a world-beater and I would dearly love to bring him to Sheffield.' The lad's name was Maradonna.

Unfortunately for Harry, he was unable to halt United's slide. We fell into the Third Division for the first time in the club's history at the end of his first full season in charge and, although we made a good start to the following campaign, things never worked out as we hoped.

It was not without irony that the turning point in the 1979–80 season was our match with Sheffield Wednesday on Boxing Day. We went into the game looking firm promotion favourites after an excellent run, while Wednesday had been having a fairly thin time. Alas, we lost 4–0 and it was the Owls who went on to climb back into the Second Division while we ended up in twelfth place.

Incidentally, the 49,000 crowd at Hillsborough that day was a record for the Third Division—but I was not among the spectators. Of course, my son Martyn went to the match and cheered for the Owls. As you can imagine, he took great delight in filling me in with the details when he arrived home from the game!

The circumstances of our fall into the Fourth Division in May 1981 were traumatic and it was a desperately cruel twist right at the end of a season during which Harry Haslam had packed up in January and handed over to Martin Peters. We only needed a point from our last match, at home to Walsall, to be safe, and with about five minutes left we looked set to earn a goalless draw. Then John MacPhail was adjudged to have fouled Alan Buckley and Don Penn put Walsall in front from the penalty spot. Incredibly, with barely a minute remaining, referee George Flint ruled that Horne, the Walsall substitute, had handled in the area and we were offered the unexpected chance of a dramatic reprieve. All we needed to do was to convert the penalty. Alas, Don Givens directed a tame shot straight at the goalkeeper and it meant we were relegated.

I'll wager that even twenty years after the event there is not a single Unitedite in the whole of Sheffield who is unfamiliar with the fact that Givens was not the man nominated to take the most ill-fated spot-kick in the club's history. Before the game, John Matthews had volunteered to do the job if we got a penalty but, sadly, when the moment came he decided he couldn't do it.

I still remember the sadness and the atmosphere of sheer disbelief which swept around Bramall Lane that afternoon. Moreover, I have never forgotten that the player who could have saved us was not even on the pitch. Tony Kenworthy had succeeded with six penalties during the season but manager Peters had not picked him in the team and instead the lad was sitting in the stand.

Inevitably, perhaps, the fact that United had reached the lowest point in the club's history prompted changes. This was the moment when John Hassall chose to resign, with Reg Brealey stepping up to become chairman.

Dooley the Blade!

Chapter Thirty

Director Derek

When Reg Brealey first mentioned that he was thinking of making me a director of Sheffield United my initial reaction was to say to myself 'That'll be the day!' because I didn't really believe it would happen. I was not surprised when nothing more was said on the subject for quite a while, but then, out of the blue, Reg popped his head round the door of my office one morning in April, 1983, and announced I was being invited to join the board.

It meant I became only the second paid director in the Football League and the first in Sheffield's football history. Such a step had not been possible before, but the recent introduction of rule changes that many considered revolutionary, left clubs free to adopt a new policy which enabled them to make fuller use of professionals familiar with the management of day-to-day activities.

To say I was flattered and honoured is putting it mildly. It gave me a kick to think I would now be involved in football matters as well as being responsible for the club's commercial operation. I knew my voice would be just one among several in the boardroom but it felt good to be in a position to make a contribution and have a bit of influence in the running of the club.

It is intriguing now to recall that the season in which I joined the board had started with a setback that might so easily have signalled the end of my working days. Indeed, when I suffered a sudden heart attack in August 1982 there was a moment when I feared my life might be over. I have never forgotten how, as I lay in an ambulance which was rushing me to hospital, I pleaded with an ambulanceman 'Don't let me die in here, will you?'

Whether I had been overworking I am not sure because I never found my job as commercial manager a toil or too much of a strain. Indeed, I revelled in my role and my enthusiasm never waned despite the long days. If I had a fault it was that I was never very good at delegating responsibility. I tended to think it was necessary to do everything myself because nobody could do the job as well as me and, of course, this is a mistake. Happily, I learned more sense in later years.

No doubt I must have been pushing myself rather harder than was necessary because something induced a heart attack which was certainly not a mild one.

That morning I rose from my bed as usual and, still minus my artificial leg, hopped into the bathroom. After shaving it was my custom to jump into the bath, but on this occasion I decided not to bother because for some reason I didn't feel too good. When I returned to the bedroom I said to Sylvia: 'I don't feel very well', and she suggested I should get back into bed. 'No' I insisted, 'I must go into work.'

Moments later I had just started to put on my artificial leg when I felt a pain in my chest. I knew then there was no way I could go to the office and the next thing I remember is finding myself stretched out on the bed helplessly listening to Sylvia calling an ambulance.

On my second day in intensive care at the hospital my heart missed a beat during the night. This prompted the immediate fitting of a temporary pacemaker in an exercise all the more scaring because I was lying there wide awake while a wire was pushed into my heart—and I watched it all happen on a television screen alongside my bed!

I remained in hospital for about four weeks, but when the doctor finally sent me home his list of things I was not allowed to do for some time included driving my car and watching football. It was three months before I was considered fit enough to go to a match.

As Andy Daykin had recently joined the Blades, at the start of what was to prove a long and successful spell at the club for him, I knew United's commercial activities were in good hands, so in those weeks of enforced inactivity I was able to relax, make a full recovery and count my blessings.

When I eventually returned to my post I don't think I worked any less hard than I had before but I certainly had a different outlook on life. I became a bit more health conscious and this was the time when I threw away my pipe for good. I had always enjoyed smoking a pipe, especially when I was fishing, and I had also savoured the occasional cigar. However, following my heart attack I suddenly lost the taste for tobacco.

In terms of work, of course, it was soon business as usual and I knew there was no way I could give anything less than total commitment. It

Reading the 'get well soon' cards while recovering from my heart attack.

Andy Daykin, a key member of the backroom team at Bramall Lane and the man who succeeded me as commercial manager.

helped that my input was obviously appreciated at the club and it was a tremendous fillip when I was rewarded with a seat on the board because it showed that chairman Reg Brealey not only recognised my efforts but believed I had still more to offer.

Reg, a businessman with roots in the Sleaford area of Lincolnshire, had joined United as financial director in June, 1980, and, though I didn't know it until much later, he had not been long at Bramall Lane when he decided I was being under-used

What happened was that John Hassall asked Reg to study the operation and management of the club and produce a report with suggestions for improvements. In the course of his investigations Reg spent some time with me and looked closely at what I was doing. Apparently he told the board: 'Dooley is being wasted as commercial manager. He has more to offer and should be in a more senior role'.

So, I suppose, I should never have doubted Reg when he first mentioned his idea of making me a director, for he clearly planned to act when he thought the time was right. What I didn't know until later was that while Reg was pursuing his plan my colleague, 'Dick' Chester, who served as the company secretary from January 1979 until he left to join Sheffield Wednesday in October 1983, was also harbouring hopes of joining the board.

The rules concerning paid directors permitted only one at a club and it never occurred to me that Dick had been viewing me as a rival for the solitary seat now being made available on the board. Whether at some stage Reg had promised him anything I don't know. However, when I was called into the boardroom and confirmed as a director I could see Dick was disappointed.

It was largely down to his intervention that I was appointed an associate rather than a full director at the outset, although the word 'associate' with its implications of a diluted status was removed from my title within a month.

When it came to discussing the announcement of my appointment, Dick suggested we wait until the next edition of the club's official monthly newspaper, the *Blades News*. As the current issue had only just appeared, this would have meant a delay of three weeks. Reg Brealey didn't want that and insisted the news should be released immediately. He arranged a prompt telephone call to the *Sheffield Morning Telegraph* so the paper could use the story the next day.

A week or so later when I called into his office, Dick told me: 'You know that as an associate director you haven't got a vote, don't you?' I replied: 'If I haven't got a vote, Dick, I might just as well remain the commercial manager'. I returned to my own office and rang Reg, who fortunately was not away on one of his frequent foreign business trips. I was relieved when Reg confirmed I not only had a vote but all the privileges of a director.

Six months later I was enjoying a break in Spain when my daughter Suzanne relayed a message from Reg saying he wanted to speak to me as soon as possible. When I telephoned him he revealed that Dick Chester had resigned and suggested I had better rush back to sort things out. I knew there was no need for anyone to panic, told the chairman I would finish my holiday, and promised to take the appropriate action on my return to Sheffield.

When I came home Reg wanted to make Geoff Smith acting secretary of the club while we looked for a permanent successor to Chester. However, I knew there wasn't a better man for the job than Geoff, who, while his background was in industrial accountancy rather than football, had already shown he had the ideal qualities for the role.

Happily, Reg accepted my view and Geoff was our secretary for five years until he retired in December 1988, when we recruited Dave Capper from Stoke.

I did not always agree with Reg Brealey and we crossed swords on many occasions, but I got on with him all right and found him good to work for.

Of course, the best of the Brealey years coincided with Reg's first spell at the helm between 1981 and late December 1990 when, frankly, nobody did more to revive the club's fortunes. He put money into the club when it was desperately needed, at a time when nobody else was prepared to offer the same financial backing, and he continued to make funds available, often buying players with money out of his own pocket without considering whether he would ever get it back.

The pity is that things never went quite so well after circumstances conspired to induce his reluctant return in 1992, barely eighteen months after he thought he had sold his controlling interest in the club. There were times in this later period when I questioned the wisdom of some of his decisions, but I must confess that when some people were hounding him ahead of his final departure in 1996, I felt many of his critics either did not know or had forgotten what Reg had done for United.

I have never forgotten the positive reaction Reg showed following our relegation to the Fourth Division in 1981 because it was exactly the lead we needed at a time when things might so easily have gone from bad to worse. Goodness knows what might have happened without him.

When he took over as chairman we had just suffered a record trading loss of £725,000 and the club was around £1 million in debt. The outlook could not have been more bleak and nothing seemed more certain than that we would have to postpone, or even abandon, plans to complete the South Stand development with the creation of new dressing rooms, offices, an executive suite and a social club, etc.

However, Reg was adamant. He insisted the work would proceed. I think he knew that without the job being finished the club would always be handicapped and he saw completion of the work as a crucial practical and psychological step in the right direction.

Reg felt the key to any upturn in United's fortunes was the creation of facilities which would generate essential income and, in this context, he devised a redevelopment scheme for Bramall Lane which, had it come to fruition, would have transformed the club's finances and ensured long-term progress. It is fair to say that Sheffield United's history over the past twenty years might have been very different if Reg had been allowed to turn his dream into reality.

Unfortunately, his wish to redevelop the ground into a super sports stadium and exploit the potential of the adjoining spare land did not meet with the approval of the City Council. Reg was bitterly disappointed when the local authority threw it out in October 1983 and his subsequent appeal to Westminster failed to overturn the Council's decision.

Reg knew there was the space and capacity to turn Bramall Lane into an international stadium and, had his plan succeeded, it would not only have done wonders for the welfare of United but benefited the city of Sheffield. A new-look stadium so close to the heart of the city centre would have been a tremendous boon to the Council and the community.

Perhaps the greatest irony of all was that within a few years the Council spent millions on building the Don Valley Stadium in the east end of Sheffield when agreeing to Reg's plan would have rendered it unnecessary.

Looking back it is difficult not to feel that the Council's rejection of the Brealey plan marked a critical turning point in United's history. This was probably the moment when Reg first wondered about pulling out of Bramall Lane although, in fact, it was another four years before he first put his majority shareholding up for sale.

If it is intriguing to speculate on what might have happened if Reg had been allowed to do what he wanted, it is just as relevant to ponder on the difference it would have made to the subsequent pattern of United's history if he had never had cause to want to quit.

Of course, we might also wonder what might have happened had he found a buyer sooner than actually happened. As we know, it took Reg far longer than he expected to sell his shares and finally depart the scene. In the meantime, while we cannot say we didn't enjoy some good days, with a memorable spell back in the top-grade, in the longer term the well-being of the club suffered for a variety of reasons which many will always feel stemmed from missing the chance to redevelop Bramall Lane.

Unfortunately, back in the early 1980s, nobody could see into the future and, sadly, Reg's plan got caught up in all sorts of politics. No doubt there were faults on both sides but I always felt Reg made the mistake of not going about things with the kind of diplomacy the situation demanded. Instead of saying 'We'll go and ask' and encouraging some debate with the Council, he chose to formulate his plan and adopted a 'this is what we are going to do' approach which provoked stout resistance from the Town Hall.

Of course, before all this happened, Reg had acquired control of United. I am sure it was part of his strategy to become the club's owner and he achieved his goal following the floating of a new shares issue in the summer of 1981. It was sad to see the ownership of the Blades pass out of Sheffield people's hands in the way it did, but, unfortunately, there were insufficient local people interested in buying a stake in the club.

I remember a meeting at which someone asked Reg what would happen if all the new shares were not sold. Reg said in that case he would buy them. The man said if more than fifty per cent were unsold and Reg bought them it would mean he owned the club. 'Yes' said Reg, 'that's right, but if you buy those shares you'll own the club.'

The loss of local control was, perhaps, a down side, but it is worth noting that Reg always wanted to have Sheffield people on the board at Bramall Lane, and this happened when some owners might have chosen to bring in business associates from beyond the region. Reg also preferred to see local lads playing for the Blades where possible.

He promoted a lot of good ideas including a travel club, Junior Blades, a club newspaper and a future players fund. Indeed, when we formulated 'Blades '83' to cover these developments, he was so anxious to see the operation up and running that he told me he wanted everything in place before I started a summer holiday which was barely four weeks away.

Reg revelled in travelling abroad with the Blades. One of the earliest trips he organised was to Brunei, where he knew the Sultan. We took a youth team to play in a match to mark the opening of a new national stadium and Reg ensured it was a great experience for everyone in the United party. Later there was a memorable Far East tour with the senior squad when Reg dipped into his pocket to pay for the players to switch hotels because our original base lacked air conditioning. We ended up with an hotel which boasted a swimming pool and overlooked a beach instead of being stuck in overheated mid-town premises.

Once, when we were in Beijing, Reg learned that some of the lads were missing their English food, so he promptly organised a buffet at the British Embassy where the staff laid on pork pies, sausage rolls, salads and other 'home' produce more to the players' tastes. It transpired that Reg was able to set up the surprise because a relative of his worked at the embassy.

Reference to Beijing reminds me that during this trip I started having pains in my chest and feared I might be about to suffer another heart attack. I hoped I was wrong because I certainly didn't want to die in China! I thought the wisest course of action was to retire to bed early, but reaching my room proved more of an ordeal than I anticipated because the hotel lift was out of order. I have never been more grateful to reach my bed than I was after struggling up several flights of stairs, an exercise which did little to ease my chest pains.

When I awoke the following morning I couldn't remember where I was, and for a moment I felt I was either in a dream or I had died during the night and gone to heaven. Then I opened the room curtains, looked out and knew I was definitely in the land of the living. In the streets below there were hundreds of people rushing off to work and every one of them was riding a bicycle.

I had never seen so many bikes in one place in my life and, before we left Beijing, I was to see what seemed like several thousand more. Indeed, when we played at the local stadium later in the day there were about forty thousand spectators present and the sight of so many bikes parked twenty deep all round the outside of the ground was an unforgettable image.

It seemed a long way from Bramall Lane!

Chapter Thirty-one

Mixed Fortunes
1983–1987

My initial year as a director coincided with our second promotion in three seasons. We had bounced back from the Fourth Division at the first attempt in 1981–82 and gone up as champions, and now, in 1983–84, we climbed out of the Third Division by pipping Hull City to the last promotion place on goal-difference. It was a phase during which our progress seemed to suggest we were on course for continuing success, but unfortunately, instead of going forward we found ourselves caught in a rut and starting to slip backwards.

When Reg Brealey took over as chairman following our fall into Division Four in 1981, one of his first acts was to recruit thirty-five-year-old Ian Porterfield as manager. Ian, a product of Dunfermline, was famed as the scorer of the goal that won the FA Cup for Second Division Sunderland against Leeds at Wembley in 1973, but most local people remember that he later had a spell with Sheffield Wednesday before going into management. At the time of his arrival at Bramall Lane he had just marked his first full season as a manager by guiding Rotherham United into the Second Division.

All credit to Ian, at Bramall Lane he promptly produced a team which won the Fourth Division title and by 1984 he had led us out of the Third Division. Sadly, for some reason, he then seemed to lose the plot. It is difficult to say whether this was due to the unique security of a ten-year contract having induced him to start taking things for granted, or whether it was simply a case of Reg Brealey allowing him too much freedom when Ian might have benefited from firmer control. It was undoubtedly a combination of several factors, but, unfortunately, Ian seemed to change and a climate developed in which his departure became increasingly inevitable.

The fact that Reg gave Ian a ten-year deal was always a bone of contention with the other directors, I don't think there was another manager in the game who enjoyed such a long contract, and I was not alone in feeling Reg made a mistake which did neither him nor the club any favours in the long term. However, in the beginning, I don't think it particularly troubled any of my boardroom colleagues because the club didn't have to foot the bill as Ian was sponsored by Reg Brealey's company, Epicure, for the first two or three years.

It was a different story when the burden was transferred to United's books, and all the more so when Ian tended to get his own way on many occasions when some directors did not feel it was always the right thing.

When we shot out of the Fourth Division in style in 1982 Reg regarded what our new manager had done as a miracle. True, Ian worked hard and invested well, but I think it helped that the chairman ensured he had abundant funds to aid his cause. It spoke volumes that Ian's 'miracle' meant we ended up with a record trading loss of £835,975 on the year! No disrespect to Ian is intended when I say there were many people at Bramall Lane who felt he could hardly have failed with the team he had.

Reg Brealey (centre) with the club's managerial and training staff.
On Reg's right are Denis Finnigan, Jeff Lees and John Stubbs, while on his left are
Ian Porterfield, John McSeveney and Jim McGuigan.

In his time with United Ian was fortunate in always having Reg Brealey's full support when it came to buying players. If the kind of fees he spent on individuals were not huge compared with what some bigger clubs were paying, the sums were invariably substantial in the context of our financial situation. Moreover, with big wages, hefty signing-on fees and generous contracts, especially for the high-profile players Ian signed, it added up to a very costly exercise.

Ian brought in some good players during his five years in charge, including a few like Keith Edwards, Colin Morris and Paul Stancliffe who proved particularly successful and became big favourites with our fans. However, a fair number of his buys were men who were nearing the end of their careers. Veterans like Joe Bolton, John Burridge, Kevin Arnott, Phil Thompson, Peter Withe and others certainly didn't lack experience and most of them did well for us. However, they came on high wages and, sadly, in the majority of cases there was no way we were going to get a long-term return on our outlay. The progress we could expect was always going to be short term and invariably at an excessive financial cost.

Ian's major signings in 1981–82 included winger Colin Morris from Blackpool and goalkeeper Keith Waugh from Peterborough at a joint cost of £190,000, plus striker Keith Edwards, who was brought back to Bramall Lane from Hull City for £100,000. Edwards notched a club post-war tally of thirty-six goals and his arrival in late September coincided with the start of an unbeaten run of seventeen games. As I remember, we finished the season with another unbeaten sequence of nineteen matches.

We had a fairly modest first season back in the Third Division in 1982–83 and finished in mid-table without ever promising a promotion push. Keith Edwards chalked up another twenty-four goals and Colin Morris's tally of nineteen included eleven penalties, but we conceded more goals than we scored and our away form let us down.

This, of course, was the campaign during which I was sidelined for a time following a heart attack and then joined the board a few months after returning to full duties. It was good to be more involved and especially satisfying when my first year as a director just happened to be the one in which we returned to the Second Division after an absence of five seasons.

Ian made a number of major signings, including Paul Stancliffe, who cost £100,000 from Rotherham United, and Glenn Cockerill, who arrived from Lincoln City for £110,000 just before the transfer deadline in March 1984. Stancliffe, who was made team captain in mid-season, was an immediate hit with our fans and a key figure in a defence which conceded only eighteen goals at home. However, once again we owed much to the clinical finishing of Keith Edwards who bagged another thirty-three

League goals. In fact, Edwards and club captain Colin Morris shared fifty-three of our eighty-six Third Division goals.

The records show our 1983–84 promotion success was never a foregone conclusion. It was always a tight race and I have not forgotten that when we completed our programme of matches we feared we might have missed the boat because in the final analysis our destiny was not in our own hands. We knew that Hull City, who had one game left to play, could pip us into third place in the table if they could win 3–0 at Burnley. As it happened they managed a victory but the margin was only 2–0, which meant we clinched the final promotion place by virtue of having scored more goals. Thank goodness for Edwards and Morris!

While United's fate was being decided across the Pennines at Turf Moor I was at Bramall Lane watching a local cup final in which my other team, Rowlinson YC, were playing. As I have mentioned elsewhere, I revelled in my involvement with the Rowlinson lads and it was good to be in a position to ensure they could use the home dressing room for their big game. Unfortunately, they lost the match but as we had paid for a buffet at the ground afterwards, at least we were able to compensate by celebrating United's promotion success. Moreover, a bonus the Rowlinson lads appreciated came when some of the United players popped in to share in the post-match get-together.

Having won promotion twice in three years I suppose it was only natural that we anticipated maintaining at least a steady pattern of progress. Sadly, it didn't happen. Somehow we lost a lot of impetus and the focus never seemed as sharp as it had been.

Some people suggested it was at least partly because Ian was allowed too much freedom, while others felt the success he had achieved had induced a detrimental effect on his approach to the job which ultimately undid his earlier good work. Regrettably, Ian considered himself above criticism and there came a time when he said he was not concerned what anyone else thought because, in his view, he and the chairman were running the club. Later, of course, he learned to his sorrow that this was not the case.

When Ian first arrived at Bramall Lane, he worked hard and did a fair job. Moreover, he and I got along all right. Unfortunately, his management style and philosophy seemed to change and one of the consequences was that our personal relationship subsequently deteriorated.

One of the things which soured my view of him was an attitude best illustrated in the way he dealt with Reg Brealey. The chairman had backed Ian to the hilt, dipping into his pocket without a murmur on countless occasions so the manager could buy the players he wanted. Ian didn't often fail to get his way, but, of course, there did come a time when funds were not quite so readily available and some constraints became essential. Sadly, when this happened Ian responded by having a go at Reg.

I have to admit I was not impressed when Ian seemed to think he could ride roughshod over someone who had given him so much support. Call me old-fashioned if you will, but if there is one thing that really upsets me it is people being disrespectful to others, especially when it occurs in public as well as in private. I didn't like the way Ian spoke to Reg and, when it kept happening, I think it hinted at a situation which could only lead to the manager's departure sooner or later.

None of the directors were happy at the way things were going, and it didn't help Ian's cause that he also lost the confidence of the club's supporters. In this context, I suppose the writing was on the wall from early in the 1985–86 season, six months before he finally went.

One development which put Ian and the supporters at odds was his decision to leave Keith Edwards out of the team. I have never forgotten the day he dropped Edwards for a match at Fulham because, even though we won the game, our fans insisted on singing and chanting the name of their hero throughout the ninety minutes. Ian was, to say the least, deeply resentful of what he saw as public criticism of his team selection. Alas, worse was to come in October when he found himself being barracked at a home match.

I regret to say that my relationship with Ian got so bad towards the end of his time at the club that I used to communicate with the manager through his assistant, John McSeveney. This was ironic because it was around this time that I had been elevated to managing director, and it was far from ideal for the two of us to be on non-speaking terms.

One morning, in early 1986, when I arrived at the ground to start work, I saw McSeveney as I walked past Porterfield's office and he said: 'We're selling Keith Edwards'. I asked: 'Since when?' and McSeveney replied 'Last night'. I mentioned that it couldn't happen because the chairman was away in Gibraltar, but McSeveney explained Reg had arrived home the previous evening and this was when he and Porterfield had discussed the sale of Edwards.

I telephoned Reg who confirmed Porterfield wanted to sell Edwards and had lined up a deal. 'It can't be done like that, Reg' I said. 'Ian will have to wait until after Thursday's board meeting because at this moment none of the other directors have had the chance to discuss the matter.'

To cut a long story short, I then telephoned each of the other directors in turn and discovered that none of them wanted Edwards to be sold. I relayed the information to Reg and the consequence was that Ian had to call a halt to the sale he had arranged.

I cannot now remember the name of the other club involved in the deal that never was. However, seven or eight months later, by which time Billy McEwan was the manager, we did agree to let Edwards go and he joined Leeds for £125,000.

Ian Porterfield's contract as United's manager was terminated in late March 1986 on the day when Norwich came to Bramall Lane and beat us 5–2. It was not without irony that, although Ian and I had not been seeing eye to eye for some considerable time, I had no formal part in the decision to sack him. I must admit, however, that I would have voted for him to go if circumstances had not prevented me from getting into the boardroom before the decision was taken.

Ian's departure had been on the cards for some time and it is history now that the situation was resolved at an impromptu meeting shortly before the end of the match against Norwich. The game was still in progress when I noticed that, one by one, my boardroom colleagues were leaving the director's box. They were so keen to meet and agree a decision before the Norwich directors joined them that everything was done and dusted by the time I arrived on the scene!

It was Paul Woolhouse, then the newest member of the board, who told me: 'We've sacked him, Derek'. As I recall, soon after the final whistle had been blown out on the pitch, Paul said to Reg Brealey: 'Hadn't you better go downstairs and tell Ian the news?'

Reg said he would do so once he had finished his cup of tea but, moments later, someone looked out of the window and noted that Ian was just driving out of the car park. It meant Ian was able to say he learned of his sacking on the telephone, but he only avoided hearing the news in the presence of the chairman because he left the ground earlier than he had ever done after a match. I have no doubt Ian knew what was coming and chose not to hang around for confirmation.

I would like to be able to say that we solved our problem and got it right when we appointed Billy McEwan as Porterfield's successor. Unfortunately, although Billy showed great determination and worked very hard, he didn't get the results and, within less than two years, we were back to square one.

After Porterfield left, Reg preferred to make an appointment from within the club and persuaded the board to give Billy a chance. Billy, who was then thirty-four, had done an excellent job with the reserves and juniors. Also, while this was his first managerial position, he had the experience of some 340 games as a player with six clubs over a span of more than a dozen years since moving into English football from his native Scotland. To enable Billy to concentrate on running the team, I was asked to look after contracts.

Billy was good on organisation and he was also a strict disciplinarian. He was desperately keen to do well and if he had a fault in his dealings with the players it was that he was sometimes rather too strict. There were occasions when I was tempted to mention this to him but I refrained for fear he might feel I was interfering. Nobody could ever doubt Billy's dedication to the job and he was an excellent coach, but I think he was probably unlucky in that his first managerial role coincided with circumstances which sometimes exposed his inexperience. The pressure was on him to ensure our fortunes resumed an upward trend just at a time when our financial position was becoming more difficult. In truth, the situation required a manager with the knowledge and experience to exploit every opportunity of a bargain in the transfer market.

There were a couple of instances which illustrated the point. We missed out on Leicester's Mark Bright and Brighton's Dean Saunders, two players who went on to enjoy great success in the game. In both cases, perhaps, the deals might have been pushed to a successful conclusion by a more experienced manager.

Billy McEwan.

Billy's first full season in charge was hardly a memorable one, and, unfortunately, we followed this with a poor start to the 1987–88 campaign. I think we won only one of our first nine games and, although we then managed four successive victories, the next seven games brought six defeats. In fact, between late October and the first Saturday in January we played fifteen games, won only two and lost ten.

It was a situation which suggested the decision to give Billy his chance had been a mistake and I recall that by mid-December my fellow directors had reached the conclusion that it was time for our young manager to go. They were all for acting without delay, but, while I did not disagree that we needed to bring in an experienced manager sooner rather than later, there was no way I was going to support the sacking of Billy McEwan so close to Christmas.

I told my colleagues that if they sacked Billy just before Christmas I would make public the fact that it had been done without my vote. 'I am not shirking my responsibility as the club's managing director' I said, 'but, having been sacked as Wednesday's manager on Christmas Eve fourteen years ago, it is something I would not wish to happen to my worst enemy. Billy is certainly not my enemy but someone who has worked very hard and for whom I have a great deal of respect.'

Billy's departure was deferred until after the New Year, and it was precipitated by the 5–0 defeat by Oldham on the second day of January.

I felt sorry for Billy and I felt the least I could do was to ensure he went out with the sort of pay-off which reflected the hard work he had done. In truth, I had a bit of an argument with my boardroom colleagues over the size of the payment. When they mentioned a figure I told them that if they had offered that to me I would consider it an insult. Happily, Reg Brealey supported my view and we ensured Billy got a fair and reasonable settlement.

Incidentally, a few weeks ahead of Billy McEwan's departure, Reg Brealey, who had by then invested around £2.5 million in United during his time as chairman, announced he was putting his sixty-three per cent majority shareholding on the market. It was to take him rather longer than he expected to find a buyer and a saga that was destined to feature a number of curious and frustrating twists was not finally resolved until 1996.

Back in early January 1988, however, our priority was to find a manager who could revive our playing fortunes. We didn't know it then, but at last we were about to get lucky when we found a diamond called Dave Bassett.

Chapter Thirty-two

A Weekend
in Bournemouth

When I studied United's fixture list for the 1987–88 season and saw we were scheduled to play at Bournemouth in mid-January, I suggested to my wife Sylvia that it would be a good idea to fix up a weekend winter break at the south coast resort to coincide with the match. Sylvia was delighted and arranged for her sister Joan and brother-in-law Derek to join us on the kind of occasional short holiday we have always enjoyed.

Naturally, all this was organised long before the departure of Billy McEwan from Bramall Lane and we could not have anticipated that the quest for a new manager would turn our weekend break into a working holiday and cause me to leave Sylvia feeling rather neglected. Fortunately, over the years, she has grown all too familiar with football's frequent habit of disrupting the best-laid family plans and I think she forgave me!

When McEwan left and the club advertised for a new manager, we received just under fifty applications. However, less than half were from people who could be considered serious contenders with a background in the game, and perhaps as few as ten of the applicants had managerial experience. When the directors met to discuss the vacancy, we narrowed the number of possibles down to three but, frankly, there was not one candidate who stood out.

There was no way we were going to consider anyone whose career had not gone beyond a coaching role because we knew our situation required a man well versed in management and preferably someone with a proven track record plus a talent for motivating footballers without needing to spend a lot of money. All the people who fitted the bill appeared to be settled in jobs with other clubs, and I suppose if we were honest we knew the majority of those we fancied for the post were unlikely to be lured to Sheffield.

When we held a second meeting to discuss the subject, Reg Brealey announced 'I've got somebody in mind' in a tone that suggested he was being mysterious about a well-known manager whose name was sure to surprise the other directors.

'Come on, then, Reg, tell us who it is', I said.

'Dave Bassett' he announced.

I must admit I didn't think he was serious. I commented: 'But Reg, the man only joined Watford in the summer and he's not going to quit them to come up here'.

Reg smiled: 'Ah, but I've heard on the grapevine that things have not worked out and Watford will sack him next week'.

Every director sitting round the table agreed that if Dave Bassett became available he was exactly the sort of man they would rate as an ideal candidate for the United job. He was experienced and he had not only worked wonders in taking Wimbledon from the Fourth to the First Division but, significantly, he had succeeded on a very limited budget. The question was whether we could persuade a London man who had always stayed close to his roots to move north.

Reg was quite right about Bassett's fate at Watford and news of his formal departure from Vicarage Road, after only twenty-three League games in charge, broke on the Monday following our discussion. His sacking came shortly after Watford lost 1–0 at home to Manchester United and two days after the Blades, with Danny Bergara in temporary charge of the team, had scraped a single-goal victory over non-League Maidstone in the FA Cup third round.

Our next game was at Bournemouth and, looking back, I might have known that the omens for our family break were far from good when an extended Friday board meeting delayed our departure from Sheffield until the middle of the afternoon. We had intended to leave by car before lunch but ended up struggling to reach our hotel in time for dinner.

Naturally, after we had eaten, I took time off to telephone Danny Bergara at the Round House Hotel where the United party was staying. The players had travelled down by coach and I wanted to check they had arrived safely. That duty completed I had no sooner turned my attention to family matters when I received a call from Reg Brealey.

Reg revealed he had fixed a meeting with Dave Bassett at the Chewton Glen Hotel the next morning and said he would pick me up at ten o'clock to take me with him. 'So much for our holiday' said Sylvia when I told her the news.

I have to admit that the moment I met Dave Bassett I knew he was someone with whom I could work. 'He's the man for me', I told myself within seconds of him joining us for morning coffee. There was something about him that won me over immediately. He was so positive and it was evident he knew where he was going. At that stage I didn't know a great deal about him other than that he had played at Wimbledon before taking over as manager in early 1981, and, of course, I was aware of what he had done in nearly seven years in charge. Meeting him helped me appreciate that he had a natural talent for management.

Frankly, Reg and I had already made our minds up about Dave long before the other travelling directors, Michael Wragg and Paul Woolhouse, joined us following their drive down from Sheffield. To be fair, Michael and Paul were sharing our enthusiasm within minutes of meeting the man.

Of course, nothing was formalised at this get–together and we arranged for Dave to meet the full board in Sheffield on the following Monday. In the meantime we all dashed off to Dean Court to watch the Blades in action, with Dave electing to stand among the United supporters behind one of the goals. Remarkably, none of our fans discovered they were standing alongside the guy destined to become one of the most familiar and popular figures in the club's modern history.

It was quite a rush reaching the Bournemouth AFC ground where I was supposed to be helping Danny Bergara with pre-match preparations, and Reg and I arrived in the car park barely ten minutes before the kick-off. Arriving in the dressing room so late was not my normal style but I could only apologise to Danny, I could not tell him or anyone else what had delayed me.

I must admit I felt a touch of guilt after the game because, when we won 2–1 with goals from Tony Philliskirk and Paul Stancliffe, Danny was all smiles when we returned to the dressing room. Indeed, when he suddenly said 'Derek, you and me are a good management team, we could be just like Joe Mercer and Malcolm Allison', I didn't know how to reply. Of course, I could honestly admit that I had no desire to be involved in running the team for any longer than necessary, but I couldn't reveal that a new manager was set to be appointed within a couple of days.

Dave Bassett's appointment was confirmed as expected. As I recall, he came on a two-year contract and the wages we gave him were peanuts compared with what most managers in the game were getting. He readily agreed to Reg's request that the existing backroom staff should be retained for the time being.

Dave didn't enjoy instant success in his first few months and, indeed, he was unable to save us from relegation, but I never had any doubt that he would not take long to prove he was the right man for the job. I saw enough in the early weeks of the Bassett era to feel sure he had exactly the qualities we needed.

When he came we were at the bottom and had fifteen games left. We won five and lost nine, doing just enough to earn the chance of a reprieve through the play-offs. In those days the clubs which had just missed automatic relegation were pitted against teams bidding for promotion from the lower grade. On paper we thought we had a fair chance against Bristol City, who had finished fifth in the Third Division. Alas, after losing the away leg 1–0 we could only manage a 1–1 draw in the return at Bramall Lane.

Some managers might have blamed relegation on their predecessor, especially after taking over a troubled team in mid-season, but Dave Bassett insisted United's fall into Division Three was as much his fault as Billy McEwan's. He said he had had enough games in which to turn things round, and he always felt he failed because he made the mistake of trying to do too much too quickly.

I have never forgotten how, once the dust had settled and the reality of relegation had registered, Dave came to see me and said he would quit without any strings if that was what the club wanted. Some managers in the same situation would have been looking for a way out with a financial incentive to go. However, that was not Dave's style and his attitude told me a lot about him.

He said he had initially been planning to move his wife, Christine, and their two daughters up to Sheffield, but now he wondered how the directors viewed the situation and whether he still had a job. 'Look' he said, 'I'll walk away if that's what you want and I don't expect a pay-off.'

I replied: 'Dave, you've still got a job and we definitely want you to continue, so bring the family up from London and let's start preparing for next season'.

Chapter Thirty-three

Dave Bassett and a Promotion Double

Dave Bassett is definitely the best manager with whom I have ever worked. Indeed, apart from my time as a player, the eight years Dave and I spent together at Bramall Lane were the best of my career in football. We had a wonderful working relationship, and it was not only fulfilling to share a great mutual trust and friendship with a very remarkable guy but fascinating and rewarding to be able to watch him operate.

After becoming a director I always travelled with the team but I had never attended team talks or training sessions. In truth, most managers would consider it was not my place and never dream of inviting me along to watch them work with the players. But with Dave it was different. On away trips, especially, he encouraged me to be there and ensured I never felt I was encroaching on his territory. Right from the start he made me feel welcome and insisted I was an integral part of the team.

Of course, I didn't get directly involved and was always content just to watch as a trusted observer. However, it was a privilege I appreciated, not least because it brought me much closer to the playing side than I might have expected. The experience gave me a greater understanding of Dave's management style and methods and, frankly, I enjoyed his team talks so much I sometimes used to think he had only to throw me a number nine shirt and, even at the age of fifty and with only one leg, I would go out and run through a brick wall for him!

Dave was always bubbling with energy and enthusiasm, it was impossible not to warm to him because he was invariably open, straight and sincere in all his dealings with other people. Being a typical Cockney, he promptly decided my name was Del not Derek, and I soon found the players and coaching staff were all following Dave's lead in calling me Del. It meant

I developed a close relationship not only with Dave but with his players and backroom team.

As both a man and a manager the Dave Bassett I knew was very different from the image often portrayed in the media and perceived by the public at large. He was far more thorough, dedicated, intelligent, knowledgeable and perceptive than many people recognised. Listening to him talk about football and watching him at work, I soon appreciated that his reputation as being nothing more than a long-ball merchant was totally unjust.

One of the first things I discovered about Dave which left a lasting impression was his remarkable knowledge of players. Somewhere in his head he seemed to have an encyclopaedic print-out of every detail of every player in the game. If you asked him about the most obscure footballer at any League club he would astonish you by relating all the key facts and figures almost before you finished posing the question. What is more relevant is that he could back up this knowledge with an astute judgement of a player's strengths and weaknesses and, as we soon discovered, he also had the knack of making the best use of the transfer market to ensure the majority of his deals were to the club's advantage and at minimal cost.

The time I spent working with Dave Bassett was one of the happiest periods of my life in football.

It didn't take long to learn that Dave invariably knew what he was doing and preferred to get on with it without always having to discuss every detail with others in authority before doing so. Indeed, I have never forgotten how he took us all by surprise when he made his first signing before telling anyone about it.

We were playing at Portsmouth in an FA Cup tie, and when someone walked into the boardroom at Fratton Park and said 'I see you've signed Wally Downes', I had to admit it was totally unexpected news to me. Only later did it emerge that Downes had been snapped up on a free transfer and we had no need to fear Dave had committed us to a fee without asking.

Early in his time with United, Dave signed Tony Agana and Peter Hetherston from Watford in a deal which typified his talent for negotiating a bargain. When he arranged for Martin Kuhl to move from Bramall Lane to Vicarage Road as part of the package, I felt sure we would have to make a cash adjustment. I was pleasantly surprised, and most impressed, when Dave persuaded Watford to give us some money as well as Agana and Hetherston!

Tony Agana in action.

In the event, Hetherston did not prove a success, but nobody could say the deal was a failure when you consider that Agana, who had both speed and skill, not only scored over forty goals for us but was eventually sold to Notts County for £750,000.

It is history now that, within a few months of coming to Sheffield, Tony Agana established an outstanding partnership with fellow striker Brian Deane, and no Blades' fan will ever forget how the pair shared ninety-five League and Cup goals in their first two seasons. The way those boys hit it off together and helped shoot United from the Third to the First Division is an episode which has passed into club folklore.

Deane, of course, became a tremendous favourite with United fans following his arrival from Doncaster Rovers in the summer of 1988, and, at a cost of little more than £30,000, he was an outstanding bargain. He went on to score 106 goals in 239 games before he was sold to Leeds for £2.7 million in the summer of 1993 in controversial circumstances which I will discuss later.

It is amusing to reflect that when Dave Bassett took me with him to watch Deane in action in a game at Belle Vue some months before we

Welcoming Brian Deane to Bramall Lane. He was one the Dave Bassett's most inspired signings.

signed him, I was not especially impressed with the tall, lean striker. However, Dave insisted 'This lad will get a lot of goals, you'll see'.

It was while we were on a pre-season tour of Sweden ahead of the 1988–89 campaign that I suddenly recognised what Dave had seen in Deane. In training and in those initial friendly matches 'Deano' displayed such remarkable skills and a natural scoring knack I was left wondering why I had not spotted his potential when I watched him playing with Doncaster. As I recall, we played four games and finished up scoring thirty-two goals while conceding only two, with Deano prominent among the marksmen. I never questioned Dave's judgement of a player again!

Bob Booker, who arrived at Bramall Lane in November 1988, provided a classic illustration of the way Dave's encyclopaedic knowledge of players benefited United by enabling him to react quickly and recruit exactly the right man when circumstances demanded an urgent decision.

Dave had negotiated an astute deal seven or eight months earlier when he bought Simon Webster from Huddersfield for £30,000, but in the autumn of 1988 the lad suffered a broken leg in an FA Cup tie at Mansfield. It was an especially cruel blow because Simon had been in outstanding form and we knew it would not be easy to find a replacement.

Then Dave announced: 'I've got Bob Booker coming up and I'm going to sign him'. I have to admit I did not know who Booker was and Dave had to fill me in on a midfielder or defender who had made about 290 appearances for Brentford. When I asked Dave how much the lad was going to cost, I was relieved to learn no fee would be involved. In fact, it transpired that Booker, who was then aged thirty, had been on the point of quitting football and the move to Sheffield signalled a remarkable revival in his career and personal fortunes. Bob took time to win some United fans over, but soon everyone recognised him as of those players with the capacity to make marvellous use of modest talents. He missed only eighteen of 127 League games in his years at Bramall Lane and, much to his surprise and delight, he became a cult figure with our supporters.

I think Bob expected his stay with United to be shorter than proved to be the case and I have not forgotten how genuinely thrilled he was when we gave him a new one-year contract at a moment when he had been anticipating a free transfer. He knocked on my door and insisted on thanking me profusely for extending his stay, but, of course, I had to say it was Dave Bassett who had urged us to keep him on.

That 1988–89 campaign in the Third Division was one in which we got off to a good start and never looked back. We won nine of our first twelve games and between August and May we lost two successive matches only twice. Deane and Agana shared forty-six League goals, and on a memorable day in September they each scored a hat-trick in a 6–1 defeat of Chester to become to first United pair to achieve the feat for sixty-two years.

Somehow, right from the summer of 1988, there was a mood of optimism in the Blades' camp, and it was all down to the way Dave set about his task with renewed enthusiasm and great determination after our chat about his future following the club's relegation. The day I told him there was no way we wanted him to leave marked a positive turning point which led to a memorable phase in United's history.

As I mentioned earlier, at the time of his arrival Dave agreed to keep the coaching staff he had inherited, but in the close season of 1988 he was able to make changes when Danny Bergara moved on to become manager of Rochdale while Phil Henson and Ian Bailey left to join Rotherham.

Dave brought in Geoff Taylor as his assistant, recruited Keith Mincher as his youth coach and Derek French as the club physiotherapist, and, with the appointment of John Greaves as the kit man, he created a backroom team that provided a crucial key to the success we enjoyed in the next few years.

Geoff, Keith, Derek and John formed a quartet of backroom boys whose dedication was total and, when you talk about team spirit, I doubt if I have ever known a group of people who provided a better example of the true meaning of that phrase. I don't think I am overstating the case when I say it was a joy to be able to spend so much time in their company and to share in the unique atmosphere they generated.

With Dave as their leader, they ensured a tremendous spirit prevailed in the United dressing room and I shall always treasure the memory of those days when there was not a single individual on the football staff who didn't genuinely believe we had the capacity to overcome any obstacle or adversity.

This self-belief was probably never better illustrated than in the 1989–90 campaign when we probably surprised even ourselves by winning a second successive promotion and clinching a return to the old First Division after a fourteen-year absence. We also enjoyed our best FA Cup run for twenty-two years, and, if we were disappointed when Manchester United knocked us out at the quarter-final stage with a controversial goal, we had the consolation of being free to concentrate on the last lap of what proved a desperately tight race for a place in the top grade.

When we started off the season with a ten-match unbeaten run and lost only one of our first eighteen games, those people who had predicted we might struggle on our return to the Second Division belatedly began to view us as serious promotion contenders.

Dave Bassett with his back-up team (left to right) John Dungworth, Geoff Taylor, Derek French and Keith Mincher.

There was a time when we fancied our chances of going up as champions, but, in the event, we were pipped to that prize on goal-difference by Howard Wilkinson's Leeds. In fact, the two automatic promotion places were not decided until the last day of the season and we went into our final game, at Leicester, knowing we had to win to be sure of going up and avoiding the play-offs.

That sunny Saturday, in May 1990, was one of the most unforgettable days of my football life. These are the sort of episodes you savour all the more because they only come along at infrequent intervals in your career, and when they happen they compensate for all the disappointments and setbacks. They certainly make every ounce of blood, sweat and tears seem worthwhile.

We faced Leicester without the injured Paul Stancliffe and John Gannon, and, symbolically perhaps, Bob Booker deputised as captain. There were a few frowns when Leicester scored the first goal, but the way the United lads bounced back and ended up romping to a 5–2 victory with goals from Tony Agana(2), Brian Deane, Paul Wood and Wilf Rostron was an intoxicating experience. It was a display which summed up the character and spirit which Dave Bassett had instilled in the players, and I can hardly

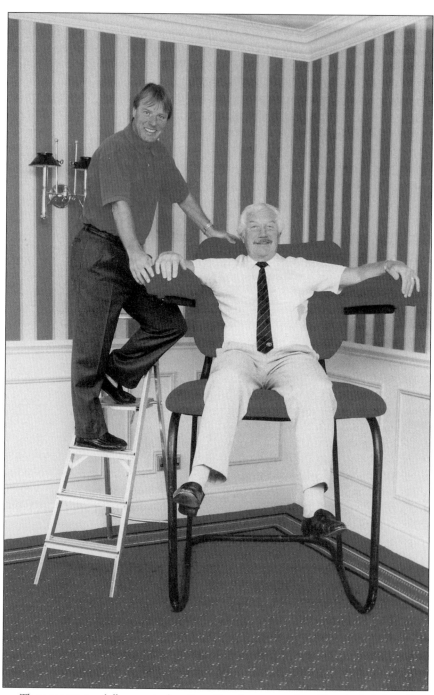

There was never a dull moment when Dave Bassett was around, and here he finds himself needing steps to reach me in a rather huge chair at Bramall Lane.

find the words to describe the pride I felt when the final whistle signalled a famous victory.

While Leeds were winning at Bournemouth on the same afternoon, Newcastle, the other club who could have pipped us to promotion, ended their programme with a 4–1 defeat against Middlesbrough. It meant the Geordies, who were then managed by a famous footballing Sheffielder called Jim Smith, went into the play-offs, and, unfortunately, they were destined to miss out on promotion. Smith, by the way, is a Wednesdayite who started his career with United.

For the record, the top of the Second Division table looked like this:

1. Leeds	P46	85 pts (GD +27)
2. United	P46	85 pts (GD +20)
3. Newcastle	P46	80 pts

Ahead of the trip to Leicester, I had consulted with Dave Turton, who was in charge of the Bramall Lane Executive Club, and arranged a promotion party for Saturday evening. Of course, we knew it would only take place if the result at Filbert Street was the right one, but I had to make sure everybody knew about the party, well, everyone that is, except Dave Bassett. I knew I dare not let Dave hear a whisper about what was being planned because he might have accused me of tempting fate to put a banana skin under our feet!

I doubt if anyone in the United squad will ever forget the remarkable scenes which greeted us when we arrived back at Bramall Lane that evening. The car park at the ground was jammed with thousands of ecstatic Blades fans who were singing, shouting and dancing. It seemed as if everybody was chanting Dave Bassett's name. The joy on the faces of those supporters is a memory I shall always treasure, just as I will never forget the elation and happiness I witnessed among the players in the Filbert Street dressing room after the game.

Not surprisingly, a memorable afternoon was followed by an unforgettable evening and night of uninhibited celebration, and I have to admit I ended up having rather more to drink than I had planned. This may explain why I never did know how I got back to the Dooley house at Norton in the early hours of Sunday morning! All I can recall is that, after leaving the party at the ground, I joined some friends for a pre-arranged meal at the Moat House at Meadowhead where the champagne continued to flow.

An unfortunate footnote to the day was that United's moment of triumph coincided with a black day for Wednesday. I was sipping champagne in the boardroom at Leicester when someone told me Wednesday had lost at home to Nottingham Forest, which meant they were relegated. At first I could not believe the news because nobody really thought they were in serious danger of going down. After a bad start to the season they had staged a great recovery and seemed to have saved themselves from the drop. Alas it transpired that Luton had saved themselves with a shock last-day victory at Derby.

Football can be a very cruel game, and even while I was feeling so good about United's promotion I felt sad about what had happened to the Owls. My thoughts were especially with my son Martyn and those friends of mine who were so devoted to the Wednesday cause. Moreover, the fact that the Sheffield clubs had swapped divisions meant we would again be denied any city derby games in the League in 1990–91.

It was late in the 1989–90 promotion campaign that one of the most curious episodes in United's modern history occurred when an Iraqi-born man called Sam Hashimi, then aged thirty-two, suddenly appeared on the scene and was announced as our new owner.

He arrived out of the blue one day in March but finally disappeared over the horizon in June, and I must admit I was grateful for his departure because he told a local radio station that once he took control of the Blades he intended making it his first job to give me the sack!

Everybody knew Reg Brealey had been trying to sell his 62.5 per cent majority shareholding since 1987 but, when a Press conference was called at short notice on a morning in March 1990, it took everybody at the club by surprise to learn our chairman had apparently agreed a six-million pound deal with this unknown man.

Anyone who attended that meeting will confirm how baffled and mystified all the other directors looked as they listened to Hashimi talking of his great plans for the future. His view of the way ahead for the Blades sounded wonderful, even fantastic, but, frankly, we all thought everything Sam said was far too good to be true. It didn't take us long to decide there was something not quite right about what was going on and we were not surprised when it eventually emerged that our suspicions were not without foundation.

I should mention that this was the season when we had agreed to let the BBC television cameras into the club to produce a fly-on-the-wall documentary. The fact that we ended up clinching promotion in dramatic style on the last day of the season must have delighted the film-makers, but they must have viewed the Hashimi bombshell as a tremendous bonus in terms of lending unexpected colour and conflict to their series of programmes.

As far as we at the club were concerned, the Hashimi mystery could not have arisen at a more inopportune moment. Here we were pushing for promotion and, just when things were going really well, we were hit by the distraction of a supposed sale of the club in circumstances which, to say the least, were puzzling.

In the light of subsequent events some of us have often looked back on the Hashimi episode and wondered whether Sam was brought in by Reg to create a climate which would prompt director Paul Woolhouse to make a bid for the Brealey shares.

I don't think any of us were surprised when it transpired that Hashimi did not have the resources or background he had suggested, and I doubt whether Reg Brealey viewed it as an unexpected development when the other United directors put pressure on him to withdraw from the deal. Every member of the board expressed alarm about the deal and reiterated their fears when our inquiries fuelled our suspicions that young Sam was not quite the man he said he was.

Reg eventually sent Hashimi packing and by June the episode was history. However, in the meantime, I had one or two run-ins with our would-be owner.

One day he came to the ground and said he wanted to study the club's books. I refused his request. I told him he could do what he liked once he had actually bought the club, but, until that happened, it was my responsibility as managing director to do what I considered the right thing for Sheffield United, and, in my judgement, Sam was not yet in a position to qualify to see the books.

Soon after this incident, I saw Hashimi and a colleague walking about on the Shoreham Street Kop where they were taking measurements and recording details. Sam was not best pleased when I told him they were trespassing and ordered him and his pal to leave.

When we played Manchester United in the FA Cup sixth-round, Hashimi rang up and ordered four directors' box tickets for the game. He also talked about arranging for an open-topped car to take him on a 'meet the fans' ride around the perimeter of the pitch before the match. I turned him down on both counts. When I said all the box tickets had been allocated, he insisted he was definitely coming to the game. I said if he did come he would have to stand on the Kop.

Some years later I met up with Hashimi again in Dubai and we had a chat which could be described as friendly. What had happened in 1990 was firmly in the past, and anyway, as I was in a foreign country and conscious of being an ambassador for United, there was no way I wanted to be anything but civil, even to someone who had once talked of kicking me out of Bramall Lane!

Chapter Thirty-four

Life at the Top

The Blades were destined to spend four years in the top grade following our promotion in 1990, with two years in the old First Division and another two in the new Premier League. It is not overstating the case to describe this as a particularly eventful period which seldom lacked interest or incident. Indeed, it not only proved to be another remarkable phase in the club's history, but, on a personal level, the second half of this spell was especially notable but not always for the happiest of reasons. For the moment I will concentrate on our two years in the First Division.

We did not find life at the top an easy adventure but, in the context of difficult circumstances in which the club's ownership saga tended to distract focus from the football, Dave Bassett continued to produce a team which had the capacity to defy the odds and keep bouncing back from the dead just when the pundits had prepared United's obituary notices.

Our initial season back in the First Division was a classic tale of extremes, rather like a game of two halves. We kicked off the 1990–91 campaign with a nightmare run of sixteen matches without a win, and there was one spell when we did not score in six successive games. When we had to wait until three days before Christmas for our first League victory the gloom merchants predicted we were already doomed. However, between late January and mid-March we registered seven successive victories, our best top-grade sequence for eighty-seven years, and we actually lost only three of our final sixteen fixtures. We finished in thirteenth place in the table, twelve points clear of relegation.

People hailed our 'great escape' as a miracle but it was down to the faith and spirit inherent in everything associated with Dave Bassett. Somehow you always felt that Dave could achieve what some managers might find impossible. Even when the outlook seemed to be at its bleakest I never stopped believing he would get us out of trouble.

Dave recruited lads like John Pemberton, Jamie Hoyland, Paul Beesley, Brian Marwood and Glyn Hodges in 1990–91, but if there was one thing he did which could be said to have proved the most crucial key to our survival in the First Division in that initial season, it was signing Vinnie Jones. I feel sure we would have been relegated if we had not bought Jones from Leeds in September 1990. I know some of our supporters never took to Vinnie because of his name and the public perception of the man but, in my view, he was the victim of an image which was false and unjust.

Nobody knew Vinnie better than Dave Bassett, who had plucked him from non-League football at Wealdstone and launched his career at Wimbledon in 1986. Dave assessed our situation and said: 'What we need at Bramall Lane is Vinnie. I know what he can do for us and if we get him we'll not go down'.

Vinnie had done a good job for Leeds United in the season when they pipped us to the Second Division title but, after Howard Wilkinson signed Gary McAllister in the summer of 1990, the Jones boy found himself surplus to requirements at Elland Road. Wilkinson told Bassett that Jones was available and the two managers agreed to leave formal negotiations to myself and the Leeds managing director, Bill Fotherby.

Dave told me not to pay any more than £400,000, a sum which the Blades' board approved, but, unfortunately, Fotherby initially said there was no way we could have Jones at that price. He insisted: 'If you want Vinnie it will cost you a lot of money'. I replied: 'It won't cost us a lot of money, Bill, because I'm making you one offer, £400,000. I'm not going to barter with you and the fee we're prepared to pay will be the same next week as it is today'.

Fotherby said 'We're not selling him for that', but eventually this was exactly what he did. Moreover, we got a bargain because Vinnie made a tremendous contribution to our cause both on and off the field. He was a rare character who was like a breath of fresh air. In the dressing room, on the pitch, on the team-bus and everywhere he went, he had the ability to lift people. He made his team-mates perform and it was exactly the kind of example and leadership we needed.

At Christmas Vinnie organised a party for the lads. He called it a 'jolly up' and it was certainly one of the jolliest social events of the season thanks to the unique Jones humour. He bought everybody a present which could be described as unexpected but appropriate, and it certainly provoked much mirth. For instance Simon Tracey, our goalkeeper, was given a pair of spectacles and most of the other gifts had particular significance for the recipient. One of the guests, incidentally, was entertainer Joe Elliott, and, naturally, Vinnie made sure he went up on stage and performed 'a turn' for the lads. In those days, of course, we didn't known that Vinnie had any particular leanings towards show business and we could not have imagined he might one day become a film star!

Few people ever knew the human side of Vinnie Jones, his good deeds were seldom considered newsworthy by the media, and, in any event, Vinnie always preferred to let gestures which reflected his generosity pass unnoticed. For instance, one day he went out and bought some toys, then took them up to the Sheffield Children's Hospital. However, it was all done without fuss because he didn't want it to get into the newspapers that the guy with a reputation as an uncompromising hard man was really a big softie at heart!

When Vinnie came to Bramall Lane he took a big cut in his wages. He told me: 'Nobody but Harry Bassett could have got me to come and play for him for less money, but, of course, Harry has always been able to talk me into anything'.

After a year with United Vinnie moved on to Chelsea and, once again, I respected Dave Bassett's judgement even though I didn't really think the manager wanted to sell him. The way Dave saw it was that Vinnie had done the job he had come to do and Chelsea's offer presented a timely opportunity to reward him with a return to London plus the chance of better wages than we could afford. The bonus for us was the fee meant we would recoup what we had paid Leeds.

The 1991–92 campaign has passed into football history as the last season before the launch of the Premier League, and, because of the implications of the impending changes, we knew it was vital for us to retain our top-grade status. In the event, we finished ninth in the table, but, yet again, our upward climb was preceded by a poor start to our programme when we won only one of our first twelve matches.

This, of course, was the season in which, following Wednesday's prompt promotion in 1991, the Sheffield clubs staged their first city derbies in the top grade since 1968. Moreover, to the delight of every Blades fan, we claimed a double over the Owls.

The first date with Wednesday was on a memorable Sunday in mid-November when a 31,803 crowd packed into Bramall Lane and we defied the form book with a 2–0 victory. Even some of our own supporters considered a comfortable triumph for the Owls the likeliest outcome, for they were on a good run while we had managed only two wins in fifteen games. It was very much a case of Bassett's boys producing all the passion and we well deserved a success sealed with goals from Dane Whitehouse and Brian Deane.

The return at Hillsborough, in March 1992, was even more unforgettable, not least because this was the evening when I attended a Wednesday match at the ground for the first time since the club sacked me as manager on Christmas Eve 1973.

I have already referred to this emotional return to my professional roots, but what I did not mention was how I was finally persuaded to end my self-imposed exile from Hillsborough. Without the prompting of friends who felt the time was right to go back it might never have happened.

It was, perhaps, a happy coincidence that during this season I had rather more personal contact than normal with Wednesday chairman Dave Richards and Owls secretary Graham Mackrell because we often travelled together on the same train to London to attend meetings in connection with the formation of the new Premier League. I got on very well with both Dave and Graham, and they were always telling me how welcome I would be at Hillsborough. Indeed, they were very keen to have me as their guest and kept pressing the point.

I appreciated their friendship and I certainly did not harbour any ill-feeling towards them for what had happened many years before they arrived on the Wednesday scene. However, while I knew they were sincere in wanting to encourage me to put the past behind me, I still found it difficult to accept their invitation and break a vow I had made so long ago.

Naturally, as United's visit to Hillsborough drew near, many people started to speculate on whether I would attend the match. Frankly, I could not make my mind up, and in the end, it was Dave Bassett who persuaded me to go. He kept saying: 'Get down there, Del, and don't worry about the result because we're going to win'. Even when I finally said yes I remained apprehensive, and, as I noted earlier, when I first arrived at the ground I found myself wrestling with my emotions so much that I was sure I had made the wrong decision.

I must admit I felt much better when the crowd received me so warmly when Dave Richards took me onto the pitch before the match. Indeed, the moment when the Blades and Owls fans were united in greeting me with cheers and generous applause was an experience I knew I would always treasure.

There were tears in my eyes when I disappeared back down the tunnel, but I had to smile when I approached the away dressing room and heard the United players' ghetto blaster pounding out music. Once inside I

The night I went on the pitch at Hillsborough before seeing my first Wednesday game at the ground for nearly 20 years. Owls' chairman Dave Richards presented me with a picture of Hillsborough, and I also saw the Blades clinch a famous victory.

Another souvenir of my Wednesday years is an oil painting of me in action during my playing days.

could hardly hear myself think, but I could see the lads were fired up for the match. When somebody shouted 'Don't worry, Del, we'll be all right tonight, we'll win it for you!' I knew they could not fail to succeed.

Dane Whitehouse, who had been raised as a passionate Unitedite from his earliest years, gave us a great start when he scored after four minutes and striker Bobby Davison, who was on loan from Leeds, notched a double in a tremendous 3–1 success.

The triumph at Hillsborough came midway through a spell in which we lost only twice in sixteen games and, as I recall, soon after beating the Owls we embarked on an eight-match unbeaten run which featured six wins and shot us from the bottom half of the table into the top seven.

Unfortunately, we ended the season with a couple of defeats, including a home setback against Leeds United on the day Howard Wilkinson's team clinched the League Championship. However, considering our poor start to the campaign we had every reason to feel pleased with our record and the fact that we finished in the top nine was no mean achievement.

We looked forward to the new Premiership era with enthusiasm and felt sure our time in the top-grade promised a few more golden days. We could not have predicted that the following season would bring an FA Cup run which would take the Blades all the way to the semi-final and a unique Wembley date with neighbours Wednesday.

As for myself, in the late Spring of 1992 I could never have imagined that the next twelve months would produce such a mixed chapter of personal pleasure and pain.

Chapter Thirty-five

Premature Retirement

The 1992–93 campaign has a special place in Sheffield football history because United and Wednesday reached the FA Cup semi-final together for the first time and when they were paired in the draw the game was staged at Wembley.

It was an unfortunate twist of fate for me that the pattern of events which produced this unique fixture just happened to coincide with a season when not only was I pushed into a premature and reluctant retirement but I was prevented from travelling with the team. In fact, the break turned out to be temporary, but the situation meant spending months enduring the frustration of not being directly involved and having to view all the drama and excitement distanced from the heart of things.

For me, the period between August 1992 and the summer of 1993 was a curious, bitter-sweet phase. There was a long spell when I felt hurt at the way the situation developed, but in the end I had cause to feel justice was done.

There are times in all our lives when we are the victims of the actions of other people and it is a case of circumstances which we cannot influence affecting our careers for better or worse. What might be called the Woolhouse episode in the long-running ownership saga at Bramall Lane provided a classic example.

When Paul Woolhouse took over and almost immediately started running into personal financial difficulties, he decided to make himself chief executive and force me to resign as managing director. However, within less than twelve months of getting his way, he had no choice but to return control of the club to Reg Brealey, who promptly brought me back in the role of temporary chairman.

Now when I look back on this episode I can say that while I did not think Paul was as fair to me as he might have been, I have never harboured any lasting rancour towards him. In fact, his departure from Bramall Lane was not the end of his misfortunes, and I must admit that these days when I think of him I do so not without a certain sympathy.

Woolhouse, a businessman with interests in metals, computing and property, was forty-one when, in December 1991, he agreed to buy Brealey's majority shareholding for a reported £2.75 million. At the time he had been on the board for about five years and, because everybody knew he was a local lad and a lifelong Blades fan, the step was greeted with great enthusiasm. Indeed, as this happened during the Christmas period, many of the club's supporters cast Paul as a kind of modern Santa Claus!

When the Hashimi business had arisen some eight months earlier and been viewed as a development likely to leave the club in the wrong hands, nobody fought harder than Paul to persuade Brealey to withdraw from the deal. Whether Reg had contrived the Hashimi episode with the intention of prompting Paul to react in exactly the way he did was something we all wondered about, but Paul, who was already the club's second largest shareholder, left nobody in any doubt about his passion for the Blades when he fixed up the deal which seemed to have put control of United back into local hands.

Certainly Paul's heart was in the right place and I think most people would concede that he started out with the best intentions when he undertook to pay for Brealey's shares in instalments. Unfortunately, it transpired that he had bitten off rather more than he could chew. He made the mistake of allowing his heart to rule his head, undertaking a financial burden he must have known he could not really afford. Perhaps he was anticipating an early upturn in his fortunes, but alas, his personal and business circumstances took a sudden dip, so, with his difficulties unexpectedly compounded, he found it impossible to keep up his instalments.

By the following October, barely ten months after he had taken over, it not only became public knowledge that Paul had defaulted on his payments but everyone was aware that Brealey intended taking legal action to reclaim his shares. In the meantime Paul had to hand over the chairman's job to Alan Laver and the role he had created for himself as chief executive became untenable. In February 1993 the High Court ruled in Brealey's favour, and two months later, after Paul's resort to the Court of Appeal met with failure, the Woolhouse era was brought to a formal and undignified conclusion.

All this, of course, formed an unwelcome backcloth to a season in which United fought another tense but successful battle against relegation while confounding the critics by reaching the last four in the FA Cup. Moreover, for me, it coincided with ten months or so in the wilderness when I watched the unfolding drama on and off the field as a reluctant outsider until Reg Brealey brought me back. I was temporary chairman from mid-May until the end of June, when Reg resumed his old role.

After Paul took control midway through the 1990–91 season, he and I got along very well, just as we had done before. Indeed, I liked the guy. The two of us did not always agree, but we had a board that was united and we were all pulling in the same direction with the club's cause our sole concerns.

For some time I was under the impression Paul had paid Reg the money he owed him, but, frankly, I didn't consider what went on between them as any of my business. When it began to emerge that Paul was having problems, I still didn't feel it was anything which should concern me. However, it was a different story once it became clear that what Paul wanted to do affected me and raised serious implications which I could not ignore.

From the day I became a United director back in 1983 I had always been prepared to say my piece at board meetings. I took my responsibilities

Paul Woolhouse.

seriously and felt it only right and proper to contribute to the debate and question proposals with which I did not agree. I was never a rebel but I was a bit of a stickler for doing what I thought was right.

When Paul took over, I didn't change my style. Indeed, there were instances when he wanted to do something and I pointed out that he couldn't, but, if I knew he was not happy about my opposition and clearly did not like the stance I sometimes took, I hoped he would appreciate that my objections were not personal but in the interests of the club.

However, matters did ultimately get a bit more personal when Paul started wanting to make himself chief executive, and it quickly became obvious that his plan included showing me the door sooner rather than later. He eventually lined up a contract for himself which would guarantee him £100,000 a year and, in the meantime, much of what he said and did served to confirm that my own position was increasingly under threat simply because he wanted me out of the way.

I must stress that throughout this episode I never lost any of my feeling for Sheffield United. This was essentially a conflict between me and Paul Woolhouse and I was saddened that a situation developed which could have been handled better on Paul's part.

He seemed to think I was being awkward just for the sake of it when this was not so. I remember one occasion when Paul said I knew it had been agreed he was to become the club's chief executive, and he was angered when I pointed out that nothing had been discussed at any board meeting and there was no confirmation of any appointment in the minutes.

At an early stage during this phase there was talk between Paul and myself about a new contract for me, but he was not pleased when I turned it down each time it was put in front of me. Frankly, I found every version of the contract totally unacceptable and if I had signed any it would have added up to an early departure on terms considerably short of what I was entitled to expect. So the situation developed into a battle in which Paul was frustrated by my stubborn resistance to his wishes, but I stuck firmly to my principles and felt I had right on my side. It was, as you might imagine, a time when I knew I had to be on my mettle.

On one occasion I received the minutes of a board meeting I had attended and, to my astonishment, saw they included an item which mentioned my contract and identified my apparent retirement date. As my fellow director, Alan Laver, agreed when I telephoned him, the subject had not been discussed by the board. It was pure fiction, and, of course, when I insisted on the item being removed from the minutes it did not improve relations between Messrs Dooley and Woolhouse.

At another board meeting Paul reported I was ready to sign my contract, but I promptly interjected: 'That's not quite true, Mr Chairman, because I'm not going to be signing it'. He asked if the problem was the need to tie up a few loose ends, and I said: 'Yes, a lot of loose ends'. When he asked what I didn't like about the contract, I told him: 'All of it'.

Naturally, perhaps, I eventually grew tired of all the fighting with Paul. I had always hoped to stay on until I was sixty-five, and for me the ideal format would be one in which I could always remain involved in some capacity, but at nearly sixty-three years of age I felt I could do without all this aggravation. I was ready to go if that was what they wanted. However, it was important to ensure I was treated fairly and there was no way I was going to let Paul ride roughshod over me.

The situation reached a climax at around the time I went with the team on the 1992 pre-season trip to Norway. Indeed, my retirement was confirmed shortly after our return to Sheffield, but, ironically, when the announcement was made it offered no hint of the tense and unpleasant atmosphere in which the decision had been formalised.

I had no idea of what the immediate future held in store for me while I was savouring the pleasure of being on another foreign trip with Dave Bassett and the players. Indeed I was just glad to escape from the scene of my battle with Woolhouse for a few days. However, even in Norway, there was no getting away from Paul's influence.

One night when Dave and I were relaxing over a few glasses of wine and discussing Bramall Lane business, Paul's name cropped up in conversation and Dave said: 'Why don't you start taking it easy and stop opposing and upsetting Woolhouse?' I replied: 'He's asked you to have a word with me, hasn't he?'

I doubt whether Dave would have attempted to play the peacemaker if he had known that things were happening back in Sheffield which were designed to remove me from United's board before the new season kicked off.

When I arrived home I found a letter awaiting me. It was from the chairman, who said the board had met during my absence and decided it was not in the best interests of the club for me to continue as managing director. I was required to hand in my notice, and, if I didn't, I would be sacked.

It is not necessary to rake up all the contents of that letter now, but I have never forgotten the shock and dismay I felt because, apart from having decided my fate while I was abroad on club business, Paul made several allegations and statements which were not only untrue but outrageous and libellous.

My disappointment was compounded by the knowledge that my fellow directors had obviously discussed the matter, yet nobody appeared to have supported me and said 'hang on a bit' or spoken in my defence. Soon after reading the letter, I rang Alan Laver to ask whether he was aware of the contents. Significantly he said yes.

I attended my final board meeting in the Woolhouse era on the 11th of August 1992. Considering the circumstances, with my departure a formality, I envisaged my colleagues would want to discuss my situation first and have me leave the room ahead of the rest of their business. I said as much to Paul but he insisted I stayed and went through the motions as if it was just another meeting. So I delivered my usual managing director's report and then sat patiently awaiting the inevitability of the fateful final item on the agenda.

Once we began discussing my situation Paul made it clear it was a case of accepting the decision and leaving quietly or going to court. I said 'well if you want to go to court, that's fine by me' but I always knew that, even if they did not agree to pay up my contract, there was no way I would force the club into a legal battle. That was not my style.

Paul's first words to me that day were: 'If you worked at my company I would have sacked you', and, in my inimitable style, I responded 'Well, sack me then'. I told him again what he already knew, that I was not a 'yes' man but someone who said what he thought. To cut a long story short, in the end Paul came up with severance terms which I considered acceptable.

I had to smile when my departure was announced in the local paper the next day. In the report Woolhouse was quoted as saying:

> *Derek has decided after eighteen years with Sheffield United to take early retirement. At yesterday's meeting the directors reluctantly agreed to accept his request and granted him a testimonial season in respect of the services he has given to this club and to football in general over the years. Derek will still be retaining a connection with the club and a close relationship with our manager Dave Bassett.*

For the sake of diplomacy I gave out some comment to the effect that the decision pleased me and I was looking forward to being able to spend more time at home. Of course, people who knew me well were aware that this didn't ring true and none of my friends really believed I considered myself ready for retirement.

At least I had the consolation that the settlement terms had included a verbal agreement which afforded me a number of privileges such as two tickets in the directors' box for life plus the facility to travel with the team to away games whenever I wished.

Unfortunately, within weeks, Paul suddenly reneged on the travel arrangement. It was not the only promise to me which he failed to fulfil, but, in this instance, it added insult to injury that neither Woolhouse, nor any of his fellow directors, could bring themselves to tell me the news personally.

One day when I had packed my bag ready for an overnight trip to Chelsea I received a telephone call from Nick Strafford at the offices of the club's solicitors, Clegg & Sons. Nick said: 'I don't know how to start telling you this, but I've been told by the board to tell you that you can't travel with the team tomorrow'.

Travelling with the first-team was a part of the job I had always enjoyed, all the more so during Dave Bassett's term as manager, and it was a blow to be denied the privilege. It was not without irony that, over the previous nine years, no United director had done more travelling with the club's various teams. Indeed, unlike my colleagues, I had not only been an ever-present with the first-team but with the reserves.

Going with the reserves to some distant ground on a wet and wintry night in January is not something every football club director views as a pleasure, indeed it is a duty some consider a chore. I actually enjoyed undertaking the responsibility with any of the United teams. Whenever the presence of a director was required, home or away, I had always been happy to oblige and I often relieved a colleague whose business or other commitments prevented him from undertaking the task.

I must admit that this was a phase during which I didn't feel comfortable even at home games. Some of my former boardroom colleagues nodded to me when I took my place in the directors' box on match days, but others ignored me, and even in the guest room before and after the games I never felt at ease. I sensed that certain people did not want me there and that hurt, not simply because I knew I had done no wrong, but because I had the knowledge and experience to be able to operate in an unofficial public relations role for the club. What made it all the more embarrassing was the way so many visiting directors would emerge from the boardroom, spot me standing on the far side of the guest room, and greet me with the words: 'What are you doing out here?'

The situation did not remain like that for long because Paul Woolhouse's period at the helm came to an abrupt end and my status within the club suddenly changed again.

In the meantime, the 1992–93 season developed into one of the most remarkable campaigns in local football history. Both Sheffield teams had a place in the new Premier League and the success the Blades and the Owls enjoyed on the Wembley trail was a wonderful bonus for supporters.

United finished fourteenth in the table, but they had a long fight to beat the drop and it was not until early May that they were sure of retaining their top-grade status. Their progress in the FA Cup, meanwhile, included a famous fifth-round home victory over Manchester United, when they came from behind to win 2–1, and a memorable triumph over Blackburn Rovers in a quarter-final replay settled by a penalty shoot-out.

When the semi-final draw paired the Sheffield clubs the game was initially scheduled for Elland Road, Leeds, but the Football Association was persuaded to switch the tie to Wembley which meant a crowd of over 75,000 was able to witness a unique occasion on a fine afternoon in April, 1993.

Naturally, it was a particularly emotional day for me. This would have been so in normal circumstances, but my feelings were heightened by the knowledge that I was merely a spectator and the fates had conspired to deny me closer involvement. Here were the two clubs which had meant so much to me in my professional career yet I was sitting on the sidelines, and the situation hurt because I felt I ought to have been part and parcel of it all.

In fact, United had arranged stand tickets for me, and these were used by my wife Sylvia and my daughter Suzanne, but my role on the day was confined to watching the game as a guest of Sky Television. I cannot say I enjoyed the occasion because it was a curiously painful experience to be in the role of spectator. Moreover, it didn't help that United went a goal down after only sixty-two seconds when Chris Waddle hammered a free-kick past Alan Kelly, and, though Alan Cork equalised just before half-time, Mark Bright clinched victory for Wednesday with a headed goal in extra-time.

It was in the same month as the semi-final that I received an unexpected honour when I was made a Freeman of Sheffield.

How can I begin to describe the pleasure and pride I felt when, out of the blue, I learned my home city had chosen to reward me in this way? To say I was overwhelmed would be an understatement for it was such a tremendous thing. For a lad from the humble streets of Pitsmoor, a mere football man at that, to be singled out for so great a public prize was something very special.

I had always thought being made a Freeman was a privilege reserved for politicians and people of high rank. Indeed, when I looked at the illustrious names on the list of Freemen I was staggered to think anyone

A proud moment…the day I became a Freeman of Sheffield.

With my grandson Del and United's Bob Booker ahead of my testimonial match at Bramall Lane.

would feel Derek Dooley merited a place alongside them. I was the only sportsman on that list, and I must confess I felt there must have been many others in my field over the years who had been far more deserving of the honour.

At least I could say I had always been proud of being a Sheffielder, Sheffield is a place I have always loved and never wanted to leave. For me it is the greatest place in the world and I have never ceased to sing my home city's praises on my travels around the globe.

When the ceremony was staged at the Town Hall I had to make a speech. I have never been one for making speeches, but, although this was an occasion when I felt very emotional, I found it much easier than expected to say what I wanted.

I had only one regret, and that was that my mother and father had not lived to share in the proudest moment of my life. I think even my dad would have been lost for words, but I could well imagine him saying 'Well done, Derek' and doing so without his normal reluctance to offer praise!

A trio of Dooleys...me with son Martyn and grandson Del.

Chapter Thirty-six

Brealey Brings Me Back

I don't suppose I am alone in being one of those people who cannot really settle to retirement. I have enjoyed the freedom of those spells when I have been 'pensioned off' and had the chance to spend more time at home, but the pull of football is such that I much prefer to be active and involved. So long as I remain fit and able I will always feel much happier when I am encouraged to make a contribution and use my knowledge and experience.

In fact, apart from the short spell which followed my reluctant early retirement in August 1992, I have maintained my links and kept doing my bit in some way or other at Bramall Lane. Indeed, on three separate occasions I have been called back to fill rather more than a part-time role, and I must admit I have revelled in the challenge of returning to the front-line. Nothing gives me a greater sense of fulfilment than having a part to play and giving it my total commitment.

My first 'comeback' was in May 1993 when Reg Brealey resumed control and he asked me to return as chief executive and temporary chairman. I remained in the chair for a month and, at the time, my plan was to continue in my administrative role for twelve months or so and then start winding down towards formal retirement. In the event my stay lasted a little less than three years.

I cannot say they were vintage years because the club's financial situation had worsened under Woolhouse, and when Reg came back he was not the gambler of former times. Now, with the club having accumulated a number of hefty debts which required urgent attention despite our lack of funds, he was a man rather more conscious of the need to restore some stability and balance the books. Moreover, it was in the context of this climate that the first season of the second Brealey era saw us fall out of the Premier League.

Soon after Reg succeeded me in the chair, in late June 1993, he said something which had implications that I did not fully appreciate at that moment. 'When you are chairman, Derek', he commented, 'there are some decisions you have to make that people will not like, so my coming back means you will not be put in that situation.'

Only later did I realise he had already made up his mind to sell Brian Deane. It was a decision with which I did not agree, all the more so when we ended up getting much less for him than we should have done. Like some of my colleagues and the majority of our fans, I feared Deane's departure would cost us our place in the Premiership. Alas, my resistance failed to persuade Reg to change his plans.

The Deane saga began when the Blades' board held a breakfast meeting at the Moat House in Sheffield at which Reg revealed that Leeds United had made a £2 million offer for our popular striker. Manager Dave Bassett, who was due to go to Italy for a short holiday within a few days and so missed the climax of this traumatic episode, was present. Dave obviously didn't want Brian to go and he supported the view of the majority of the directors that if we had to sell the lad there was no way we could do so at under £3 million.

Unfortunately, as is so often the way with these things, news of the Leeds bid got into the newspapers and the transfer speculation continued to dominate the headlines on the sports pages. Leeds subsequently raised their offer to £2.7 million, which I said was still not acceptable, and, in the meantime, Chelsea were in touch and intimated they were prepared to pay £3 million.

In an attempt to find a meeting place where we could be sure of anonymity, we held our next directors' get-together at a Wakefield hotel just off the M1 motorway. This was the famous occasion when the formal decision to sell Deane to Leeds was taken and three of the directors walked out in protest—with me leading the way.

Reg began proceedings with the comment: 'You'll never guess who has also come in for Deane'. I said 'Wait a minute, Reg' and wrote 'Sheffield Wednesday' on a piece of paper. He looked at it and asked how I knew. I said I had been contacted by Owls' chairman Dave Richards and manager Trevor Francis but I had kept the fact secret in an attempt avoid the news leaking to the Press.

'Well, anyway, Leeds is Deane's home city and he'll not want to go anywhere else' said Reg, who was clearly all for accepting the Elland Road club's £2.7 million offer.

I didn't feel any amount of money would compensate for the loss of Deane, but I knew we could get at least another half-a-million, so I said:

'It's tough on Brian if he wants to go to Leeds because we want a lot more than they have offered'.

Reg said Bill Fotherby, Leeds United's managing director, had stopped behind at Elland Road and lost a day of his summer holiday in order to be free to complete the transfer. Moreover, Fotherby had apparently intimated it was a case of 'take it or leave it' in the next twenty-four hours because if we didn't accept their offer now the deal would be put on ice.

I said in that case I would telephone Fotherby myself, tell him to go off and enjoy his holiday, and say that if this was their final offer he ought to know we were not accepting it. I told Reg: 'I don't want to sell Deane, others sitting here don't want to sell him, and the manager doesn't want to sell him, so we have a problem'.

This was when we took the vote. Myself, Bernard Procter and Alan Laver opposed the proposal to accept the Leeds offer. The directors who voted for it were Reg's brother, Len Brealey, who had become a director when Reg reclaimed his shares in May, John Plant, who had joined the board in late June, and Reg.

It was a straight split, three for and three against. I looked at Reg and heard him utter the words I didn't wish to hear: 'Unfortunately, I have the casting vote, and, as we need the money to square the bills we owe, the vote goes for the sale of Deane'.

I said: 'If that's it, Reg, I've resigned, and, what's more, you've just got us relegated'. When I stood up and walked out, Bernard Procter and Alan Laver followed me.

My decision was a spur-of-the-moment thing, an instinctive reaction, and I must admit I didn't start reflecting on the implications of my response until later. I drove straight to Bramall Lane and, as I started to clear out my desk, I thought 'That's it, I'm off'. I had only gone back to help Reg out, but, while I was happy to be a director again, I felt I didn't need the hassle of trying to run the club.

Then I started thinking: 'Do you know what you've done? The start of the season is coming up, you've resigned, and if Reg should choose to turn awkward he could say don't bother coming here anymore'. Deep down I knew that if I were ever to be denied access to the game I loved and a club which meant so much to me, it would be a devastating blow. If it happened now, I might have to admit it was self-inflicted. I consoled myself by saying I had at least had the courage to back my convictions.

Of course, by now the news of my walk-out was already making headlines on local radio and it soon became common knowledge once the early editions of the local evening paper reached the streets. I have not forgotten how, as I went out into the car-park after leaving my office, a young fan came up to me and said: 'Tha's done reight, Derek. They've done it again, 'aven't they, selling our best player just at the start of the season'. He added: 'You've resigned on principle and this is what I think of them'. Then he promptly started tearing up his season ticket. I said: 'Don't do that. It's important that true fans like you should keep supporting the team'. I had just resigned, yet here I was trying to be diplomatic on behalf of the club!

Dave Bassett telephoned from Italy and urged me not to resign, and over the next few days I received a lot of calls and letters from friends and supporters with the same message. I was flattered that people cared enough to suggest I had again shown I had United's cause at heart and my action confirmed I had not been converted into a 'yes' man. At that stage, however, I felt the deed was done, although I had not put anything in writing.

In the end I did elect to stay, and on reflection it was probably the right thing to do. Sometimes you have to stay and keep fighting from within instead of walking away, and I recognised that I had a responsibility to people at the club who had always been loyal to me. In my heyday at Bramall Lane one of the most rewarding things for me was always the enthusiasm and dependability of the office staff, people whose dedication and commitment matched that of the playing staff. I didn't want to betray their faith in me.

Even so, it was touch and go until after I had spoken to Reg, who called a meeting at an hotel in Southall. This, incidentally, was another instance when we chose a venue where we thought nobody would know us. Amusingly, we had barely taken our seats in the lounge and started drinking our coffee when someone came up and asked: 'Are you ready for your room yet, Mr Dooley?'

When we started the meeting, Reg's first question to me was: 'Have you resigned or haven't you?' I said if he wanted me to resign I would do so and go immediately. But he insisted: 'No, I don't want you to resign, I'd prefer you to stop'. Later in our discussion he repeated that he wanted me to stay and continue in the job I was doing. I said I would, although I did add that in the long term I wished to hand over my present duties to someone else while remaining a director.

Reg wanted to know what the situation was with Alan Laver and Bernard Procter. Neither of us had heard from them since they followed me out of the Wakefield meeting. I undertook to telephone them and when I did so I urged them not to resign. When they said they would stay I thought well at least I have two allies on the board!

As I had feared the loss of Deane and his scoring knack proved costly. I always said that Brian would score enough goals in a season to save us from relegation, and without him we won only eight of our forty-two

League matches in 1993–94. We averaged only a goal a game and we managed three in a match just twice all season.

By drawing eighteen games we equalled a club record which had stood for seventy-three years, but many of those draws could have been turned into victories if only 'Deano' had been in our attack. It was very frustrating to dominate games but end up earning only one point.

We had a spell when we won only two of thirty games, but, ironically, by the end of April we had managed a run in which we had suffered just one defeat in twelve matches. When we came from two-goals down to beat West Ham 3–2 at the end of March and then followed this with our first victory at Liverpool for twenty-six years I think we felt another famous escape from relegation was on the cards.

Our final match of the campaign, at Chelsea, was a real heartbreaker, a classic example of just how cruel football can be. We led twice with goals from Norwegian Jostein Flo and Glyn Hodges. Even when Chelsea pulled level at 2–2 we looked to have done enough to beat the drop, but then Mark Stein made it 3–2 with an injury-time strike and the players returned to the dressing room to learn a combination of results meant we had been relegated by a single point.

It was a day when the fates seemed to delight in conspiring to push us over the brink, because we could have lost and still stayed up. Ipswich escaped by gaining an unexpected point at Blackburn, while Everton hauled themselves to safety with an astonishing comeback in their home game with Wimbledon.

Everton looked doomed when they went two goals down after only twenty minutes. However, they reduced arrears when Anders Limpar won a very dubious penalty and they equalised halfway through the second half. Then they clinched a dramatic 3–2 victory nine minutes from the end when Graham Stuart, who was later destined to have a spell at Bramall Lane, grabbed his second goal of the game with a shot which he somehow managed to squeeze past Hans Segers.

At the time of our fall from the Premier League we had just made plans to demolish the John Street stand, and, unfortunately, circumstances which subsequently developed meant completion of the new structure took rather longer than expected. The hold-up was somehow symbolic of a spell when the future of the club was shrouded in uncertainty, with Reg again putting his shares on the market in November 1994 and a situation unfolding which could hardly be described as positive.

Reg eventually sold out to a Manchester businessman called Mike McDonald, and within about eighteen months of our drop from the top-grade the Bassett era was over and I had stepped down as a director.

Sitting proudly with the United squad ahead of our trip to Australia in 1994.

Chapter Thirty-seven

Changing Times

It is a fact of life that things seldom remain the same for long. Change is inevitable and, whether you like it or not, it is something you have to accept. When you look back there are always some good years to remember with affection and I suppose it is only natural to wish things could have stayed as they were for longer. However, time keeps moving on, one thing leads to another, then one day you suddenly realise something special has gone forever.

As I have said, the period in my career at Sheffield United which gave me the most pleasure and the greatest sense of fulfilment was the spell that coincided with Dave Bassett's time as manager. Those were the days when we had a good team and a unique spirit not just on the field but in every area within the club. I was sorry when it started to break up because, with the best will in the world, it is impossible to recreate the same situation once so many of the leading figures have departed the scene.

In truth, the beginning of the end of an era can probably be traced back to before Reg Brealey returned to the helm. By the time Reg came back the climate had started to deteriorate, and, what with the sale of Brian Deane, our fall from the Premiership, the delay in rebuilding the John Street stand and a few other things, he found himself under fire from supporters who blamed him for the decline in United's fortunes.

The lack of progress on the John Street stand was seen by many as a symbol of the slide and as evidence of diminishing hopes of an immediate upturn in our prospects. It was not without irony that when the old stand was demolished we anticipated an early start on rebuilding, indeed, all the necessary provisions for the supply of water, electricity and similar essential services were quickly put into place in readiness while Reg tried to raise the necessary finance. Then, to our dismay, we found it impossible to get the money. There were times when Reg was desperately close to succeeding in his efforts, and I recall one instance when we were, quite literally, just a thumb-nail away from a breakthrough. Alas, we ended up with more disappointment and frustration, and in the context of the overall situation at the club perhaps it was inevitable that another setback simply compounded the mood of gloom and disenchantment.

Once Reg made it plain that he wanted to pack up and sell his shares as soon as possible, everybody hoped the buyer would prove to be a Sheffield man or at least a local consortium made up of people boasting a lifetime's devotion to the Blades. Unfortunately, that didn't happen. One day in the early autumn of 1995 Reg announced he had agreed a deal with a Manchester businessmen called Mike McDonald.

It didn't help when the transfer of the shares turned out to be a protracted affair. This meant that for about three months we didn't really know what was happening, which was hardly in the club's best interests. A situation arose that cried out for someone to get it resolved quickly so everyone could know where they stood.

Of course, once everything was finally in place we knew it was the end of a chapter. Once again the club was at a crossroads. Because there had been several false beginnings before, many people viewed the development with caution and even a touch of cynicism, but everybody with the club's interests at heart hoped the latest change of ownership might finally signal a genuine turning point and see the Blades set on a positive course. In the meantime, whatever the future held, most of us recognised there would be changes which would have more significance for some individuals than others.

I don't think anybody was really surprised when, in early December 1995, Dave Bassett came to accept that, with the eighth anniversary of his arrival just weeks away, this was the right moment to depart the scene. Dave had developed a tremendous affection for Sheffield, for United and for our supporters. Everybody knew he had always hoped to complete ten years as manager. However, he was ever the realist and he felt he had taken the club as far as he could in the context of a climate and financial circumstances which I am sure he did not feel would significantly improve in the immediate future.

I must admit I was saddened by Dave's departure. Indeed, over the previous three or four years it was probably the thing I had dreaded the most. I had kept thinking to myself that one of these days Dave was sure to get so fed up with the way things were going at Bramall Lane that he would seek a fresh start somewhere else.

I shared his frustration when his better players were sold and he had all my sympathy when he didn't get the funds to invest in the kind of quality

Peter Springett, who was my goalkeeper when I was Wednesday's manager, joined the police force after his playing days ended and became community policeman at Bramall Lane. His early death was a terrible blow to many people who knew him as a friend and a good and genuine man.

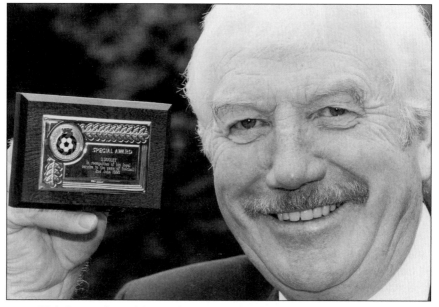

With the special award I received in 1995 recognition of my long service to football.

needed to push the club forward. I was annoyed when certain things didn't happen and promises were not kept, but while I expressed my opinions at board meetings mine was too often a voice in the wilderness.

On many occasions over the years Dave had turned down opportunities to join clubs where he would have enjoyed much better resources. With hindsight he probably had moments when he felt his loyalty was not appreciated by some people, and, in the end, a time came when he knew that a change was in the best interests of himself and the club. Perhaps what eventually happened was inevitable, but, all the same, I didn't find it easy to see things that way because it signalled the end of a very special period in my life.

Long before Mike McDonald arrived on the scene, there was a sense in which the Dave Bassett era was winding down. Dave grew increasingly disillusioned and after Brian Deane was sold and we were relegated in particularly painful circumstances things were somehow never the same again.

It hurt because, to me, United had been much more than a football club during the Bassett years and it was upsetting to see things breaking up. Dave had a unique backroom team and we had shared so many good times, created so many happy memories and savoured such a terrific camaraderie. Of course, my own position at Bramall Lane came under review once the transfer of ownership was completed. Frankly, I was more than ready to cease being a full-time employee and resume my retirement, but I did hope I might be able to remain a director.

By the time of McDonald's arrival, I was already starting to reduce my working week. Instead of doing six days full time I had cut back to four, although sometimes I felt as if I was still doing six! However, McDonald knew I was looking to retire sooner rather than later and I had no problem with his decision when it transpired that he planned to bring in his own man, Charles Green, as the new chief executive.

I would have liked to have remained on the board because I felt I could still make a useful contribution, but when McDonald eventually asked me to step down I understood and accepted his reasons. He was bringing in new directors, people who were putting money into the club, and I suppose it was considered incongruous for someone with no financial stake in the business to be raising pertinent questions and voting at meetings. Things were not what they had been in Reg Brealey's heyday!

I was made a vice-president and, to be fair to McDonald, he ensured I retained my director's privileges. He chose to keep me involved with match-day duties which included looking after visiting directors and VIPs, and I also continued to help out in various other ways, such as representing the club on a number of committees where my knowledge and experience were useful.

Frankly, at the outset I don't think McDonald knew enough about me and my background to appreciate what I had to offer. However, to his credit it didn't take him long to see that because I was known to so many people in a range of different fields I could be a useful guy to have around. My new role suited me because it kept me involved, and it was important to feel I was still part of the scene even if I was now on the periphery rather than at the heart of the action. Of course, it would have been more fulfilling to be a director but, if I am honest, there were to be times over the next two or three years when I was pleased I was no longer a member of the board. My tendency to speak my mind might not have gone down too well with the other directors!

The McDonald era, which was destined to last until late 1999, was certainly colourful but, sadly, it failed to bring the long-term upturn in our fortunes that we had hoped to see. Of course, what happened in those three years was no longer within the scope of my responsibility or influence, but, naturally, I still had deep feelings for the club and I must admit there were many times when I was unhappy and concerned at the way things were going.

At least McDonald got the new John Street stand built and I have to say there were spells when I believed we were moving in the right direction. Indeed, we did reach the play-offs twice. Moreover, on one of those occasions we were only beaten by virtually the last kick of the Wembley final, and I felt that if we could maintain that sort of impetus we would be all right. Sadly, this didn't happen.

When the club was converted into a plc I thought it would be good in terms of generating money which might enable us to push things in the right direction. Unfortunately, we proceeded to spend the money on players and wages at levels which we could ill-afford at that stage. We needed to get back into the Premiership pretty promptly to justify the investment and, of course, missing out meant we were back to square one and poorer into the bargain.

In the meantime, there were further changes behind the scenes which, for me at least, compounded the feeling that things were no longer the same. I have mentioned the sense of loss I felt when Dave Bassett's backroom team broke up, and it was a similar blow when Dave Capper, Andy Daykin and Mick Rooker, key figures in the administration of the club for many years, departed one by one.

They were people who had always been passionate about United, and, like the boys in the old boot room, they had contributed to a very special atmosphere within the club. Moreover, they had such a tremendous depth of knowledge and experience, and because they knew the club inside out I felt it could only be a significant loss to United when they went.

I had been responsible for recruiting Dave Capper midway through the 1988–89 season when Geoff Smith retired and I found myself combining my managing director's duties with those of club secretary until we filled the vacancy. Happily, Peter Coates, who was then chairman of Stoke City, told me they had an assistant secretary at the Victoria Ground who would be an ideal man for the Blades. Over the next nine or ten years Dave definitely proved an inspired choice.

Andy Daykin's links went back even further. He had been brought in by Reg Brealey as the club's marketing manager and came under my wing when he succeeded me as commercial manager after my elevation to the board. With Daykin handling commercial matters and Mick Rooker looking after the pools while doing various other jobs to back up Andy's projects, we had two lads who were not only among the best operators in their specialised fields but a pair of lifelong Blades' fans.

Dave, Andy, Mick and a number of other people who had worked with me behind the scenes at Bramall Lane boasted a loyalty which money cannot buy. They had the kind of know-how and instinct for the job which is difficult and probably impossible to replace, and, as I have said before, you can only view the loss of such people with regret.

It was during the last year of the McDonald era that I was called out of retirement for a second time when I was invited to return to Bramall Lane for three months to take temporary charge of the club's administration.

One day, in the early spring of 1999, I received a telephone call from my former boardroom colleague Bernard Procter, who said the directors had asked him to ascertain whether I could be persuaded to go back to my old job for just long enough to sort out a few things which needed early attention. At the time, for various reasons, the chief executive's role was vacant, and it meant some important decisions were being kept on hold simply because there was nobody operating on a day-to-day basis with the authority to take the appropriate action.

Once Bernard had confirmed that the board was unanimous in wanting me to go back, I said I would do so. I did, however, insist there was no way I was going to work full-time, but, of course, once I returned to action the hours I ended up putting in were hardly those of a part-timer. It was a period towards the end of the season when there is invariably so much extra work to cope with, and this is also a phase during which a range of essential tasks have to be completed to ensure everything is made ready for the following campaign. My duties, incidentally, were not connected with the football side of the club's operation.

It was a six-days-a-week challenge but, knowing I was not going to be saddled with the job indefinitely, I enjoyed it and it was good to be making use of my knowledge and experience again. I went back without a title but I never felt I needed one. I was charged with the task of making decisions and getting things done, and that is exactly what I did.

Once I had completed my three-months stint it was time for a holiday, and in June 1999 when Sylvia and I flew out to spend a couple of weeks in Jersey I thought this was a break which would finally mark the beginning of a proper retirement.

It had always been my custom to take my summer break in June, and what made this holiday different from so many in the past was being spared the usual telephone calls and faxes from Bramall Lane. The lack of communication seemed to confirm I had finally reached the point when I was no longer needed, and at that moment I firmly believed I would never be called back to Bramall Lane again to serve in any formal capacity.

I did not imagine that within less than six months I would complete a hat-trick of comebacks and find myself appointed Football Club Chairman.

Chapter Thirty-eight

Chairman Derek

Like everybody with the interests of Sheffield United at heart, by the autumn of 1999 I was growing increasingly concerned about the direction the club was taking. However, while I was not happy with the way things were going, I was in no position to influence matters. Nobody in authority at Bramall Lane asked for or seemed to place any store by my opinion and I did not anticipate a situation arising in which I would ever again have a leading role with the Blades.

In truth, although I wanted to continue making a contribution and felt I had more to offer than I was being invited to give, I had reached a stage in my life when I no longer seriously aspired to get deeply involved again. Of course, that didn't mean I didn't wish I could help the cause, but as this didn't seem likely to become possible as things stood, I just hoped that those who had inherited the responsibility for running the club would be able to begin reversing the present trend and start improving United's fortunes.

Yet, as the late John Harris often said, football is a funny old game which never ceases to throw up frequent and often unexpected surprises. You never know what is just round the next corner, and Tuesday the 23rd of November was one of those days when the fates chose to create another dramatic twist in the eventful tale of the Blades.

A personal consequence of the events of that day was to suddenly find myself back in business as chairman of the Football Club and I had not been in the job for more than a few hours when the first major task I faced was to organise the recruitment of a new manager.

As I mentioned earlier, the Mike McDonald era was certainly colourful and abundant in incident, however, as I was on the outside anyway for much of this period, I was not directly involved. Naturally, I had my views, but when I look back now I don't feel it necessary to detail every little twist and turn connected with the control and management of the club. Suffice to say that there were times when the situation in the boardroom appeared rather complicated and chaotic, also, by the summer of 1999 Steve Bruce had become the third team manager to leave since Dave Bassett's exit less than four years earlier. The others were Howard Kendall and Nigel Spackman, and, of course, Steve Thompson had had a brief spell in temporary charge.

Like Spackman before him, Bruce had quickly become disenchanted with a policy which forced him to sell his best players while lacking the funds to buy quality replacements. Although the United job had been Bruce's first managerial position, many people felt the former Manchester United captain confirmed he had the potential to progress a long way as a manager, and it was a source of regret that someone with his talents was lost to the Blades.

While Bruce was quickly snapped up by Huddersfield, Adrian Heath, who had managed Burnley for a short spell, was recruited from a coaching job at Sunderland as the replacement who got McDonald's vote at Bramall Lane.

Plc chairman McDonald, having come under fire from supporters, had been threatening to quit for some time and, without quoting chapter and verse, I think it is fair to say there was a sense in which his departure became increasingly inevitable following a further deterioration in both United's playing fortunes and the atmosphere at Bramall Lane in the early months of the 1999–2000 campaign. Certainly things were said which did not suggest he would regain the support of many Blades fans.

By the time of United's home match with fellow strugglers Port Vale in late November we had lost nine of our eighteen games and won only four. We were facing a battle against relegation and the situation did not promise much cause for optimism.

I knew that meetings of the boards of the plc and the football club were scheduled ahead of the Port Vale game, and, indeed, I was aware of the speculation which suggested this was the day when McDonald would finally resign. All the same I was not sure whether this would really happen, and I remember that when I drove into the Bramall Lane car park a couple of hours or so before the game I did not appreciate the significance of seeing McDonald's car pulling away from the ground at the same time. I simply assumed Mike wasn't stopping for the match, which was not unusual because he had not attended a game for some months as a consequence of the criticism he had been getting from supporters.

However, as I walked from my car towards the Platinum Suite, where I was expecting to fulfil my normal pre-match duties, I overheard a number of people saying 'He's gone' and nobody needed to explain who they were talking about.

I didn't think McDonald's departure would have implications for me and I had no intimation of what might happen in the wake of his exit. It was true that, some twelve months earlier, Kevin McCabe and Bernard Procter had mentioned the possibility of my returning to the board but, frankly, I had not taken it seriously. When nothing happened I began to view it as pie in the sky and put the whole business out of my mind.

Sylvia and I were having a meal and entertaining guests in the Platinum Suite, and I remember that, with the kick-off less than half-an-hour away, I was just about to finish my coffee when one of the stewards arrived to announce that Kevin McCabe and Bernard Procter wanted to see me in the boardroom.

Kevin asked me if I had heard that McDonald had gone and I said yes. 'Well', he said, 'we want you to be chairman of the football club.' I replied: 'But, Kevin, you are the chairman of the football club.' He explained that he had resigned from the position but was remaining on the board, then added: 'I feel we need a fresh face—you'.

I turned to Bernard and asked: 'What about you?' Some time earlier Bernard, with whom I had always had a close connection, had intimated that he wanted to leave at Christmas. Now I found myself thinking that if he carried out his plan, I could end up being chairman without the presence and support of a good friend.

It was Kevin who spoke. 'Bernard has succeeded Mike McDonald as chairman of the plc.' I looked at Bernard and asked: 'Does that mean you're stopping?' He replied: 'Yes, for now'.

So I accepted the job of Football Club Chairman. Later, when I told Sylvia what had happened, I don't think she was surprised by my decision to say yes but, all the same, she said she thought I was either mad or just plain daft. Thank goodness she loves me enough to understand and forgive my foolishness!

Once the decision was taken, I asked Kevin whether anyone had seen or spoken to Adrian Heath since McDonald's departure. Adrian had been appointed by Mike and I don't think I was surprised when Kevin said the lad had looked a bit shell-shocked when told the news about the chairman.

I felt I ought to pop down and see Adrian myself but, with the kick-off in the Port Vale match barely fifteen minutes away, I didn't want to walk into the dressing room unannounced. As it happened, Adrian was sitting in his office so I knocked on the door and went in. He looked a bit down in the mouth and I could see he was on edge and obviously felt the sudden turn of events had left him exposed and vulnerable. Having explained that I had been appointed chairman of the football club and stressing that I wanted to help and did not intend to interfere, I tried to put him at ease. I said that whatever happened against Port Vale his position would not rest on this one result. Adrian didn't need telling that four defeats in the previous five games had created a situation which needed an early improvement, but we left it that he and I would have a much longer discussion about things on the following morning.

When I returned to the boardroom ahead of going out to watch the game, I told my fellow directors I had taken it upon myself to promise Adrian that whatever the result he would not be sacked because of it. We all knew that things could not go on as they were, and if we kept losing matches something would have to be done sooner rather than later.

Frankly, having suddenly found myself doing the chairman's job, I felt the need to ensure any major decisions were based on proper judgements. It was important to take time to think things through and not rush into making dramatic gestures simply for the sake of it. I had been on the receiving end of that kind of situation myself following the boardroom changes at Hillsborough in 1973. Indeed, somewhere at the back of my mind I was conscious that Christmas was only a few weeks hence.

Sadly, we did not play well against Port Vale. In the second half our performance was particularly poor. We lost 3–1 with Brian Horton's side claiming only their second victory in eleven games and their first away success of the season. After the game some of our supporters staged a demonstration in the car-park and were calling for Adrian to go.

Within five minutes of the final whistle, one of the stewards brought a message to the boardroom from Adrian. He wanted to see me. Kevin and Bernard went with me and we had barely walked into Adrian's office when he said: 'I think I should leave this job, I think it is in my interests and the club's interests that I leave'.

I asked him 'Don't you want to sleep on it?' He said 'No, I've made my mind up'. Was he sure? I asked. 'Yes' he said.

I did not enjoy seeing him looking so shattered and upset, but I felt his decision was the right one and I did not feel there was any sense in trying to persuade him to change his mind.

I asked: 'What do you want to do? Do we wait until tomorrow morning to announce it?' He replied: 'No, I'll go up and see the Press now'. He declined my offer to join him in meeting the journalists who were waiting upstairs for what they thought was going to be a normal post-match Press conference. The Press corps soon found themselves with a bigger story to report than just another game of football, and for the morning paper men it meant some hurried re-writing to catch the last editions.

My first few hours as chairman could hardly have been more dramatic and I knew that, whatever my initial thoughts about my likely working schedule, the job would definitely be a full-time, hands-on task at least until we had sorted a few things out and got everything ticking over again. It was some years since United had had a chairman who worked six days a week at the club, but I didn't believe there was any other way that the challenge could be tackled. In any event, it is not in my nature to give anything less than total commitment to a job.

Of course, the top priority was to find a new manager and I spent my first full day as chairman setting in motion all that was necessary to advertise the vacancy. Even before that formality was dealt with, there were the usual nods and winks and telephone calls from people who were interested in the job. As is invariably the case in these circumstances, a few callers suggested they might be interested in talking to us if we wanted to offer them the job without them actually applying!

We had about eighteen serious applications and the majority of the people involved were out of work. In the event the man we chose was Neil Warnock, who was working at Bury without a contract. I think it is fair to say he got our vote because he had the right credentials in terms of experience. He also had the advantage of being a lifelong Unitedite who understood better than most the history and background of the club and what the Blades meant to their supporters.

Once we had sorted out the applications, Neil had only one serious rival and that was Gary Megson, the former Wednesday player. This was the job Neil had always wanted. Many years earlier, in Dave Bassett's time, he had often said to me 'Don't forget, I want Harry's job when he goes'. That hadn't happened, but now circumstances had conspired to give him the chance.

Like me, Neil is a realist and we didn't need telling that the immediate future promised nothing less than a huge test for the new manager and his chairman. However, at least nobody could doubt that we both shared a great passion for the Sheffield United cause and, with a new century just weeks away, we could only trust that our partnership would push the Blades forward in the year 2000.

I accepted that time alone would tell whether we reached our goal. My hope was that we might at least start progressing along the right lines before I stepped back into retirement for good.

The happiest team in the world…Sylvia and Derek Dooley!

Chapter Thirty-nine

Time for Reflection

Football has been my life and it has been my good fortune to enjoy a career in the professional game in my home city for more than fifty years. Naturally, I have suffered a few setbacks and disappointments along the way but I have no regrets. If there are one or two things I might wish had not happened, nevertheless I consider myself a lucky man because I have been blessed with a life which has been happy and fulfilling.

I may never have been a wealthy man but my reward has been the kind of riches that money cannot buy. There are some things which are beyond price, like the joy of a wonderful family, the lasting friendship of so many people in my private and professional worlds, and the satisfaction of working in the business that has always meant the most to me.

I suppose I was born lucky, for nobody could have had better parents or have been given a more stable and contented start in life. Then, as if to discover the sheer pleasure of playing football just for the fun of it wasn't enough, there was the delight of a dream coming true when I found myself wearing the colours of my boyhood favourites, Sheffield Wednesday and actually getting paid for the privilege. That was a golden phase indeed, and to have claimed a club scoring record which still stands will always be a source of special pride.

When my playing days were ended with the loss of a leg at the age of twenty-three, it seemed as if my world had collapsed. Here I was, newly-married, short on funds, lacking a trade and suddenly deprived of the only career I was equipped to pursue. In 1953 the view from my hospital bed in Preston could hardly have been more pessimistic. Feeling desperately depressed and facing a bleak and uncertain future, I could never have imagined I would have the good fortune to do all the things I was destined to achieve over the next forty-seven years.

Some twenty-one years later, in 1974, when I joined Sheffield United shortly after my sacking as Sheffield Wednesday's manager, I was delighted and grateful to get a job as the Blades' commercial manager. I thought that modest role would be my lot in life for the rest of my working days. If someone had said then that one day I would become United's managing director and touch other heights of office at Bramall Lane, I would have found it hard to believe.

I could not have predicted that my home city would bestow upon me the honour of being a Freeman of Sheffield. Was this really possible for a kid from Pitsmoor whose chief claim to fame had been as a dashing centre-forward forty years earlier? That it happened only served to emphasise the gratitude and sense of wonder I felt at the way life had continued to be so kind to me.

I have had so many golden moments to savour and to remember with pride, and, as I have said on countless occasions down the years, the real hero of the Derek Dooley story is my wife Sylvia. I could not have achieved anything without her constant support and the strength I have drawn from her example and encouragement. The luckiest day of my life was the day we met.

Sylvia has always known me better than I have known myself. Her patience and understanding, the way she has never resented and always encouraged my love affair with football, has served as a constant reminder that our marriage is the best thing that ever happened to me. Sylvia has shared the pain of the setbacks I have suffered in the game, but, while there have been times when she has questioned my sanity, she has never once prevented me from doing my own thing by responding to the pull of football.

I love football and I love Sheffield, and to have been involved at different stages in my career with both clubs in my home city is something for which I am grateful. I have been a United man for a long time now but a large chunk of my life was spent with Wednesday and my ideal would be to see both the Blades and the Owls together in the top grade and thriving.

In these early months of the 21st century the prospect of a renewal of Sheffield derby fixtures in the Premiership looks rather remote, but I remain the eternal optimist and I hope I shall see it happen again in my lifetime. As a realist I recognise that United and Wednesday will find it increasingly difficult to compete with the very top clubs in terms of financial strength, but I feel there will always be room for two clubs in the city and there is every reason to believe they can both have a place in the top grade. At the moment, following Wednesday's fall from the Premiership, we have to settle for First Division fare on both sides of the city.

Perhaps it was inevitable that, during the 1999–2000 campaign when the city's clubs were both involved in relegation battles, the hairy old chestnut of a United–Wednesday merger should be revived yet again. Had Wednesday been in the Premiership's top six and United been pushing for promotion from the First Division nobody would have dreamed of suggesting the idea. It was amusing the way some people found themselves under the illusion that they had discovered a brand new idea when, of course, it is almost as old as the seven hills of Sheffield.

Frankly, whatever the circumstances, I think the majority of supporters, not for the first time in local football history, viewed the merger talk as plain daft. Most of us who are familiar with the history, tradition and nature of the Sheffield football scene would insist a merger will always be a non-starter. True enough, you can never say never because nobody can know what might happen in the distant future, but I cannot see it happening in my lifetime. There are enough people in Sheffield to support and sustain two clubs and, unless there is a dramatic and unexpected change in attitude and emotional commitment, the supporters will surely ensure United and Wednesday long continue to retain their own separate identities.

Of course, we live in a world in which the ruthless climate of economics can create circumstances that influence developments we might regret but cannot resist, and we can hardly begin to imagine how a future generation might react. The modern Blade and Owl might prefer to play in the Conference as United or Wednesday rather than join up with 'the other lot', but who is to know whether fans will feel the same way in another fifty or a hundred years? After all, my own generation has witnessed changes in attitudes in so many areas of life which would have been considered impossible just a couple of decades ago.

I have never been opposed to change, but I am not keen on change for its own sake and I feel that a lot of the change we have experienced in modern times has not always been for the better. There are so many things we have lost, things which had merit and value, and the irony is that there are people growing up who are unaware that these things ever existed. Once something has been changed and a new situation becomes the norm, it is surprising how soon people forget the way things were. I hope they never have cause to be in a situation where they might forget that our great city once had two famous football clubs!

Sheffield football fans of today would not even consider the possibility of ground sharing and, as both United and Wednesday have invested heavily in developing their grounds at Bramall Lane and Hillsborough, the prospect of the Blades and the Owls operating from the same headquarters looks like remaining as remote as any merger.

Long before the two city grounds were redeveloped, Eric Taylor suggested a single stadium for both Sheffield clubs, but, like the latest merger idea, the subject was never taken to the point of serious or formal discussion because the separate parties viewed it as an impossible dream. Indeed, rival fans saw it as a nightmare scenario!

More recently, at the time the Don Valley Stadium was being built at Carbrook in the east end, the City Council asked officials of United and Wednesday to see for themselves how the development was shaping. The place was then little more than a dustbowl, but both clubs showed genuine interest and recognised that the finished stadium would offer modern facilities plus ample parking space and the advantage of being served by the new Supertram system.

A switch to Don Valley might have seemed like good business sense but, once news leaked that Blades and Owls officials had been invited merely to have a look, the outcry from supporters on both sides of the city ensured any talks about ground sharing would be doomed to fail.

Custom and emotional commitment will always influence attitudes but the world today is already a very different place from the one we knew only a few years ago, and, if predictions about the tremendous changes to come are accurate, who can say what the effects will be on the way we view our football and our sporting heritage? Perhaps a shared stadium will not only become a reality but be welcomed by fans in the future, and, goodness knows, there may even be a time when Sheffield supporters agree to a merger. If it happens, I hope they will ensure that nobody ever forgets about the history of the Blades and the Owls and perhaps someone will erect a memorial to the good old days of Sheffield football!

The problem with football nowadays is that too much money is going out of the game and the trend is guaranteed to compound the problems of many clubs and hasten the kind of long-term change which the modern supporter will regret. Everybody is chasing the golden pot and the danger is that too many clubs are overstretching their resources. You cannot keep spending what you haven't got, and when speculation and investment is not subsequently matched by success it can only spell disaster. At the very least some clubs will end up becoming part-time operations, but others, I fear, could go to the wall.

I hate to keep mentioning the good old days but that was a time when money used to circulate in the game. A big club would buy a player from a small club, who would use a part of the fee to buy a couple of players for modest sums and invest the rest in the running of their club. There was a sense in which everybody benefited. Now the rich get richer while the poor get poorer and the gulf just keeps on widening, with the wealthy untroubled by the fate of the clubs at the bottom of the pile.

Of course, in the old days every club knew what its wage bill would be in the immediate future and could budget accordingly. In modern times wage bills are astronomical, and while, thanks to the huge television deals, much more money is coming into the game, the bulk of it is going straight into the pockets of the players.

I have never been opposed to the concept of players being able to earn good money, but the way it is going will surely ruin the game. Too many clubs are paying wages they cannot afford and the expense, already crippling, can only lead to the demise of long-established clubs in many communities steeped in the history and folklore of football.

There have been many examples of clubs getting into difficulties because they have spent big money on players and paid higher wages than they could afford, then failed to generate the success required to make the investment viable. It is rather like trying to walk up a fast-moving down escalator—there comes a time when you realise you have not only made no progress but actually moved backwards, Moreover, you have used up all the resources you need to keep trying to climb!

In Sheffield, both United and Wednesday have suffered the trauma inherent in the philosophy of seeking to speculate to accumulate. To gamble is great when it succeeds, but when it doesn't you can end up facing far more problems than you started with.

We have to be bold and positive but we need to be realistic and sensible too. We have to live in the present and accept the circumstances in which we exist, and, of course, we must learn to adjust to whatever the future holds. However, we shall only survive and thrive if we choose the right route and make the best use of our resources, preferably in a climate in which common sense and a more reasonable approach to spending prevails.

That is the challenge facing our local clubs and the game at large. If they succeed then perhaps future generations will be able to savour the sort of joy which football has given me.

It's always good to meet up with some of my old team-mates, and here I am enjoying myself in the company of Cyril Turton, Jackie Sewell and Redfern Froggatt.

This get-together took place at the dinner celebrating 100 years of football at Hillsborough. My drinking partners are Ron Springett, Jackie Sewell and Keith Bannister.

Appendix

DOOLEY'S FOOTBALL LEAGUE RECORD

With Lincoln City

Apps & Date			Opponents	F–A	Goals
1947					
1	May	24	Wrexham (h)	3–1	1
2		26	Barrow (h)	1–0	1
2 apps					2 goals

With Sheffield Wednesday

Apps & Date			Opponents	F–A	Goals
1950					
1	Mar	11	Preston (h)	0–1	–
1951					
2	Jan	13	Charlton (a)	1–2	–
3	Oct	6	Barnsley (h)	2–1	2
4		13	Hull City (a)	1–0	–
5		20	Blackburn (h)	2–0	–
6		27	QPR (a)	2–2	1
7	Nov	3	Notts County (h)	6–0	5
8		10	Luton (a)	3–5	2
9		17	Bury (h)	2–1	2
10		24	Swansea (a)	2–1	2
11	Dec	1	Coventry (h)	3–1	2

Apps & Date			Opponents	F–A	Goals
12		8	West Ham (a)	6–0	3
13		15	Doncaster (a)	1–1	1
14		22	Everton(h)	4–0	4
15		25	Nott'm Forest (h)	1–1	–
16		26	Nott'm Forest (a)	1–2	1
17		29	Southampton(a)	4–1	2
1952					
18	Jan	5	Sheff United (h)	1–3	1
19		19	Leeds United (h)	1–2	1
20		26	Rotherham (a)	3–3	1
21	Feb	16	Barnsley (a)	4–5	1
22	Mar	1	Hull City (h)	6–0	4
23		12	Blackburn (a)	0–0	–
24		15	QPR (h)	2–1	–
25		22	Notts County (a)	2–2	2
26	Apr	2	Luton (h)	4–0	2
27		5	Bury (a)	2–1	1
28		11	Brentford (a)	3–2	3
29		12	Swansea (h)	1–1	–
30		14	Brentford (h)	2–0	–
31		19	Coventry (a)	2–0	2
32		26	West Ham (h)	2–2	1
33	Aug	23	Newcastle (h)	2–2	–
34		27	Liverpool (a)	0–1	–
35		30	Cardiff (a)	0–4	–
36	Sep	3	Liverpool (h)	0–2	–
37		13	Tottenham (h)	2–0	–
38		17	Middlesbrough (h)	2–0	1
39		20	Burnley (a)	1–1	1
40		27	Preston (h)	1–1	–
41	Oct	4	Stoke City (a)	3–1	2
42		11	Arsenal (a)	2–2	–
43		18	Derby County (h)	2–0	–
44		25	Blackpool (a)	1–0	–
45	Nov	1	Chelsea (h)	1–0	–
46		8	Man United (a)	1–1	1
47		15	Portsmouth (h)	3–4	–
48		22	Bolton (a)	1–1	1
49		29	Aston Villa (h)	2–2	2
50	Dec	6	Sunderland (a)	1–2	–

Apps & Date		Opponents	F–A	Goals
51	13	Wolves (h)	2–3	1
52	20	Newcastle (a)	5–1	2
53	26	West Brom (h)	4–5	1
54	27	West Brom (a)	1–0	1
1953				
55	Jan 1	Middlesbrough (a)	2–2	–
56	3	Cardiff (h)	2–0	2
57	17	Charlton (a)	0–3	–
58	24	Tottenham (a)	1–2	1
59	31	Wolves (a)	1–3	–
60	Feb 7	Burnley (h)	2–4	–
61	14	Preston (a)	0–1	–
61 apps				62 goals

Dooley scored 64 goals in 63 Football League games for Lincoln and Wednesday, plus one goal in two FA Cup matches for Wednesday, making 65 goals in 65 League and Cup matches.

His one FA Cup goal for the Owls came at Bradford in January 1952.

He bagged more than 105 goals for Wednesday in 96 Yorkshire League and Central League matches.

A Wednesday line up in 1952. Back row: Eric Taylor (secretary-manager), Gannon, Bannister, McIntosh, Curtis, Witcomb, Turton, Alan Brown (coach), Rickett. Front row: Froggatt, Sewell, Dooley, Quixall, Marriott. You will note that we had two mascots on duty that day.

FROM DEREK'S SCRAPBOOK

Some Press Comments

From the *Sheffield Telegraph*, Monday October 8th 1951

DOOLEY CAN REACH TOP IF HE WORKS HARD
By Richard A. Sparling★
Wednesday 2, Barnsley 1

Because 21 year old Derek Dooley scored two splendid second-half goals to become Wednesday's match winner, it is proclaimed that he has solved the club's centre-forward problems On one showing I do not care to commit myself.

His style is ungainly, his heading ability and capacity to link up with the wings limited, but of his possibilities there can be no doubt.

If he is willing to work hard and consistently he can remove his deficiencies and become a power. Dooley has everything in his favour—years, physique and a gift for shooting. Above all he has a wonderful opportunity.

The former Sheffield YMCA player, 6ft 2in tall and weighing 13st 81b, scarcely knows his own strength. Since he was signed as a professional by Wednesday in June 1947 he has scored 108 goals in 102 matches of various grades. This was his third League outing.

His shooting ability is exceptional. It was conspicuous not only when he so ably turned passes from Gannon and Sewell to account but when he registered several near misses.

I was struck by his correct body stance and admirable timing. The ball flew from his foot like a shot from a gun without any display of exertion. Seldom was he more than a few inches off the target. Possessing such an asset he should develop other phases of a centre-forward's needs.

Here I would acknowledge the selfless support accorded him by colleagues, Sewell placed the interests of the youngster in front of his own. In fact all the forwards made it their business to give the ball to Dooley whenever possible.

Maybe they overdid it and hesitated to shoot on their own account when opportunities came their way. In the circumstances, however, that is passed over. After all, it was a young line. Finney is only 17, Quixall 18, Sewell 23, Dooley 21. Despite errors, the team spirit was good.

When Dooley left the field he was applauded. So was goalkeeper McIntosh whom many regarded as Wednesday's match-saver. I do not recall McIntosh making a mistake and but for his work Barnsley would have had more than Baxter's penalty goal after nine minutes.

Barnsley were unlucky when Taylor's header in the second half struck the crossbar and, perhaps, when off-side was blown when Baxter netted the ball. But Barnsley's defence was ill-at-ease owing to Dooley's potentialities, though Pallister was cool and stylish as ever. McNeil, who invariably stood alongside Dooley, was always on pins and needles.

Barnsley have yet to win an away match, but they will not always be balked. The match contained nothing finer than the combined efforts of McCormack and Smith, especially in the first half.

Satisfaction for Barnsley was the happy return to action of Scottish international winger Johnny Kelly. Despite having been out of the game since Christmas he played with all his old skill.

Bannister, back to duty, played quite well, and I thought Wednesday's defensive covering showed improvement. Turton had occasional rounds of applause for effective interventions. Curtis had to stand down at the last minute owing to a poisoned foot.

The teams lined up as follows:

Wednesday: McIntosh; Bannister, Kenny; Gannon, Turton, Davies; Finney, Sewell, Dooley, Quixall, Rickett.

Barnsley: Hough; Hudson, Pallister; Ward, McNeil, Glover; Smith, Taylor, McCormack, Baxter, Kelly.

★*'Dick' Sparling was sports editor of the* Telegraph *for many years and highly regarded in local sporting circles. Incidentally, while this manuscript was in preparation, in late 1999, the deaths occurred of two of the men who figured in this game, Wednesday's Cyril Turton and Barnsley's Gordon Pallister.*

Writing of the above game in the *People* on Sunday October 7th 1951, Phil King commented:

Derek Dooley is the name, and if you can imagine a well over six-foot individual with broad shoulders and a shock of ginger hair who plays soccer in the style of a rugby football forward you have a very fair picture of Wednesday's two-goal hero. This almost cumbersome-looking centre-forward, scorer of 13 goals this season in the reserves, has unbounded dash and enthusiasm and he caused a whole heap of trouble for a Barnsley defence which was never too happy under pressure. My man of the match is that Hero of Hillsborough and Bachelor of Bustle, Derek Dooley. He has got a long way to go, but seems to know the way.

From the *Sunday Pictorial*, November 3rd 1951

DOOLEY'S FIVE SHAKES NOTTS COUNTY
Wednesday 6, Notts County 0

Derek Dooley, the Wednesday centre-forward, scored five—yes, five—in succession in the second half of a never-to-be-forgotten game. Did ever a local boy make good in such a big way?

Dooley stole the limelight from Tommy Lawton and gave the shock of his football lifetime to ex-England centre-half Leon Leuty, who could do nothing to curb the appetite for goals of the red-haired giant. Leuty will never have a more miserable match. In the first half, he was worried by Dooley's speed and weighty challenges, and in the second period he simply did not know what to make of the young giant.

Dooley is surprisingly quick off the mark for such a big fellow and his first goal, a dream effort, advertised his power of shot.

A Jackie Sewell header from a Rickett corner a minute before half-time transformed a game that was running against Wednesday and paved the way for an avalanche to strike County in the form of Dooley, who scored on 50, 63, 68, 79 and 83 minutes.

From the *Sunday Express*, December 9th 1951

DOOLEY 'HAMMERS' A HAT-TRICK
West Ham 0, Wednesday 6

A voice bawled out in broad Yorkshire at half-time: 'You can have your Lofthouses and your Milburns, but give me Dooley every time'.

Few in the crowd would have disagreed, having just seen Derek Dooley, the young Sheffield giant, bang home three goals in the first half-hour, with a wonderful goal from Redfern Froggatt thrown in for good measure.

In these days when you can almost count on one hand your real goal-scoring centre-forwards, Dooley must stand out as the wonder find of the season.

With his long, loping, deceptive stride and his ability to crack the ball into the net with either foot from every conceivable angle, Dooley's price tag must be out of this world.

This was West Ham's worst home defeat ever, but although they were outplayed it is only fair to say that they were denied goals on three occasions when Bannister kicked off the line.

From the *Sheffield Star*, December 13th 1951

DOOLEY MAY LEAD ENGLAND AT HAMPDEN
By Fred Walters★

Derek Dooley, in only ten matches, has become the joint top scorer in the Second Division with Rotherham's Jack Shaw. His three first-half goals at Upton Park brought his total to 19, an almost incredible record.

West Ham supporters were all agog about him after Saturday's game, and the position now is that there are far more unlikely things in this game of football than that Dooley will be strongly considered as leader of the England attack against the Scots at Hampden next April.

People can laugh this off if they wish. The thing the selectors have to decide is what kind of centre-forward they want—one of the stylists, or one who can get goals.

Dooley has not yet come up against a Barrass or a Jack Froggatt but the Second Division has yet to produce a centre-half who really looks comfortable against him.

Dooley, within the space of two months, has lifted Wednesday right into the promotion race. He is well capable of keeping them in it and he is well capable of getting goals for England.

There is only one risk, that someone may come along—we hear a lot about tactics before big games in these days—who may try to show him how to play football according to the theories of the game. That may be fatal.

Dooley is developing into a footballer according to his own inclination. There is nothing haphazard about the way he moved into position for Wednesday's first goal at West Ham, or how he took the centre from Finney with his left foot to score his third. As for his second it was just sheer determination to hold on to the ball that carried him past Allison and Wright.

★*Fred Walters was sports editor of the* Star *and widely regarded in his era as one of the most influential sports journalists in the Sheffield region.*

From the *People* Sunday December 30th 1951

TWO MORE FOR THE AMAZING DOOLEY
By Maurice Smith
Southampton 1, Wednesday 4

Take a red-haired giant of 6ft 2¼ in, weighing 13 stone and a bit, load him into size twelve boots, lace those boots with high explosive… and there you have Derek Dooley, latest centre-forward scoring sensation of Sheffield Wednesday.

I went to Southampton yesterday specially to size up this bargain-basement footballer whose thunder-jet feet have made the headlines week after week. I was not disappointed.

DD—Double Dynamite. That's Derek Dooley. That's how goalkeepers see him. That's how Southampton saw him yesterday. They had the great men watching him and still couldn't keep him quiet.

True, they cut his chances down to six. But he took two of them, made a third goal for colleague Finney, and also twice hit the crossbar.

It's Dooley's quick seizing of half-chances which must make him a definite 'possible' for England's team against Scotland next April. These two goals bring his total to twenty-seven in fifteen matches. If there's another centre-forward in England with a better shooting record than that, lead me to him. There is the answer to those who ask whether Dooley is yet ready for the big time.

True at first glance he does not look a footballer. Physically he resembles nothing more than a Danny Kaye on stilts. He moves with the gangling air of a farmer's son going out to feed the pigs, and ploughing through this ankle-deep Southampton mud just added to that illusion.

When he dribbles he seems to shuffle with the ball. It looks awkward, but he keeps it close under control on the ground. He is always in position and knows where to find his colleagues, too. What's more, he will never accept that he is beaten. That's what I like about Derek Dooley.

They are going places these Sheffielders and believe me Dead-shot Derek Dooley will take them there.

Finney got Wednesday's other goals, and Dudley scored for Southampton. But the crowd didn't seem to care about the scores. Everyone was watching Dooley. It was his day.

From the *Daily Express*, January 7th 1952

DOOLEY'S SIZE 12s PACK PUNCH BUT NO MAGIC
By Terence Elliott
Wednesday 1, Sheffield United 3

Now I've seen everything. How do you like your football? Let me tell you what is happening Sheffield way. A tremendous hunk of a fellow swinging a size twelve boot at the ball in shooting range threatens to put the Jimmy Hagan school of perfection in the background as a thrill-maker. How do you like that?

I saw it happen in this great Yorkshire scrap. Derek Dooley's flying enterprise is doing something to the game. A shot in the arm for football that is stereo-typed? Certainly. But…

There was little, dapper outside-right Alan Finney, an eighteen-year-old who caresses the ball in and out with his precise feet. That was soccer artistry.

There was magic in Wednesday's left-wing combine, boyish-faced, fair-haired little Quixall pulling out Mannion tricks in grand harmony with Jackie Marriott.

On the spot with two rapier goal-thrusts was perky Irish winger Alf Ringstead, and Hutchinson got a dazzling goal.

Then there was the leaping goalkeeping of Ted Burgin, and a Continental-style penalty save from Redfern Froggatt. Enough for anyone's money, surely.

But who turned the 65,000 crowd into a heaving, roaring mass of electrified fans? Right. Goal-snatcher Dooley, 13st 8lb and 6ft 2¼ ins, the Carnera of Soccer.

Is it true what they say about Dooley, the man they call 'the greatest discovery since penicillin'? Hardly. But if it's goals you want, this auburn-haired giant who crashes down the middle will keep on getting them. I'm sure of that.

Just one Dooley goal this time when he swung his boot round centre-half Harry Latham. A 'lost' ball to most players. That's how he gets them. He does something different. He forgets to dribble and swerve. Straight for the target… then crash! That's Dooley.

But Wednesday carried the Dooley fetish too far. This time there was Latham, who, despite being a Wednesday fan before joining United, enjoyed limiting Dooley to a single goal.

It proved a blackout match for winger Jackie Marriott, banished to a dark room with concussion. There he tried to remember the match he had forgotten by half-time.

But for Graham Shaw, United's seventeen-year-old full back, it was a day he will always remember.

Picked for the reserves, who were lunching with the seniors at mid-day, local boy Graham was asked by manager Teddy Davison: 'How would you like to play in the big game?'

Said Graham: 'I'd be very pleased if it could happen'. Said Davison: 'You're in'. What more could a lad wish for?

From the *Sheffield Telegraph*, April 3rd 1952

40-GOAL DOOLEY SETS UP CLUB RECORD
By Richard A. Sparling
Wednesday 4, Luton Town 0

Creation of club scoring records by 22-year-old Derek Dooley, who obtained two goals at Hillsborough yesterday, coincided with Wednes-day's return to the Second Division leadership on goal-average.

The hope is that, just as the Second Division championship was won in season 1925–26 when Jimmy Trotter blazed a 37-goal League trail, promotion will follow in the wake of Dooley's feats.

In 1926–27 Trotter established Wednesday's League (37) and Cup (2) aggregate record with 39 goals and Jack Allen (33 and 6) equalled it in 1929–30.

Both Trotter and Allen played in over forty matches for their figures, whereas Dooley has played in only twenty-four League matches and one Cup-tie, and he has scored in all but five.

From the *Manchester Guardian*, September 22nd 1952

DOOLEY STAGGERS BURNLEY
By an Old International
Burnley 1, Wednesday 1

Burnley and Sheffield Wednesday drew their Football League game at Turf Moor on Saturday. Burnley had the most brilliant forward in Elliott, the finest half-back in Attwell, nine-tenths of the play, and all the bad luck going. But the

Yorkshire team had Dooley and that made all the difference.

As a centre-forward Dooley defies conventional classifications. He hurls himself into the fray like a man possessed. Tall and big boned, he carries a tuft of red hair at one end of his anatomy and a pair of genuine 'beetle crushers' at the other. Woe-betide the centre-half back who has no previous warning of his coming. To face him must be like trying to stop a runaway steer. His ball control at most times would shame a baby and he seems just about as innocent of deceit, but once let him get his eye on the ball and away he goes. 'Hark, Forrad!', 'Tally Ho!', 'Tantivvy!', and all the rest of it.

His football strategy is no more subtle than this, the great thing is to get there first. Should two or three attempt to bar his path a crash will occur, bodies will reel in all directions, then lie disordered, like shattered trunks in the track of an avalanche. And, after all, you cannot blame Dooley for cutting straight to the heart of things any more than you can blame a snow-plough or a Centurian tank, or even a hippopotamus. That is the way they are made. Finesse, or the art of circumvention is no part of their function. Frontal attack is all.

For real artistry we had to turn to Elliott, Burnley's international outside left, or to Attwell, their left half-back, a player who, on this form, might well become an international himself should any mishap overtake Dickinson.

Attwell anticipated shrewdly, tackled strongly, and sprayed passes all round like a master, and his example seemed to bring the best out of a junior colleague, Adamson. As for Elliott, he is as characteristic

of his locality as a piece of millstone grit and about as awkward and sharp-edged to run up against. His play was a fascinating mixture of subtlety and bite.

Meanwhile, with Sewell and Quixall showing only a pedestrian talent in the Sheffield forward line, and with Finney and Woodhead both fussily ineffective on the wings, there seemed no hope for Wednesday unless Dooley did his stuff. For an hour he seemed blankly incapable of doing so and many present who had not seen him before wrote him off as a complete failure, if not, indeed, a hoax.

How rash they were, and how foolish they looked, when Dooley proceeded in his own mysterious way his wonders to perform. Suddenly he picked up a loose ball and charged away down the right wing. Attwell and Cummings bravely opposed their bodies but in vain. Dooley's momentum carried him along, reeling and stumbling, until, near goal, a metamorphosis, tantamount to a miracle, set in. Dooley's ball control assumed, momentarily, the delicacy and certainty of Milburn's. A feint, a sidestep, a neat flick, and the ball was side-footed gently into the Burnley net. The incongruity of it all quite startled one, as might, in Welssian fancy, 'the dexterity of a hippopotamus picking up a pea'.

And this, if you please, after the Burnley forwards had done everything with the Wednesday defence except riddle it with goals. One great shot from Holden, striking the Wednesday crossbar, set it trembling and vibrating like a plucked G string. It needed prodigies of anxious effort, of persistent pressure, of angry shouting, before Shannon found a way to head an equaliser. Of the impact which Dooley made on Burnley, one example only need be cited. 'They keep calling him names' said one elderly observer, 'but he keeps ramming 'em in. Ah wish we had a mug like him'.

From the *Daily Mail*, November 10th 1952

UNITED TAKE THEIR EYES OFF DOOLEY—THEN WHAM!
By J.L. Manning
Manchester United 1, Wednesday 1

Some folk, judged by their noisy demonstrations, regarded this match as a heavyweight contest between the Dooley Kid and the Chilton Champ.

In a way it was, for this particular bout caught the eyes of most of those present, including the referee's.

But those season ticket holders who jumped up to applaud when Dooley was upended and, for his pains, lay still upon the ground, must be chided. This was ringside behaviour more easily tolerated at Belle Vue than Old Trafford.

This in no way detracts from the conclusion that in between rounds there was good clean fun and quite admirable football.

For half an hour teamwork was spurned and a few contests promoted. And it was during this period that pushings and punches threatened the players' right to assemble without interfering with their right to strike.

Dooley hits a team hard. It took two of United's men to watch him all the time. One could say he's dangerous without being dainty. He never trips the light fantastic but he certainly lights upon fantastic trips.

Only once did Chilton take his eyes from him. And what happened? Jackie Sewell lobbed him a pass and the Dooley head carefully aimed at goal and scored in-off the bar.

No one was near him. He was well out of distance, as the boxers say.

And as that occurred after half-an-hour, the United spirit spent the next hour fighting desperately to avoid their fourth successive home defeat—which would have ruined Manchester's weekend.

They succeeded with only three minutes to spare when Pearson, who had driven his forwards with splendid spirit all the match, sprang to head a ball into the goal which but for a sudden deflection would have been easily saved by Wednesday goalkeeper Capewell.

From the *Sheffield Telegraph*, January 2nd 1953

DYNAMIC DOOLEY AT HIS BEST
By C.M. Marston
Middlesbrough 2, Wednesday 2

No one contributed more to the drama of this match than Derek Dooley with a centre-forward display that was more virile, clever and challenging than any I have seen him give,

Perhaps he was especially eager to make an impression on his first appearance in the rain and gloom of Teesside, or, perhaps, he wanted to reward his young wife for the 100-mile journey she made to see him play.

In any event, it was highly satisfactory for Wednesday. Whitaker, a highly experienced centre-half, could never hold Dooley nor subdue his terrific determination. In fact, several times it took not only Whitaker, but two more men, and once four men, before his bulk could be shackled.

The two passes which Dooley gave for the goals, and his unconquerable spirit not only drove his own team to maximum effort but also Middlesbrough so that the match became a memorable clash of two teams with a rare will to win.

There was an abundance of incident and a lively movement of the ball not encouraged by the thick and sticky mud. Much of Wednesday's approach work was delightful but at the start they looked less likely to score than Middlesbrough, who were rewarded with a goal by McCrae after 34 minutes. That goal might have been prevented. The mud was partly to blame but there was also a partial clearance by Curtis which opened up the danger.

Middlesbrough enjoyed that success for only three minutes for the swiftly-moving Wednesday attackers tore such gaps in the home defence that Sewell's equaliser looked a simple affair. Witcomb swung the point of attack, Dooley gave the ball to Sewell in open space and Ugolini could only pick it from the net.

The second instalment of the drama was even more thrilling than the first and this time it was Wednesday who went into the lead after 60 minutes. Again Dooley gave a good pass for a goal scored with a splendid cross-drive by Marriott. Seven minutes later Middlesbrough were again level when Delapenha crashed the ball home from just inside the penalty area.

For Wednesday team work and hard work won a good point.

From the *News Chronicle*, January 26th 1953

'I NEVER LET CROWD WORRY ME' SAYS DOOLEY
By Peter Campling
Tottenham 2, Wednesday 1

Spurs scored in the fourth minute and were always in the lead thereafter but the home crowd had no time to enjoy the pleasure of victory. They were too busy booing Derek Dooley almost every time he touched the ball.

Spurs' skipper Ron Burgess was addressed by the referee for some time after he had been in contact with the Owls centre-forward, and he was not the only home man to whom the referee spoke.

As the final whistle sounded, a section of the crowd surged on to the pitch. A spectator who appeared to be heading for Dooley dodged one policeman but was brought down by another with a rugby tackle as good as any I ever saw.

Why all this fuss? I cannot understand. Nor can Dooley. 'I just love the game' he said. 'I guess on account of my size I am bound to be the target, but it's all in the game, and as for the crowd I never let them worry me.'

That is what I liked about this youngster. He took as many knocks as he gave but not once did I see him appeal to the referee.

Why he should have brought bad feeling from the crowd because he tried to intercept the ball each time Ditchburn was about to clear it, I cannot understand. Dooley was within his rights.

In the first half he looked as dangerous as any centre-forward I have seen, and his header, that reduced the two-goal lead built up by Walters and Bailey, was perfect.

DOOLEY'S TESTIMONIAL MATCH, 1955

Derek Dooley's testimonial match was staged on Wednesday March 9th 1955 and has a special place in the club's records as the first game played under the new Hillsborough floodlights.

The match saw an International XI beat a Sheffield team 5–1 in front of a 55,000 crowd. Gate receipts totalled £7,500. Dooley was introduced to the teams before the game and performed the kick off. The teams in this fixture were:

Sheffield: Ted Burgin (United); Jack Martin (Wednesday), Graham Shaw (United); Jack Shaw (Wednesday), Don McEvoy (Wednesday), Joe Shaw (United); Alan Finney (Wednesday), Albert Quixall (Wednesday), Jack Cross (United), Jackie Sewell (Wednesday), Jackie Marriott (Wednesday). Scorer: Jack Sewell.

International XI: Jack Kelsey (Arsenal); Bill Foulkes (Manchester United), Roger Byrne (Manchester United); Peter Farrell (Everton, capt), John Charles (Leeds United), Alex Forbes (Arsenal); Stanley Matthews (Blackpool), Eddie Quigley (Blackburn Rovers), Tommy Lawton (Arsenal), Jimmy Hagan (Sheffield United), Tommy Eglington (Everton). Scorers: Jimmy Hagan (2), Tommy Lawton, Eddie Quigley and Don McEvoy (og).

Referee: Arthur Ellis (Halifax).

THE MYSTERY VIRUS OF 1973

As background to the mystery virus which hit Sheffield Wednesday in the first half of the 1973–74 season and is referred to in chapter twenty-six, it is relevant to reproduce an article which appeared in the *Sheffield Morning Telegraph* and was written by their No. 1 feature writer Peter Harvey.

> *When Willie Henderson, the Sheffield Wednesday forward, was taken ill on the morning of 5th September there seemed to be no cause for alarm. It looked innocent enough, a minor short-duration ailment that could have had any one of a dozen explanations, unpleasant while it lasted, but nothing to get het up about.*
>
> *The new season was only two matches old, and there were bound to be early injuries and illnesses. Henderson was sent home to bed for a*

couple of days and told to rest. His trouble was described as a 'stomach upset'.

It was later to be described as a mystery virus and it was to cause the biggest crisis in terms of manpower that the club had suffered for many years. The virus spread through the club like wildfire claiming as its victims fifteen other players, more than half the total playing staff, and most of them from the first team or reserve squads, the club manager, many of the office staff and players' wives and families.

It put two players in hospital, forced a situation in which players who were known to be less than one-hundred per cent fit had to turn out and play, and its effects lingered on at the Hillsborough ground for five months.

All this in a setting in which medical care is thorough. The physical well-being of professional footballers is overseen with great care.

By early October, by which time four first-team players had been struck by the illness, club officials knew the symptoms only too well They came in three phases:

1) First a feeling of weariness and lethargy.
2) Then stomach pains, sometimes intense, and sometimes associated with back pains.
3) Finally, a general feeling of nausea and occasionally diarrhoea.

In most cases appetite was not affected. One player remarked with some surprise that despite the illness he could still 'eat like a horse'.

Geoff Eggington, the club physiotherapist, describes it as more like a tropical bug than anything. 'If we had done a pre-season tour of one of the tropical countries it would have been easier to understand' he told me. In fact, Wednesday had played their pre-season games in Sweden.

In an effort to stop the spread of the virus players were fed antibiotics and vitamins. Immediately anyone complained of the first symptoms, he was sent home. 'It was a hectic period, we were rushing round every morning with pills' said Eggington.

But still the virus spread.

Crisis day was Thursday 25th October. By then Derek Dooley, team manager and eleven players were suffering from the virus or its after-effects. Taking account of three other players suffering from normal knocks or strains, more than half the club's playing staff was out of action,

Wednesday felt they had a reasonable case for asking the Football League to call off the match against Notts County two days later on 27th October.

'We were frantic at this time', Eric Taylor, general manager, told me. 'We wanted to close the players' habitation areas for 48 hours, but unfortunately the story broke that we wanted to close the entire ground.'

Wednesday officials believe the Football League missed the point. Wednesday wanted to stop the virus spreading inside the club. The League appeared to think that the postponement request was based on the danger of the virus spreading to the public attending the match. The League also said that Wednesday had enough fit players to field a team and the request for a postponement was refused.

The match, which ended in a goalless draw, was described as one of the season's best at Hillsborough. But, despite that, Wednesday officials still feel aggrieved at the League's refusal to give them breathing space to get rid of the virus.

Dressing rooms, showers and adjacent areas were closed on the Tuesday and Wednesday of the following week, players and staff were kept out of the ground for two days, and the rooms were fumigated from high pressure disinfectant cylinders by men of the Ministry of Health department.

In the meantime, two of the players most seriously affected, John Holsgrove and Mick Kent, were admitted to the Royal Infirmary, where blood tests and other tests established that they were suffering from a virus localised to the intestines. For a time there was concern that the virus might also affect the liver but that has now been discounted.

Wednesday carried out tests of their own to try to establish how the virus got into the club, but without success.

No investigations are needed to see how it spread. In the closed community of a football club where players change, train, bathe together and meet socially, the spread of infection is always a danger. The club doctor was convinced that the only sure way of stopping the spread was to scatter the players, empty their accommodation for two days, let the fresh air through it and disinfect it.

Certainly since this was done the virus seems to have abated. But the effects are still being felt at Hillsborough,

Several of the officials to whom I spoke felt that the virus was not taken seriously by people outside the club who often seemed to think that it was little more than an excuse for bad results. Eric Taylor said: 'The facts and figures we presented were not taken seriously by the Football League. Other people seem to think that the virus was something that affected us just before the Notts County match. In fact, it has been with us for five months'.

The club doctor added: 'The recovery period was often quite a long time. Some players reported back for training thinking they had recovered *and then had to be sent home again. It's one thing feeling fit enough to return to a job behind a desk, but it is very different being fit enough to return to playing ninety minutes of football'.*

Some players have been out of first-team football for two months. Others were out for two or three weeks at a time. Inevitably, team selection has been badly affected to the extent that it has proved impossible to play a regular, settled team.

Today Wednesday officials feel they have beaten the virus. There is relief, but no great elation. Now they have to show what they might have been without it. And the season isn't young anymore.

Harvey's piece was supplemented a timetable of the epidemic, reading as follows:

5th September: Willie Henderson ill with 'stomach upset', sent home for two days.

21st September: Jim Craig and John Sissons affected by same 'stomach upset'.

8th October: John Holsgrove, club captain, and David Sunley sent home ill and told to stay at home for a minimum of 48 hours. Alan Thompson, who shares digs with Sunley, moved into an hotel to prevent the infection spreading.

19th October: Newcomer Mick Kent, at that time on trial but later to sign full-time for Wednesday, is latest victim. Holsgrove, Tommy Craig, Peter Grummitt and Kent sent home for 48 hours, and for the first time there is talk of a 'mystery virus'.

25th October: Crisis day. Craig, Kent and Grummitt return for training and are sent straight home by the club doctor. Manager Derek Dooley sent home ill. Four more players fall ill—first-teamers Brian Joicey and Bernard Shaw, plus youngsters Gary Parker and Dave Cusack. Wednesday ask for postponement of match with Notts County.

26th October: Football League say match must be played. Youngsters Peter Fox, Alan Hill, Kevin Wilson and Steve Hancock fall victims of the virus.

30th & 31st October: Team area at the ground closed, sealed and fumigated.

After this phase, the virus gradually abated.